"Pastors get asked to do many things, but there is 'one thing needful'—preaching. Lest the 'one thing' get buried in the frenzy of multitasking, we need continual reaffirmation of the 'one thing' that as both glory and mystery anchors our vocation. Welcome Darrell Johnson as a serious and joyous preaching companion. All of us working pastors need a preacher like him in our life."

Eugene H. Peterson, translator of *The Message,* and Professor Emeritus of Spiritual Theology, Regent College, Vancouver, British Columbia

The GLORY *of* PREACHING

PARTICIPATING IN GOD'S
TRANSFORMATION OF THE WORLD

DARRELL W. JOHNSON

IVP Academic

An imprint of InterVarsity Press
Downers Grove, Illinois

InterVarsity Press
P.O. Box 1400, Downers Grove, IL 60515-1426
World Wide Web: www.ivpress.com
E-mail: email@ivpress.com

InterVarsity Press® is the book-publishing division of InterVarsity Christian Fellowship/USA®, a movement of students and faculty active on campus at hundreds of universities, colleges and schools of nursing in the United States of America, and a member movement of the International Fellowship of Evangelical Students. For information about local and regional activities, write Public Relations Dept., InterVarsity Christian Fellowship/USA, 6400 Schroeder Rd., P.O. Box 7895, Madison, WI 53707-7895, or visit the IVCF website at <www.intervarsity.org>.

All Scripture quotations, unless otherwise indicated, are taken from the New American Standard Bible®, copyright 1960, 1962, 1963, 1968, 1971, 1972, 1973, 1975, 1977, 1995 by The Lockman Foundation. Used by permission.

Design: Cindy Kiple
Images: Giorgio Fochesato/iStockphoto

ISBN 978-0-8308-3853-0

Printed in the United States of America ∞

Library of Congress Cataloging-in-Publication Data

Johnson, Darrell W., 1947-
  The glory of preaching: participating in God's transformation of
the world / Darrell W. Johnson.
    p. cm.
  Includes bibiliographical references and index.
  ISBN 978-0-8308-3853-0 (pbk.: alk. paper)
  1. Preaching. I. Title.
BV4211.3.J64 2009
252—dc22

                                                                    2009021522

| P | 20 | 19 | 18 | 17 | 16 | 15 | 14 | 13 | 12 | 11 | 10 | 9 | 8 | 7 | 6 | 5 | 4 | 3 | 2 | 1 |
| Y | 25 | 24 | 23 | 22 | 21 | 20 | 19 | 18 | 17 | 16 | 15 | 14 | 13 | 12 | 11 | 10 | 09 | | | |

CONTENTS

PROLOGUE

Something Always Happens

SOMETHING ALWAYS HAPPENS.

Whenever a human being, Bible in hand, stands up before a group of other human beings, invites the gathered assembly into a particular text of the Bible and as faithfully as possible tries to say again what the living God is saying in the text, something always happens. Something transformative, empowering, life-giving happens.

I know it is a bold claim. Some might say overly bold, even audacious. Some might say too simplistic, even naive. I understand; I often feel the same way myself. Nevertheless, I take my stand in this claim. It is the glory of preaching.

I believe the preaching of the Word of God changes the world. I believe individuals, neighborhoods, cities and nations are changed by the preaching of the gospel of Jesus Christ. For in preaching the good news of Jesus Christ (which is ultimately what any biblical text preaches), it turns out that we are participating with the living God in God's ongoing transformation of the world. Not that preaching is the only means God employs. God clearly also effects divine transformation through intentional small-group ministries, through one-on-one mentoring ministries, through music ministries, through social-justice ministries, through healing ministries, through counseling, through worship and through intercessory prayer. Yet God has certainly chosen to change the world through the ministry of preaching, through the exposition of biblical texts in the power of the Spirit who inspires the text. "God was well-pleased," writes the apostle Paul, "through the foolishness of the message preached to save those who believe" (1 Cor 1:21). God saves the world through the cross and through "the word of the cross" (1 Cor 1:18). God saves the world through the event of Jesus' passion and through the preaching of that event. It turns out that preaching itself is a saving event.

Again, I know it is a bold claim. Nevertheless, I stand on it. Through the never-perfect speech of an always-imperfect speaker, the triune God works the miracle of transformation.

The following story will help you understand why I have written this book.

A friend and I were making our way out of the chapel. I had just preached the Jesus of John 2:1-11, the Jesus who turns water into wine at a wedding in Cana of Galilee. We were rejoicing in the wonder of what the Spirit of God had worked in and through the sermon. It appeared that most of those present that day had been deeply moved, and were alive with fresh hope.

The sermon had emphasized that what Jesus did at the wedding turns out to be the most miraculous of the deeds done by Jesus, surpassed only by the deed done to Jesus on Easter morning. It is the most miraculous because unlike every other mighty deed done by Jesus, in this one he does not merely change what was there but brings into being what was not there. In all his healing deeds, for example, Jesus touches what is there, what is not working correctly, and puts things back together again.[1] For instance, in the feeding of the 5,000 (the one mighty deed recorded by all four Gospel writers) Jesus takes what is there—five loaves of bread and two fish—and makes a whole lot more bread and fish. It is a very impressive deed. At Cana, however, Jesus does not make more of what is already there; he brings into being what was not there. The way I kept putting it in the sermon was "The ingredients for the wine were not in the water pots." I noted that

---

[1] I learned this—surprisingly—from David Strauss in his 1831 *The Life of Jesus Critically Examined*, ed. Peter C. Hodgson, trans. George Eliot (Ramsey, N.J.: Sigler Press, 1972), pp. 219-27. Strauss does not believe that anything happened which the Gospel writers claimed to have happened. Nevertheless, when he reads a text he amazingly grasps what the author is claiming better than many who *do believe* what the text describes.

many preachers of John 2:1-11 have been accustomed to quoting Saint Augustine, who when wrestling with the miraculous in this deed, said something like, "The Creator is always turning water into wine, usually through a slow, natural process; at Cana, the Creator now in our flesh and blood, simply sped up the process." But, as I argued, that is not the case, not at all. The Creator is always turning water and grapes into wine through a slow, natural process, but not turning water alone into wine. At Cana, Jesus does not speed up a natural process. No natural process would ever bring wine out of water alone. The ingredients for wine are not in the water pots; no grapes are there, only water. Jesus is not simply transforming what is there. He is bringing into being something new.

I wish you could have witnessed the joy springing up in the room from the text! I sensed it especially as we came to one of the implications of the text. "When Jesus promises to do a new work in you, the ingredients of the new work do not have to be there," I said; "He can bring into being the new work without the ingredients being there."

So then, she and I were making our way out of the chapel, our hearts once again alive with hope, aware that nearly everyone present that day was now moving into "an alternative reading of reality" which engenders such hope.[2] Knowing that I had for some time been praying about responding to requests to write a book on preaching, she said to me, "Darrell, I do not think you can put down on paper what just happened in that preaching moment."

"Why?" I asked.

"Because what just happened is beyond what you as the preacher were doing, something almost 'other' than what you were doing."

My heart leapt with joy. And I asked her, "Are you saying that I should not even try to articulate what happened?"

"No," she responded in her gracious southern manner,[3] "I am saying that it may not be possible. I think you convey it well in person as you

---

[2]The phrase Walter Brueggeman uses in his teaching on the role of texts and preaching texts. See his *Cadences of Home: Preaching Among Exiles* (Louisville, Ky.: Westminster John Knox Press, 1997).

[3]My friend is Polly Long, one of our instructors in New Testament Greek at Regent College and a very fine preacher.

interact with students and other preachers face-to-face. But I do not think you, or anyone else, can convey it on paper."

You hold in your hands my attempt to do what may not be possible to do. You hold in your hands my attempt to explore and articulate the glory of preaching.

I do not write as an expert on preaching; given what I say about preaching in this book, you will appreciate why I think no one can completely be an expert. I have, at the time of writing this book, been preaching for nearly four decades (since the spring of 1970). So you could think of me as a seasoned preacher (and teacher of preaching); you could think of me as an experienced preacher, but do not think of me as an expert. The term *expert* suggests mastery of a subject, exercising a degree of control over a subject. I have not mastered preaching; and, as you will learn as you read this book, I certainly do not think I have control over the preaching moment (no human does). I would rather you think of me as a coach or an encourager. I write as a fellow student of preaching, as one who is still learning. I think of myself as, by God's grace, a disciple of the great Preacher, Jesus himself. I am his student, and always will be.

Let me lay out, in preliminary form, some of the foundational convictions from which I am working in this book.

1. *When the living God speaks, something always happens.* "Let there be light." And there was—lots of it. "Be still." And the waves and winds died down. "Lazarus, come forth." And a dead man walked out of the tomb.

2. *When the preacher speaks God's speech, God speaks.* Here I paraphrase Martin Luther's words.[4] This assertion lies at the heart of the Reformed tradition, of which I am a part. *"Praedicatio verbi Dei est verbum Dei":* "The preaching of the Word of God is the Word of God" (The Second Helvetic Confession).

3. *Therefore, when the preacher speaks God's speech, something always happens.* Always?

I will develop and defend these convictions as the book unfolds.

---

[4]I cannot find his essay/book that begins, "When the preacher speaks, God speaks."

These convictions will be the particular subjects of chapters one, two and three.

It might be helpful to say just a bit more, again in preliminary form. Something happens. What happens? I believe that whenever human beings leave a preaching moment[5] (a preaching-of-the-Word-of-God moment), they will do so with

- a clearer vision of the living God in Jesus (who, according to himself, is the subject of any text, and therefore, of any sermon on any text)[6]

- a better understanding of the gospel of Jesus, the good news of what God has done, is doing and will do in Jesus

- an "alternative reading of reality," a different, more redemptive way of understanding the concrete circumstances, challenges and fears in their lives

- a new way of thinking, feeling, acting and re-acting shaped by the clearer vision, better understanding and alternative reading

- a new power enabling them to walk in the new reality into which the preached text has brought them

I will unpack and apply these convictions as the book unfolds, especially in chapters three, four and ten.

The key term in the title of this book is *participating*. I have chosen it for two reasons. First, because the gospel of Jesus Christ is the good news that, because of what Jesus has already accomplished ("It is finished," Jn 19:30), he can, and does, invite us to participate in his life (which, it turns out, is the inner-life of the triune God). Every time I write or speak those words I feel like dancing, or at least saying, "Amen." Because of Jesus, because of his work on the cross, because of his resurrection and ascension, we mere humans, and sinful humans at that, are included in the very life of the Trinity. We are included in Jesus' own filial relationship with the one he calls Father. We are included in the relationship he has with the one he calls Paraclete, the

---

[5]By this term I am referring not only to preaching in a sanctuary in the Lord's Day service, but also to gatherings in homes midweek, or to student ministry meetings on college campuses, etc.

[6]John 5:39; Luke 24:27, 44.

Spirit of truth and life. We are included in his status[7] as "Son," and, therefore, in his ministry[8] as "Son." He invites us to join him in his ministry as Prophet, Priest and King (or, if you prefer, Revealer, Redeemer and Ruler).[9] To be called to the intercessory prayer ministry is to participate in his intercessory prayer ministry; to be called to the healing ministry is to participate in his healing ministry; to be called to the teaching ministry is to participate in his teaching ministry; and on it goes, encompassing the totality of Jesus' ministry in and for the world. And to be called to the preaching ministry is to participate in his preaching ministry.

I have chosen the word *participate* for another reason, a liberating reason, an empowering reason. In the final analysis, the burden for the success of preaching rests on the Preacher's shoulders, on Jesus' shoulders. (I know that the term "the Preacher" in the Bible usually refers to the author of Ecclesiastes; but I trust you would agree that we can more rightly use it of Jesus of Nazareth.) What makes preaching work is the Preacher, who, by his Spirit, is at work in and with the text, in and with the preacher, in and with the listeners. Preaching works because somehow the risen and ascended Preacher being preached is actually doing the preaching himself. We do not stand up before others, Bible in hand, alone; we stand up in and with Jesus. We participate in the activity of another.

It gets better than that. For it turns out that as we preach, we participate in Jesus' preaching of his Father; in the preaching moment, Jesus himself is pointing to and revealing his Father. And as we preach, we participate in the Father's preaching of his Son; in the preaching moment, the Father himself is pointing to and revealing his Son: "This is My beloved Son, in whom I am well-pleased" (Mt 3:17); "This is My beloved Son, with whom I am well-pleased; listen to Him!" (Mt 17:5). And as we preach, we participate in the Holy Spirit's preaching of Jesus; in the preaching moment, the Spirit is pointing to Jesus, bearing his own witness to Jesus, and doing so in a

---

[7]Larry Hurtado, *At the Origins of Christian Worship* (Grand Rapids: Eerdmans, 1999), p. 107.
[8]N. T. Wright, *The Lord and His Prayer* (Grand Rapids: Eerdmans, 1996), p. 81.
[9]Bruce Metzger of Princeton Seminary.

way that brings conviction and faith (Jn 16:8-15). We participate in a divine work, in a trinitarian work, the end results of which are not on our shoulders.

Now, this is not to say that the human preacher is of no significance. That would overspiritualize this liberating, empowering participation. Preachers do play a role, and are called to play it as competently and faithfully as they can. This I will seek to develop in chapters five through nine.

And after I do, I will bring us back to basics, in chapter ten, where I will define preaching as "standing in the mystery."

I have had many mentors in preaching, too many to try to name in this introduction (you will meet them as the book unfolds). I want, however, to name here, in alphabetical order, those who have most taught and encouraged me thus far: F. Dale Bruner, Maxine Hancock, E. Stanley Jones, Walter Luthi, G. Campbell Morgan, Earl F. Palmer, Fleming Rutledge, James S. Stewart, John R. W. Stott and Rod K. Wilson. I have often thought if I could just preach with the exegetical precision of John R. W. Stott,[10] the literary imagery of Maxine Hancock,[11] the joyful creativity of Earl F. Palmer,[12] the love for the Bible of F. Dale Bruner,[13] the skillful order of G. Campbell Morgan[14]

---

[10]John Stott is, in my mind, the purest expository preacher in history. I have been helped most by his works on the Sermon on the Mount, Acts and Ephesians. I would even put Stott above John Chrysostom, Martin Luther and John Calvin—the great preachers of the past—for the simple reason that Stott, unlike the three named, kept his own issues with other Christian leaders out of the tone and content of his sermons.

[11]Maxine Hancock, professor of interdisciplinary studies at Regent College, has a way with words and images that pulls one into the text and brings one to the feet of Jesus. I was reduced to tears of release and joy after her sermon on Genesis 1, "On Being Human."

[12]Earl Palmer has a way with texts that is immediately attractive and awakens joy. I first heard him in 1976 at a College Briefing Conference at Forest Home Christian Conference Center in the mountains east of Los Angeles, and continued to listen to him as he pastored First Presbyterian Church of Berkeley, California, and then University Presbyterian Church in Seattle, Washington.

[13]I first met Dale after he left the Philippines, where he taught at Union Theological Seminary, to teach at Whitworth College in Spokane, Washington. No one I know has the ability to draw out the richness of a text like Dale does; he shows us that all the illustrative material we need is right there in the text.

[14]Morgan only preached a book of the Bible after reading it forty to fifty times. His sermons are available in *The Westminster Pulpit: The Preaching of G. Campbell Morgan*, 10 vols. (1906-1916; reprint, Grand Rapids: Baker Book House, 1954-1955). See also his *Studies in the Four Gospels* (Westwood, N.J.: Fleming H. Revell, 1927).

and Walter Luthi,[15] the rhetorical flare of James S. Stewart,[16] the compassion for humanity of Charles Swindoll,[17] the cultural awareness of Fleming Rutledge,[18] and the "reality" awareness of Rod Wilson,[19] I could finally preach! Of course, I am wrong. Although I can, and do, learn from each of these mentors, I had to discover what all of us have to discover: I have to preach the way I am created and redeemed to preach, speaking with my own voice.[20] Which is to say that there are as many ways to preach as there are preachers. (I will say more about this in chapter eight.)

As you have already likely discerned, I am approaching the meaning and task of preaching from a robustly Reformed orientation. I come to the theory and practice out of the deep conviction that, as the apostle Paul put it, the word of God's message is not just the word of humans, but is "the word of God, which also performs its work in you who believe" (1 Thess 2:13). I gladly embrace a high view of preaching.

When I accepted the appointment at Regent College (I began in September of 2000), Dr. Robert Meye, former dean of the School of

---

[15]See Luthi's *St. John's Gospel: An Exposition*, trans. Kurt Schoenenberger (Richmond, Va.: John Knox Press, 1960) and *The Letter to the Romans* (Edinburgh and London: Oliver and Boyd, 1961). No one I know can take a whole chapter of a Gospel or epistle at once and preach as clear and concise a sermon as he does.

[16]Many consider James S. Stewart "the greatest preacher" (in English, anyway) of the twentieth century. See especially his two books on preaching, *Heralds of God* (1946; reprint, Vancouver, B.C.: Regent College Publishing, 2001) and *A Faith to Proclaim* (1953; reprint, Vancouver, B.C.: Regent College Publishing, 2002). I read Stewart, and my heart lit on fire with the gospel. I owe my introduction to Stewart to my uncle Emmett Johnson, a first-rate preacher, who upon my ordination, took me to the bookstore at Luther Seminary in St. Paul, Minnesota, and bought me everything of Stewart's work then available in print.

[17]Charles Swindoll is a master storyteller; he has an engaging capacity to make any text—not just narrative—a living story.

[18]I have only recently become acquainted with Fleming Rutledge's ministry; she can in very short order draw one into the heart of a text and into the redemptive connection to our culture. I wish I had met her sooner. You will want to read her collections of sermons in either *The Bible and the New York Times* (Grand Rapids: Eerdmans, 1999) or *Help My Unbelief* (Grand Rapids: Eerdmans, 2000).

[19]Rod Wilson is president and professor of Christian counseling at Regent College, having joined the faculty the same time I did. He is the finest leader with whom I have yet worked. He sees his number one job as "naming reality," which he does with courage, class and honesty in his preaching.

[20]Phillips Brooks, "Preaching is truth through personality," in *Lectures on Preaching* (New York: E. P. Dutton, 1877), p. 5. The fuller statement is, "Preaching is the communication of truth by man to men. It has two essential elements, truth and personality. . . . Preaching is the bringing of truth through personality."

Theology at Fuller Theological Seminary (and, at that time, professor emeritus), sent me an email. In it he expressed his sadness that I would be leaving the Los Angeles area, but wanted to bless me in the new call. He told me of a book he had read and reread over the past years, which he was encouraging me now to read and reread (which I have subsequently been doing). The book is *Princes of the Church* by W. Robertson Nicoll. It is a collection of eulogies Nicoll wrote on the occasion of the passing of significant preachers of his day, who were, for the most part, also his friends. In his letter to me, Dr. Meye quoted what Nicoll wrote about Charles Edwards, principal of University College at Aberystwyth, England and author of a classic commentary on 1 Corinthians:

> Principal Edwards was thoroughly convinced that preaching came before everything else, and he believed that preaching would never have its due unless it dealt with the profoundest mysteries of the Christian faith. One memorable sentence he used more than once—"A great preacher is Christ's last resource." He meant that when faith was decaying, when the Church was cooling, the hope was in the sudden appearance of a great preacher. Preaching, he said, would continue in the Church to the ages of ages, for Christ would not leave His people to die.[21]

Dr. Meye then wrote: "Darrell, I think that is your particular challenge, to make this truth known in and to the church." It is in that spirit that I offer this book.

I surrendered to the call to preach late in the evening of April 4, 1968, the day Martin Luther King Jr. was assassinated. All evening long, radio stations were playing Dr. King's sermons. I can still hear his thunderous voice declaring, "I have been to the mountain—I have seen the Promised Land—I am not afraid to die"; "I have a dream."[22] Around midnight, I rolled out of bed, got down on my knees, and said, "Lord, that is what I want to do with my life—preach your Word

---

[21]W. Robertson Nicoll, *Princes of the Church* (London: Hodder and Stoughton, 1921), pp. 128-29. Principal Edwards's bold assertion is historical fact; see Yngve Brilioth, *A Brief History of Preaching*, trans. Karl E. Mattson (Philadelphia: Fortress, 1965), pp. 161-70.

[22]See the collection of his sermons in *Strength to Love* (Philadelphia: Fortress, 1963). Two outstanding books help us learn from Dr. King: Mervyn A. Warren, *King Came Preaching* (Downers Grove, Ill.: InterVarsity Press, 2001); Richard Lischer, *The Preacher King: Martin Luther King, Jr. and the Word That Moved America* (Oxford: Oxford University Press, 1997).

in such a way that not only individuals, but nations, are changed." In the morning I called my grandmother Alina Johnson (1900–1987) to tell her what I had done. She began to cry. And then she told me that when I was a small boy, about three years old, I stayed with her for a few weeks. On a Sunday afternoon, she had scooped me up on her lap to listen with her to *The Old Fashioned Revival Hour* with Charles E. Fuller.[23] After the message, she led me in the prayer of response. According to my grandmother, I then climbed up on top of the radiator by the front window, and announced, "When I grow up I am going to preach Jesus!" She told me that from that day on she prayed that my words would come true. That April morning in 1968 she was crying because her prayer had been answered. It is to her memory that I gratefully dedicate this book.

And I dedicate this book to a man who, more than he knows, set the trajectory for the last forty years of my life. While studying (physics) at the University of California, I began to worship at Solana Beach Presbyterian Church in north San Diego County. The associate pastor at the time was H. Hollis Allen. It was he who called forth in me the gift of preaching. It was he who saw in me that I was gifted to teach and preach the Scriptures and who then gave me my first opportunities to exercise the giftings. He saw in me what I could not see myself. He has believed in me ever since.

Since I am a preacher by calling and by training, you will find me in this book often moving into the preaching mode. I have tried my best to not write like I speak; I have tried to not use one word exclamations, sentence fragments, repetitions and other rhetorical devices geared for oral communication. Where I have not made the shift to literary art form please indulge me; please press on. After all, I spend most of my time helping young graduate-school-educated preachers move from writing for the eye to writing for the ear. (More on this in chapter six.)

I want to thank a number of people who helped me with this book. A retired professor of education, Ken Nixon, and three very fine preachers of different denominational backgrounds, Brian Buhler, Mike Lee

---

[23]For a moving history of that ministry see Daniel P. Fuller, *Give the Winds a Mighty Voice* (Waco, Tex.: Word Books, 1972).

and Dick Wiedenheft, each read the entire manuscript and gave very helpful critique. Mary Romero read every page helping to correct spelling, grammar and syntax errors. Doug Hills, Regent faculty secretary, stepped in many times and helped me find bibliographical data I simply could not obtain on my own. Two anonymous authors of books on preaching, at the request of InterVarsity Press, carefully combed my work and offered insightful criticism and challenge. Emily Varner graciously and creatively helped tone down my propensity for writing for the ear. Gary Deddo, senior editor at InterVarsity Press, guided me along the way, encouraging me with his own questions and suggestions. Of course, any mistakes left in the book are mine.

I am convinced that nothing will ever take the place preaching has in God's work in the world. No matter what changes in communication theory or practice, nothing will ever take the place of a human being, Bible in hand,[24] standing up before other human beings, inviting them into a particular biblical text, and saying again what the living God is saying in and through the text. Preaching may not get the attention other forms of communication or discourse get; so be it. Preaching may be judged just as foolish and weak as the apparently foolish and weak message of the apparently foolish and weak Savior and Lord; so be it, or "not to worry," as the Canadians say. For this message turns out to be the wisdom and power of the living God (1 Cor 1:18-25); and the preaching of this message turns out to be the wise and powerful way the Creator and Redeemer changes his world.

A Chinese pastor has said, "Dare to preach . . . and watch what happens."

Something always happens.

---

[24]May I encourage you to read the text from a Bible and not off a piece of paper or off a screen; we are "people of the book" and need to model this fact.

PART ONE

Theoretical Foundations for Participating

1

WHY DOES IT HAPPEN?

A Vision: Ezekiel 37

"PREACHING WORKS BEFORE IT IS UNDERSTOOD," writes Richard Lischer of Duke University Divinity School.[1] I agree. Like all communication between persons, preaching works before it is fully understood. Yes, the better it is understood, the better it works, as any married couple that has worked at communication can testify. Yet in the mystery of things, preaching works long before we fully understand what the preacher, the hearers, the text and the Holy Spirit are doing.

THE VISION

In this first chapter, I invite you to give careful attention to a text of Scripture that helps us understand why what happens in preaching happens. It is the commonly called "Vision of the Valley of Dry Bones" given to and recorded by the prophet Ezekiel (592-570 B.C.) in the thirty-seventh chapter of his magnificent work. The longer I preach, the more I find that I throw myself on this text. What is revealed in and through Ezekiel 37 gives me courage to stand up in front of other human beings, read a text of Scripture, say again what the living God is saying in it and expect something to happen in the lives of those who hear.

Before I work with Ezekiel 37, please read it carefully, taking note of what leaps out at you and what questions you would like to ask Ezekiel.

---

[1]Richard Lischer, *A Theology of Preaching: The Dynamics of the Gospel* (Nashville: Abingdon, 1986), p. 66.

The hand of the Lord was upon me, and He brought me out by the Spirit of the Lord and set me down in the middle of the valley; and it was full of bones. He caused me to pass among them round about, and behold, there were very many on the surface of the valley; and lo, they were very dry. He said to me, "Son of man, can these bones live?" And I answered, "O Lord God, You know." Again He said to me, "Prophesy over these bones and say to them, 'O dry bones, hear the word of the Lord.' Thus says the Lord God to these bones, 'Behold, I will cause breath to enter you that you may come to life. I will put sinews on you, make flesh grow back on you, cover you with skin and put breath in you that you may come alive; and you will know that I am the Lord.'"

So I prophesied as I was commanded; and as I prophesied, there was noise, and behold, a rattling; and the bones came together, bone to its bone. And I looked, and behold, sinews were on them, and flesh grew and skin covered them; but there was no breath in them. Then He said to me, "Prophesy to the breath, prophesy, son of man, and say to the breath, 'Thus says the Lord God, "Come from the four winds, O breath, and breathe on these slain, that they come to life."'"

So I prophesied as He commanded me, and the breath came into them, and they came to life and stood on their feet, an exceedingly great army. Then He said to me, "Son of man, these bones are the whole house of Israel; behold, they say, 'Our bones are dried up and our hope has perished. We are completely cut off.' Therefore prophesy and say to them, 'Thus says the Lord God, "Behold, I will open your graves and cause you to come up out of your graves, My people; and I will bring you into the land of Israel. Then you will know that I am the Lord, when I have opened your graves and caused you to come up out of your graves, My people. I will put My Spirit within you and you will come to life, and I will place you on your own land. Then you will know that I, the Lord, have spoken and done it," declares the Lord." (Ezek 37:1-14) [2]

---

[2] I will in this book be using the New American Standard translation. Although it is for many people too "wooden," I find it the most helpful translation for sermon preparation, for it tries to covey the actual grammatical constructions of the original Hebrew and Greek texts. When I cannot understand the Hebrew or Greek, I turn to the nasb for help. I also work with the niv, tniv, esv, rsv and nrsv. I find the nrsv to be the most useful for the public reading of the text.

This text ignited hope, even in the face of utter hopelessness. For the God of this text need only speak and something happens.

Recall the hopelessness of what Ezekiel faced. It is not unlike what many of us preachers face every time we stand up to speak in our time. It was the sixth century before the birth of Jesus, before the Word became flesh and dwelt among us (Jn 1:14). Israel had been taken captive by the superpower Babylon. Jerusalem, "the city of the great King" (Ps 48:2), lay in ruins. The Solomonic temple, the center of worship of the God above all gods, was a heap of stones. The economic, social and moral infrastructure was not only in danger of collapsing; it was gone. The nation expresses its assessment of the predicament this way: "Our bones are dried up and our hope has perished. We are completely cut off" (Ezek 37:11).

Have you ever felt that way? Have you ever felt that hope has perished? I have. And I do, regularly. It is one of the most suffocating of human experiences.

While facing that hopeless situation, God brings Ezekiel, by the Holy Spirit, into the middle of a valley. Whether such a valley actually existed or was in the mind's eye of the prophet does not matter for the purposes God intends.[3] God portrays Israel's predicament using a picture of the decaying bones of a defeated army. God heightens (or should I say, deepens) the sense of hopelessness by speaking of graves. See the graves, Ezekiel? Israel was decaying, defeated, dried up. Israel was dead.

Have you ever felt that way? Have you ever stood up before a group of human beings who felt that way? Nearly every time we preach, wouldn't you say?

As Ezekiel surveys the valley and realizes it portrays him and his people, God addresses the prophet as "son of man," which in this context simply means "mortal." "Mortal, can these bones live?" (Ezek 37:3). What do you think? Can dead bones live?

Ezekiel responds, "O Lord God [literally, 'O Lord Yahweh'], You know" (Ezek 37:3), meaning, "You alone know the answer to Your

---

[3]Douglas Stuart suggests we are dealing with "a visionary visit to a visionary place." *Ezekiel: Mastering the Old Testament* (Dallas: Word, 1988), p. 343.

question." As far as Ezekiel is concerned, the situation—when considered only from the human standpoint—is utterly hopeless. There is no way he or any other Israelite, or the whole nation combined, could possibly bring those dry bones to life. Left to their own resources, they would remain dry and dead.

Is this not the nature of the human predicament? And is this not what preachers face every time we stand up before a group of other human beings? If it is all up to me to live a consistently whole and healthy spiritual life, then the dry bones of my dry soul will not live. If it is all up to preachers like you and me to keep a local congregation alive in community and ministry, then we may as well close the doors right now. If it is all up to you, me and all the other preachers alive today to bring about a moral revolution breaking the chains that bind us, then our world is doomed.

"Mortal, can these bones live?" Not by themselves. Not on their own. Left to themselves they will remain dry and dead.

"But You, O Yahweh . . . You know if they can live."

So the living God commands Ezekiel to prophesy. In this context I take the word to mean "Speak forth the word of God." Preach, Ezekiel. Yes, preaching means more than prophesying, and not all preaching is prophesying (as we will see in chapter four, which concerns the verbs of participating). For now let us assume some inherent correlation between what Ezekiel is commanded to do and what we in our time and place are commanded to do. Preach, Ezekiel, preach to the bones.

I can imagine Ezekiel saying, "But what good will that do? What possible impact can the word of God have on a national crisis? What possible effect can preaching have on dry bones? On your city and nation, on my city and nation? We are talking about a crisis of major proportions, Lord. We need more than preaching. What good can preaching do in the face of such overwhelming disintegration and decay and death?"

Yet Ezekiel obeys the strange command. Ezekiel speaks to the dry bones. He speaks to bones! "O dry bones, hear the word of the LORD!" I wonder if Ezekiel felt silly. Do you ever feel silly speaking words of life to "dead" people? I do, regularly. Yet Ezekiel does it. "Thus says the Lord GOD to these bones, 'Behold, I will cause breath to enter you that you may come to life'" (Ezek 37:5).

Next the text tells us to look what happened when Ezekiel did it, when he spoke the word of the living God. "And behold" (Ezek 37:8). It is the imperative form of the verb *to see*. That is, it is a command. Ezekiel is startled by what happened, and exhorts us to join him in his astonishment. "Look! Look! There was a noise, and look! A rattling sound, and bones came together, bone to bone. And I looked, and look! Tendons and flesh appeared on them and skin covered them" (Ezek 37:7-8 NASB modified).

Why did prophesying have that effect? Why did preaching have that effect? Was it because of something unique about Ezekiel, because of some great rhetorical and oratorical skill? No. Was it because of the responsiveness of the dry bones? Linger with the question—it is critical for preaching in our time. Did preaching have that life-giving effect because of the responsive condition of the bones? No. The bones could not respond. They had decayed. They were dead. Please mark that. The bones were dead. How could they possibly hear, let alone respond?

Then why did speaking the word have that effect? It was because of the nature of the word. The word of the Lord is living and active, powerful and creative. The word of God not only informs, it performs, it transforms. The word of God makes things happen.

This is the insight of the Roman centurion in a story Matthew tells. The text is Matthew 8:5-13, another text that encourages preachers. The centurion had gone to Jesus on behalf of a servant. He says to Jesus, surprisingly, "Just say the word, and my servant will be healed" (Mt 8:8). Who told him that? How did he know that? "Just say the word!" And Jesus says, "I have not found such great faith with anyone in Israel" (Mt 8:10).

The centurion reasons from his own experience. As a soldier he is under authority and exercises authority over others. He simply says to one of his soldiers, "Go," and he does. He says to another, "Come," and he comes. He says to a servant, "Do this," and he does. The centurion recognizes that the compassionate teacher need only say, "Be healed," and it would happen. The centurion recognizes that just as he has authority over a hundred troops, so Jesus has authority over life and death. John Calvin paraphrases the centurion's insight this way: "I have soldiers under me, as You have spiritual powers, healing angels, disease and death under you."[4] The centurion gives orders, and they are instantly obeyed. He somehow grasps that Jesus can give orders affecting the welfare of human beings which are obeyed whether he is present or not.[5]

"Just say the word." How did the centurion know this? How did he know that Jesus of Nazareth has that kind of authority? He came and threw himself on that authority, and Jesus responded, "I have never seen such great faith." And the man was not disappointed. Jesus spoke, and the servant was made whole. It is crucial to observe that the servant was nowhere near the place where Jesus and the centurion were talking. A person he does not see who spoke a word he does not hear makes the servant whole. Such is the performative power of Jesus' word.

"Just say the word." We preachers need to say that to ourselves and to one another regularly. For, as I see it, one of the greatest needs of the preaching ministry, in any era in any cultural setting, is the continual recovery of confidence in the word of Jesus Christ. Jesus need only speak and something happens. We know the power of our words. One word can change the atmosphere in a room; one word can create a whole new perspective. If our words have such power, think of the word of the Word made flesh. I know I am repeating, but I think I must: Jesus' word not only informs, it performs; his word not only announces, it accomplishes what it announces. "Be clean," and the leper is clean. "Be still," and the sea is calm. "Be gone," and the demons flee. "Lazarus, come forth," and a dead man walks out of the tomb. I believe the authors of the Gospels want us to hear in Jesus' word the echo of the original creative word, the echo of that moment, when into the darkness and chaos of nothingness there came, "Let there be light." And

---

[4]John Calvin, *A Harmony of the Gospels, Matthew, Mark and Luke*, Calvin's New Testament Commentaries, ed. David W. Torrance and Thomas F. Torrance, trans. A. W. Morrison (Grand Rapids: Eerdmans, 1972), 1:248. "Unless we allow such authority to the Word, for us to be certain that, once God has spoken by His ministers, our sins are forgiven us, and that we are restored to life, then all confidence in our salvation collapses" (p. 250).

[5]R .G. V. Tasker, *The Gospel According to Matthew: An Introduction and Commentary* (Grand Rapids: Eerdmans, 1976), p. 88.

there was. Jesus' word is the word of the Creator come into all the mess, the word that accomplishes what it announces.

Which is why we can put our weight on his promises. What he speaks will come into being. Remember the first word to Simon the fisherman? "You are Simon . . . you shall be called Cephas," *Rock* (Jn 1:42). And it happened. Remember Jesus' word to the early church? "You will receive power when the Holy Spirit has come upon you; and you shall be My witnesses" in all the world (Acts 1:8). And it happened. What Jesus speaks comes into being.

This is also how we are to understand his commandments. For example, most of us read the Ten Commandments (Ex 20; Deut 5) this way: "I am Yahweh your God, who took you out of the house of slavery. Now get on with it and have no other gods before me, keep the Sabbath, do not murder, do not covet." That is, we take the weight of fulfillment of the commandment upon ourselves. We do so because we fail to grasp the performative nature of God's word. But this, I think, is the way we are to read the commandments: "I am Yahweh your God, who brought you out of the house of slavery. You shall (not just will)[6] have no other gods before me. You shall (not just will) keep the Sabbath. You shall not murder. You shall not covet." The word empowers the obedience it commands. "You shall be holy, for I Yahweh your God am holy" (Lev 19:2 NASB modified). Most of us read it this way: "I am holy; therefore, get with it and make yourselves like me." That is not the way to read it. God's word brings into being what it commands. "You shall be holy . . . just like me." "You are to be perfect, as your heavenly Father is perfect" (Mt 5:48). Most of us read it like this: "Here is the task of discipleship—work at becoming like the Father." That is not the way to read it. God's word brings into being what it commands. "You shall be perfect." What he speaks will one day be.

Always? That is the question for preaching, is it not?

When the Word is heard, something happens. That is, when the Word is understood and received and surrendered to, something happens.

---

[6]"Shall" conveys the note of determination, inevitability; "will" the note of desire and command.

But I ask, only when heard? Does his word perform only when it is heard? Did the centurion's servant hear the word Jesus spoke?

Go back to the valley in Ezekiel's vision. "Prophesy to the bones," says God. "Speak to the bones." Speak to dry bones, to dead bones. And when he did what he was commanded to do, the bones came to life. Is this because they heard? Is that why they came to life? Linger with the question—it is crucial to ask and answer. Did the bones come to life because the bones heard? No. The bones had no life in them. They represent the Israelites who are spiritually dead, spiritually unresponsive. Then why did they come to life? It was because of the performative power of the word.

Turn in your mind to Genesis 1. There we hear the litany: "God said . . . God said . . . God said." Ten times, "God said." God creates by speech. Now, have you ever wondered to whom God was speaking? Speech is usually directed to someone. Right? To whom was God speaking in the beginning? It was to no one, to nothing. And that is the point. As Don McCullough put it: "So powerful is the word of God that nothing had to hear to be something."[7] The word of God creates what it announces.

It is happening this very moment. Do you realize that? Do you realize that you and I, along with the whole universe, are being held together, sustained, by the word of Jesus Christ? That is the claim of the author of Hebrews: "The Son is the radiance of God's glory and the exact representation of his being, sustaining all things by his powerful word," or, "upholding all things by the word of his power" (Heb 1:3 NIV). We are not, in the final analysis, being held together by some impersonal natural law. A person and his performative speech are holding us together. There is a sense in which natural law merely articulates the normal speech pattern of Jesus Christ the upholder. Were he to stop speaking, everything would crumble into chaos, into nothingness. As G. K. Chesterton suggested, each new day is not just the product of an inexorable mechanical process; rather, each new day is also the result

---

[7]In a sermon on John 1:1-18 which I heard him preach at Solona Beach Presbyterian Church, Advent 1987.

of God saying, "Do it again!"[8] To the sun, "Do it again!" To the moon, "Do it again!" To my heart, "Beat again!" To your lungs, "Breathe again!" Which is why "thank you" is the most appropriate response for human beings to speak at the beginning, middle and end of the day.

Something always happens when God speaks.

Ask Matthew. One day he was sitting in his tax office. Jesus of Nazareth walks up to him, looks at Matthew and says, "Follow Me" (Mt 9:9). And Matthew gets up and follows. He has to—the word Jesus speaks brings into being what he speaks.

Ask Andrew and his brother Simon Peter. They were mending their fishing nets by the Sea of Galilee. Jesus walks up to them and says, "Follow Me" (Mt 4:19). And they do. They have to. The word Jesus speaks brings into being what he speaks.

Ask Zaccheus. Jesus came to Jericho. As he enters the city, he sees the rich man sitting up in a tree. Jesus looks at him and says, "Zaccheus, hurry and come down" (Lk 19:5). And he does. He has to. The word Jesus speaks brings into being what he speaks.

Ask Lazarus. He had died. His body had been in the tomb for four days. Jesus stands in front of the tomb and cries out with a loud voice, "Lazarus, come forth" (Jn 11:43). And the previously dead man does. Lazarus has to come forth. The word Jesus speaks brings into being what he speaks.

What of the times when nothing seems to happen? I will wrestle with this more in the next chapter as we work through Jesus' parable of the sower, which addresses this very question.

But for now, let us take our stand here: the word of the living God is a performative word. It is the ground for confidence in preaching. Thus says the Lord:

> As the rain and the snow
>   come down from heaven,
> and do not return to it
>   without watering the earth
> and making it bud and flourish,

---

[8]G. K. Chesterton, *Orthodoxy* (New York: Dodd, Mead & Co., 1908), p. 52.

so that it yields seed for the sower and bread for the eater,
so is my word that goes out from my mouth:
    It will not return to me empty,
but will accomplish what I desire
    and achieve the purpose for which I sent it.
(Is 55:10-11 NIV)

For I Yahweh will speak,
and whatever word I speak will be performed.
(Ezek 12:25 NASB modified)

And the bones came together, bone to bone, and skin covered them.

But something is missing. More needs to happen. Ezekiel notices that although the assembled bones look like human beings, they are not yet breathing. They are like Pinocchio, the puppet who looked like a little boy but was not yet the real boy who could personally and intimately relate to Gepetto, Pinocchio's creator.

So, God commands Ezekiel to prophesy again, to speak God's performative word again. But this time he is to speak to the breath, to the wind, to the spirit. Prophesy to the *ruach*.

What does God mean? Does the noun refer to human spirit, to the breath of those who had died? Is God commanding the human breath to return and enter once again into the revived humanoids? Or does the noun refer to the divine Spirit, to the Spirit of God, whom God told Ezekiel he would put "within you and cause you to walk in My statutes" (Ezek 36:27)? I think the latter is the case. "Prophesy to the Spirit of God." "Speak to the Holy Spirit."

If it initially seems silly to speak to the bones, it seems audacious to speak to the divine breath. A mere mortal, prophesying to God's breath? Talk about the glory of preaching!

Once again the prophet does what he is commanded to do. Ezekiel obeys. Ezekiel speaks. Ezekiel preaches—to the Spirit. "Thus says the Lord GOD, 'Come from the four winds, O breath, and breathe into these slain, that they may come to life'" (Ezek 37:9). Ezekiel does it. He speaks, strange and audacious as it may seem.

Look what happens this time. "And the breath came into them, and they came to life and stood on their feet, an exceedingly great army" (Ezek 37:10). Not just revived individuals, as wonderful as that is, but a new community, so bound together they constituted a great army, ready to be deployed by the living God for his purposes among the nations.

O breath of God, breathe on us in our time.

I trust you feel encouraged by this brief engagement of this text. You probably have a host of questions, some of which I will respond to in the following chapters. Nonetheless I trust you are encouraged by this vision. The word of the living God brings into being what he declares. Not because of anything in the hearers. I want to stress this as firmly as I can. The decaying, dying bones come to life not because of anything in them. They come to life because of the inherent performative power of God's word and the breathing forth of the Spirit.

Word and Spirit. They are always together. A word cannot be separated from the breath that carries it. "By the word of the LORD the heavens were made, / And by the breath of His mouth all their host" (Ps 33:6).

When we preach, when we dare to say again what the living God says, the Word and Spirit make something happen. The going forth of the Word and the breathing by the Spirit are God coming to make something happen, to make salvation happen. As the Dutch pastor and theologian Jacob Firet put it, "The word of God is not just a vibration in the air: it breaks into a situation and creates a new one."[9] Bone came to bone, breath came into them, and they came to life.

There are many factors at work in the preaching moment, and we need to take all of them into consideration. There is no doubt that the degree to which the preacher has been and is being affected by the text plays a role in the effectiveness of the sermon. There is no doubt that the degree of the preacher's faithfulness to the text plays a role in the effectiveness of the sermon. I realize that the more people are open to the Word and Spirit, the more impact the sermon can have. Certainly

---

[9]Jacob Firet, *Dynamics in Pastoring* (Grand Rapids: Eerdmans, 1986), p. 33. This is a classic, must-read text for any preacher-pastor who wants to think theologically about the privilege of the calling.

the relationship between preacher and hearers affects what is happening during a sermon. Attention to technique also helps. Cultural dynamics surely affect the moment, either serving as a bridge to the text or as a barrier to the text. Sin and evil are clearly at work every time we preach. But the two most fundamental, essential, overriding, undergirding factors are the inherent power of God's Word and the work of God's Spirit. God's Word gives life to those who cannot hear, who are not open, who are blinded by culture and sin and evil. For God's Word brings into being what he speaks.

That is the glory of preaching. And it is the reason why we can even use the word *miracle* of the preaching event.

So I repeat the convictions I laid out in the prologue.

- When the living God speaks, something happens. Always.

- When the preacher speaks God's Word, the living God speaks. Always.

- When the preacher speaks God's Word, something happens. Always?

Gerhard Ebeling gave a series of lectures on the life and work of Martin Luther (later collected in his book simply titled *Luther*). Ebeling asked the question, "Why did Luther's Reformation, in contrast to all prior attempts at reformation, become a reformation in deed and not just in words?" How would you answer the question? Ebeling answered it this way: "Luther's Reformation became a reformation in deed and not just in words because Luther trusted only in the Word and not at all in deeds."[10]

The great Preacher puts it even more boldly: "Truly, truly, I say to you, an hour is coming and now is, when the dead will hear the voice of the Son of God, and those who hear will live" (Jn 5:25).

What's that rattling sound I hear?

---

[10]Quoted by F. Dale Bruner, *The Christbook* (Waco, Tex.: Word, 1984), p. 135.

2

DOES IT REALLY ALWAYS HAPPEN?

A Parable: Matthew 13

IN THIS CHAPTER I WANT TO WRESTLE with the question raised by the last. What about all those times when preaching does not seem to have any effect? Did the Word and Spirit not work in those cases?

The question takes us into the mystery of the preaching event, a mystery in which preachers have no choice but to stand.[1]

Yet we have to ask the "always" question. For it does not appear that something always happens when God speaks. Indeed, it often seems that for many people, nothing happens.

In a chapter titled "Preaching as the Word of God," Richard Lischer helps with this question. He shares a number of stories about people's lives being turned around through preaching. He then writes, "Having seen the Word in action, we now return to a theological rationale for its truth and power. In doing so I shall try to avoid the usual hyperbole that attends to Word-of-God talk (here I am thinking of Barth and Barthians)[2] in which the Word takes on such mystical and objective properties that it fails to keep touch with reality, especially mundane realities of inept preachers and recalcitrant listeners."[3] We know those realities all too well.

---

[1]I will develop this in chapter ten, "Standing in the Mystery."

[2]For a thorough understanding of Karl Barth's doctrine of the Word and the implications for preaching see William H. Willimon's *Conversations with Barth on Preaching* (Nashville: Abingdon, 2006).

[3]Richard Lischer, *A Theology of Preaching: The Dynamics of the Gospel* (Nashville: Abingdon, 1986), p. 66.

The best way I know to wrestle with the "always" question is to turn to another biblical text that does, as Lischer puts it, keep touch with reality. Along with Ezekiel 37, the more I preach the more I find myself turning to this text for perspective and hope.

The text is Matthew 13:1-23, where Jesus, the great Preacher, speaks of his own preaching using the word *mystery*. "To you has been granted to know the mysteries of the kingdom of heaven" (Mt 13:11). In this text Matthew the tax-collector-turned-evangelist gathers a number of Jesus' parables on "the kingdom of heaven."[4] As we read the record of Jesus' preaching, we cannot miss the fact that his preaching is all about the kingdom: the inbreaking of the kingdom, the nature of the kingdom, the God of the kingdom and the mystery of the kingdom.[5] In Matthew 13, Jesus opens up the mysteries.

First, let us step back and look at the Gospel of Matthew as a whole. Matthew, using accounting skills he learned as a tax collector, gathered five sets of Jesus' teaching and preaching. Five times in his Gospel we find the phrase, or some variation, "when Jesus had finished these words" (Mt 7:28; 11:1; 13:53; 19:1; 26:1—the last time with the addition "all these words," signaling that with the fifth section Jesus has finished his teaching/preaching ministry). Each time the phrase refers back to a body of teaching/preaching material. One could think of these five sections as five books, like the five books of Moses. Matthew portrays Jesus as the new and greater Moses. One could also think of these five sections as five sermons,[6] Jesus' preaching compiled so that the church could preach his message. The five can be titled:

The Sermon on the Mount I—Matthew 5–7
    What happens when the kingdom breaks into our lives
The Sermon on Mission—Matthew 10
    Disciples in the world

---

[4]Or as Dallas Willard rightly argues we should render it, "the kingdom of the heavens." *The Divine Conspiracy* (San Francisco: HarperSanFrancisco, 1998), pp. 14-33.
[5]For preaching Jesus' gospel of the kingdom, the most helpful resources I have found include: Mortimer Arias, *Announcing the Reign of God* (Philadelphia: Fortress, 1984); George Ladd, *New Testament Theology*, ed. Donald A. Hagner, rev. ed. (Grand Rapids: Eerdmans, 1974); Howard Snyder, *Models of the Kingdom* (Eugene, Ore.: Wipf & Stock, 2001).
[6]See F. Dale Bruner, *The Christbook* (Waco, Tex.: Word, 1984).

The Sermon on the Mystery—Matthew 13
  Understanding how the kingdom works
The Sermon on Management—Matthew 18
  Disciples in community
The Sermon on the Mount II—Matthew 24–25
  How to live awaiting the full inbreaking of the kingdom

(You can see that Matthew laid out for us a very full preaching program; we would do well simply to start in with the first sermon and preach our way through Jesus' preaching.)

Seven parables are gathered together in Matthew 13, each opening up and developing "the mysteries of the kingdom."

The Parable of the Sower (Mt 13:3-9)
  Jesus' own interpretation (Mt 13:19-23)
The Parable of the Two Sowings (Mt 13:24-30)
  Jesus' own interpretation (Mt 13:36-43)
The Parable of the Mustard Seed (Mt 13:31-32)
The Parable of the Leaven (Mt 13:33)
The Parable of the Hidden Treasure (Mt 13:44)
The Parable of the Pearl of Great Price (Mt 13:45-46)
The Parable of the Dragnet (Mt 13:47-50)

Now, whenever we study or preach any of Jesus' parables we need to do so in and from the context in which he first spoke them. That context, of course, involves the life of the first century and in particular life in first century Palestine: the Roman dominance of the world, the tensions within Judaism between Pharisees and Sadducees, the differences between life in the cities and life in the agricultural villages, the struggle to put food on the table, and all the dynamics of sin and evil with which we also live in our time.

But two contextual facts are crucial for understanding what Jesus is teaching us preachers in Matthew 13. Jesus' own gospel preaching frames Matthew 13, and a second context arises from his preaching's apparent ineffectiveness. This is why I as a preacher keep coming back to this chapter.

JESUS PREACHING HIS GOSPEL

What is Jesus' gospel? What is the gospel he himself preached?

It was, in most basic form, "The kingdom has come near." "From that time Jesus began to preach and say, 'Repent, for the kingdom of heaven is at hand'" (Mt 4:17). Matthew clearly states what he thinks Jesus means. Just before recording Jesus' first, very short sermon, Matthew quotes from the prophet Isaiah:

> This was to fulfill what was spoken through Isaiah the prophet:
> "THE LAND OF ZEBULUN AND THE LAND OF NAPHTALI,
> BY THE WAY OF THE SEA, BEYOND THE JORDAN, GALILEE OF THE
> GENTILES—
> THE PEOPLE WHO WERE SITTING IN DARKNESS SAW A GREAT LIGHT,
> AND THOSE WHO WERE SITTING IN THE LAND AND SHADOW OF
> DEATH,
> UPON THEM A LIGHT DAWNED." (Mt 4:14-16)

Matthew sees in the coming of Jesus the advent of light in the darkness and life amidst death. Thus for Matthew, when Jesus preaches that "the kingdom has come near," he makes the great declaration that in him and because of him, the reign of light is invading and displacing the reign of darkness, and the reign of life is invading and overcoming the reign of death.

Mark makes all this even clearer. He tells us that after John the Baptist had been put in prison, "Jesus came into Galilee, preaching the gospel of God, and saying, 'The time is fulfilled, and the kingdom of God is at hand; repent and believe in the gospel'" (Mk 1:14-15). The gospel according to Jesus is that the long-awaited time—the time for the living God to radically intervene in history—has arrived. This implies that Jesus moves the world into a new era in history. "The time is fulfilled." Time for what? For the kingdom of God to break into the world. It is time for God's new world order to invade and pervade all the world orders advocated and established by human beings. As David Wenham paraphrases it, Jesus "was saying, in effect, 'The longed-for revolution is now underway.'"[7] What the prophets had hoped for

---

[7]David Wenham, *The Parables of Jesus* (Downers Grove, Ill.: InterVarsity Press, 1989), p. 22.

at the end of time was now breaking into the world in the middle of time. As George Ladd writes, "Jesus came preaching the presence of the future."[8] It is time for the future to spill over into the present; it is time for heaven to invade the earth.

Thus, immediately after recording Jesus' short but explosive announcement of his gospel, both Matthew and Mark record the mighty deeds of Jesus. Jesus heals all kinds of sickness, frees people from demonic oppression and possession, repairs broken bodies. Why? These actions prove that his gospel is true: God's new world order of light and life is breaking in. But Jesus' deeds also provide a picture of his gospel.[9] God's new world order is all about healing, liberating, restoring. As Hans Küng put it, the kingdom of God is "creation healed."[10] Jesus comes into Galilee preaching his good news, and because what he announces comes into being, the kingdom starts happening.

But things do not happen in the way most people expected. This is especially so in the mind of John the Baptist. John is disappointed in Jesus and his preaching. In John's mind, Jesus' preaching is simply not effective enough.

You see, John too announced Jesus' gospel, before Jesus did: "Repent, for the kingdom of heaven is at hand" (Mt 3:2, my translation). John had spent years out in the wilderness, away from all the distracting arrogance and chaos of human kingdoms. Out in the wilderness— where we can gain new perspective—John came to realize that there was something cataclysmic in the air; the coming of his cousin meant the coming of a new day for the world. And John spells out what he expects to see happen. As people flocked to hear him preach, he said, "As for me, I baptize you with water for repentance, but He who is coming after me is mightier than I, and I am not fit to remove His sandals; He will baptize you with the Holy Spirit and fire" (Mt 3:11). Moreover,

---

[8]Ladd, *New Testament Theology*, pp. 101-2.

[9]"For the evangelists and the tradition behind them the miracles are not only signs of the kingdom of God in the sense that the fact of their occurrence is evidence of its presence; they are also signs of it in the sense that they are eloquent symbols of it, picturing it forth." C. E. B. Cranfield, *The Gospel According to St Mark: The Cambridge Greek Testament Commentary* (Cambridge: Cambridge University Press, 1959), pp. 84-85.

[10]Hans Küng, *On Being a Christian* (Garden City, N.J.: Image Books, 1966), p. 214.

John expects Jesus' baptism to involve clear signs, "His winnowing fork is in His hand, and He will thoroughly clear His threshing floor; and He will gather His wheat into the barn, but He will burn up the chaff with unquenchable fire" (Mt 3:12).

John expects a twofold baptism: with the Holy Spirit, bringing life and light, and with fire, purging evil and judging the unrighteous.

When John hears about all that Jesus is saying and doing, as he watches the consequences of Jesus' preaching, he is profoundly dissatisfied. Things are not happening the way he preached. Yes, he hears about the healing works of Jesus; I am sure he even rejoices in them. But they are not happening enough. There are still so many people unhealed. More to the point, John hears nothing about fire. Jesus is not getting rid of the chaff. Indeed, John is in prison ("Is this what it means to be a herald of the Messiah?"), held by the very chaff John expected Jesus to burn up. He hears that Jesus is partying with the chaff; Jesus is reaching out to and healing the chaff!

So John, from prison, sends a delegation to Jesus to ask him, "Are You the Expected One, or shall we look for someone else?" (Mt 11:3). The kingdom is not coming the way John expected. That is the context in which Jesus delivers his parables. Jesus is preaching his gospel, yet his preaching is not bringing about the kinds of things most people expected. The parables of Matthew 13 speak into this situation.

Jesus' parables address our own similar context as well. We preach as faithfully and as much in the power of the Holy Spirit as we know how. But things do not always happen as we hope. David Wenham says it so well: "It is all very well to say that Jesus proclaimed and brought the kingdom of God, the divine revolution. But of what value is such a claim when we look at the world around us, or even at the church? It hardly looks as though Satan is out for the count; it does not feel like the new age of God."[11]

Consider the parables in Matthew 13 in reverse order of Matthew's arrangement. I will briefly suggest implications for preaching from six of them, giving the most attention to the parable of the sower.

---

[11]Wenham, *Parables*, p. 41.

The parable of the dragnet (Mt 13:47-50). Yes, Jesus is saying to John (and to us), "fire" is coming. There is a day of reckoning for the unrighteous. But Jesus is doing something else right now. The day will come. Hang in there.

The parable of the pearl of great price (Mt 13:45-46). Yes, Jesus is saying to John (and to us), the most appropriate response to the preaching of the good news of the kingdom is to give one's all. Not everyone gets it right away. But there is, in the final analysis, no other appropriate response but wholehearted, full-on pursuit of the reign of God.

The parable of the hidden treasure (Mt 13:44). Yes, John, when we hear the good news of the kingdom, we give everything we have to buy in. "For the joy set before Him" (Heb 12:2) is the driving force of kingdom living. Your joy over the announcement of a new era for the universe is right on the mark. Do not let your disappointment rob you of the kingdom joy.

The parable of the two sowings (Mt 13:24-30, 36-43). Yes, John, the "seeds" of God's new world order are being sown all over the place and bearing significant fruit. But there is another sowing going on. Jesus has "an enemy" (Mt 13:28), who hates him and everything Jesus creates and redeems; that enemy is bent on Jesus' destruction. He too is sowing seeds of his world order. The tricky thing, the diabolical thing, is that he sows in the very places Jesus does, so much so that the roots of the enemy's plants get all tangled up with the roots of Jesus' plants. And like darnel and wheat, very different kinds of plants, one cannot tell the difference between them as they begin growing. One has to wait "until the harvest" to discover which plant is which. One has to wait until the end to make any final judgment. Just think of the consequences for the world if someone—some preacher—had judged Saul of Tarsus too soon! John, the fire cannot come until the end.

The parable of the leaven (Mt 13:33). Yes, John, the kingdom is spreading, but in a less obvious way. It is not grabbing the headlines. That is okay. For the kingdom makes its way in the world like leaven does in a lump of dough, invisibly. One cannot see the leaven. It takes time for the leaven to do its invisible work. Things are not only as they seem. You will not always immediately recognize the consequences of preaching the gospel.

The parable of the mustard seed (Mt 13:31-32). Yes, John, the kingdom is growing, in all kinds of people. But it is growing in a slower way than you expected. Often the effect of preaching is so small, so tiny, so seemingly insignificant. Often you can barely recognize it, "smaller than all the seeds." But just watch! The whole movement began so small: twelve men, a handful of women. One of the men became a traitor. One was killed as soon as the movement started to take off. But look now: billions of people have come in; there are branch offices all over the globe. The seed, small as it seems over against all the huge forces at work in the world, is more powerful than you have imagined. Trust in smallness.

The parable of the sower (Mt 13:3-23). Jesus is saying, yes, John, I am spreading the good news of the kingdom all over the place. But things are a bit more complex than you think.

Let us dwell in the parable of the sower, for here Jesus helps John and all other preachers understand what preaching is up against and why something does not always appear to happen when we preach the performative Word.

As you read Jesus' parable and his explanation of it, I trust you see and hear the word *understand.* It is the key verb of the text.

Mt 13:13—"I speak to them in parables; because while seeing they do not see, and while hearing they do not hear, nor do they understand."

Mt 13:14—"You will keep on hearing, but will not understand; . . ."

Mt 13:15—". . . Otherwise they would see with their eyes, / Hear with their ears, / And understand with their heart and return, . . ."

Mt 13:19—"When anyone hears the word of the kingdom and does not understand it, . . ."

Mt 13:23—"This is the [one] who hears the word and understands it."

Grasping what Jesus means by *understand* illuminates Jesus' teaching about the preaching of the Word in this parable (and indeed in all his parables). Mark notes that after Jesus tells the parable of the sower, the disciples ask him to explain it. Isn't that good to know—that the first disciples did not immediately understand Jesus' teaching? Jesus says, "Do you not understand this parable? How will you understand all the parables?" (Mk 4:13).

Understand. *Syniēmi*. Literally, "put together."[12] This does hold the sense of making the connections, mentally comprehending. But more, *understand* conveys the sense of "get in line with" or "yield to." The apostle Paul uses the word in this latter sense in Ephesians 5:17, "So then do not be foolish, but understand what the will of the Lord is." *Understand* means "comprehend," but also "yield to," even if you do not yet fully comprehend it intellectually.

Thus, F. Dale Bruner, commenting on Matthew 13, suggests that the most helpful translation of the key verb of the text is "stand under."[13] The way to understand is to stand under, to submit to. See how that insight changes elements of this passage (all are modified NASB):

> Mt 13:15—"OTHERWISE THEY WOULD SEE WITH THEIR EYES, / HEAR WITH THEIR EARS, / AND *STAND UNDER* WITH THEIR HEART AND RETURN, . . ."
>
> Mt 13:19—"When anyone hears the word of the kingdom and does not *stand under* . . ."
>
> Mt 13:23—"This is the [one] who hears the word and *stands under* it."

Consider now the implications of this for preaching, and especially for the "always" question.

There is, at the time Jesus was preaching and in our time, no lack of evidence for the truth of the gospel. Signs of the inbreaking kingdom are all around us. The problem according to Jesus is not enough standing under, not enough standing under the gospel of the kingdom. The problem is that not enough of those who hear Jesus' good news of the inbreaking reign of God actually yield to it.

"Joy to the world, the Lord is come." That is the gospel sung all over the world at Christmastime. The Lord is come, and come to establish his life-giving rule. "Joy to the world, the Lord is come, let earth receive

---

[12]"συνίημι," in *A Greek-English Lexicon of the New Testament and other Christian Literature*, ed. Frederick William Danker, 3rd ed. (Chicago: University of Chicago Press, 2000), p. 972.

[13]F. Dale Bruner, *The Churchbook: Matthew 13-28* (Waco, Tex.: Word, 1990), p. 491.

her king, let every heart prepare him room." There is the problem; not enough of those who hear and sing the song actually receive the king as King. Not enough of those who know the gospel actually make room for the gospelizer to rule. "I speak to them in parables; because while seeing they do not see, and while hearing they do not hear, nor do they stand under" the gospel (Mt 13:13, my paraphrase). They hear and then they go on standing under other lords, other kingdoms, other world orders, other governments.

Jesus the Preacher is saying that the reason we do not see more of the inbreaking of the kingdom lies in the human heart. "Lest they understand with their heart," lest they stand under the good news of the kingdom with their heart.

For the biblical authors, *heart* means more than the organ pumping blood through our bodies right now. *Heart* means the control center of our lives, the place where we take in all the data (whether through our brains, our emotions, our imaginations), sort it all out and make decisions. The problem, says Jesus, is that not enough of those who hear the good news with their ears are allowing the good news to take over the control center. Something—or someone—else runs the control center. The problem is not the gospel; the good news is true news. The problem is not the one who is preaching the gospel; Jesus is not failing as a preacher. If anything could be charged against him, it is that he is sowing too extravagantly. First-century farmers would counsel him to be more discriminating, more strategic: "Jesus, you are sowing seed everywhere!" The problem is neither the seed nor the sower; there is nothing defective about the seed, nothing inadequate about the extravagant way of the sower. The problem is the soil, the hearts of the hearers.

Does this then make the success of preaching dependent upon the hearers? Does this contradict what we see in Ezekiel 37? I hope not, for then there is little hope for the preaching moment, or for us!

Note that in his parable Jesus says all four soils hear the gospel, the good news of the inbreaking kingdom. This is critical to grasp. All four soils hear. All four soils hear that it is time for heaven to invade the earth, time for the future to spill over into the present, time for God's new world order to break in and take over. All four soils hear.

Note further that none of the four ask for further information.[14] That is because the gospel is not all that complicated. "The kingdom of God has come near; it is time for a regime change; you are no longer in charge here." What is so difficult to comprehend about these words? I imagine Matthew asking us, "What about the words 'change in government' do you not understand?" My wife, Sharon, calls out, "Time for dinner." It is a clear word, nothing obtuse or complex. "Time for dinner." Yet no one moves. They hear, but they do not stand under what they hear. "It looks like rain today." No one need consult a dictionary in order to grasp the meaning of the words. Yet we leave the house without an umbrella. We hear, but we don't stand under. The owner's manual says, "Change the oil every three thousand miles or five thousand kilometers." We don't have to be a rocket scientist to get it; the math is straightforward. We hear, but do not stand under. "The time is fulfilled; the kingdom of God has come near; repent, make a U-turn in the road and put your weight on this wonderfully good, good news." We hear, but do not stand under. The obvious implication is that if we do stand under, something will happen.

Notice that this word *understands* brackets the description of the four soils. Soil one "not understand"; soil four "understands." This tells us, I think, that what Jesus says about soils two and three will explain why we do not understand (in both senses). And what Jesus says about soils two and three helps us understand so we can stand under the gospel and it can bear fruit in us. What Jesus says in soils two and three helps us get in line with the inbreaking of the kingdom.

I do not think we are supposed to read the parable and then ask, "So which of the soils am I?" I think all of us have all four soils in us to one degree or another. I think we are to read the parable and ask, "So am I standing under what I am hearing?"

Soil one is the hardened heart, so the seed of the kingdom gets snatched away. Soil two is the shallow heart, so the seed starts to grow. But because of trouble the heart backs off. Soil three is the cluttered heart: the seed starts to grow, but because of worry about and the de-

---

[14]For this perspective on the parable, I wish I could recall who to thank for showing it to me.

ceitfulness of the other kingdoms for which we still want to live, the word gets choked. Soil four is the submissive heart: the seed of the kingdom is received and submitted to, and the heart bears an abundance of kingdom fruit. The hardened heart, the shallow heart and the cluttered heart can only bear fruit if they will simply follow the lead of the submissive heart. Hear and submit, and fruit is borne. Understand that the heart can be hardened, shallow, cluttered. And then choose to stand under the word. The word itself (or himself) softens the heart, deepens the heart and integrates the heart, causing the fruit to come.

Soil one (Mt 13:19). "When anyone hears the word of the kingdom, and does not *stand under* it, the evil one comes and snatches away what has been sown in [the] heart" (NASB modified). Jesus is telling us that there is objective, personal opposition to the kingdom. The universe is not a neutral place. There is a personal power of evil afoot, doing everything in his power to prevent the kingdom from breaking in and transforming the world. Why? Because it means the end of his kingdom! Jesus is warning us: whenever we hear the word of the kingdom, but do not submit to it, we lose; the evil one steals the word away. Does this mean he has power over Jesus' word? "May it never be!" as the apostle Paul would say. Jesus is saying that not submitting to his word gives the evil one room to work. If we hear and stand under the word—even in a little way—the evil one has no access. He cannot take away the word when we stand under it.

Soil two (Mt 13:20-21). "The one on whom seed was sown on the rocky soil, these are the ones who hear the word, and immediately receive it with joy; yet the hearers have no root in themselves, but is only temporary, and when affliction or persecution arises because of the word, immediately they fall away" (NASB modified). Jesus is telling us that when we welcome the inbreaking of the kingdom we are going to find ourselves in trouble. This is good news? We are going to have trouble? Yes, Jesus is saying, in this world, welcoming the kingdom will always result in trouble. Yes, welcoming the kingdom results in blessing, lots of blessing: forgiveness, peace, joy, cleansing, intimacy and eternal life. But welcoming the kingdom also means encountering trouble. How could it be otherwise? "It is time for a change in government." We are talking revolution here. And if the heart will understand this, stand under this, fruit will come.

Jesus speaks of two kinds of trouble: affliction (or tribulation) and persecution. If we understand this, we will not back off when the trouble comes.

Tribulation. The word is *thlipsis*. It is a technical word in the New Testament vocabulary.[15] It means "pressure." More to the point, it means "crushing pressure." The word refers to the kind of pressure experienced when two forces come up against one another and begin to exert their energy to overcome the other. Jesus is telling us that when we get caught up in the inbreaking of God's kingdom—and who would not want to be?—we will find ourselves experiencing pressure, maybe even crushing pressure. *Thlipsis* is the pressure experienced at the interface of colliding kingdoms. As one kingdom comes up against another, the impact creates *thlipsis*. Again, how could it be otherwise? When it happens, nothing has "gone wrong." Paul encouraged the new believers throughout the Roman Empire saying, "Through many tribulations [*thlipsis*] we must enter the kingdom of God" (Acts 14:22). Is this encouragement? Yes, because it tells us the truth. No one experiences the kingdom of heaven without some degree of *thlipsis*. It cannot be otherwise. As the kingdom of God invades a space, tension arises. To walk with Jesus in this world is to walk in that tension.[16]

Persecution. "Because of the word," says Jesus. Not because of you. "Because of the word." For the simple reason that the preaching of the inbreaking kingdom disturbs the status quo. It happened everywhere Jesus went. Not that he tried to be a rabble-rouser; in fact, he shied away from public attention (until Palm Sunday). Instead, as Jesus went around preaching and living his gospel, Jesus' announcement and embodiment of his good news automatically challenged everything not consistent with the kingdom. As Mortimer Arias says, "The coming of

---

[15]Heinrich Schlier, "θλίβω, θλῖψις," in *Theological Dictionary of the New Testament*, ed. Gerhard Kittel and Gerhard Friedrich (Grand Rapids: Eerdmans, 1964-1976), 3:139-48. This is a must-read article.

[16]I expand on this more fully in my book on the Revelation of Jesus Christ, *Discipleship on the Edge: An Expository Journey Through the Book of Revelation* (Vancouver, B.C.: Regent College Publishing, 2004).

the kingdom means a permanent confrontation of worlds. The kingdom is a question mark in the midst of the established ideas and answers developed by peoples and societies."[17] Simply by living his good news, Jesus was experienced as a subversive by the status quo. He was, therefore, persecuted. And he promises the same for all who stand with him. He promises blessings, yes—lots of blessings; but he also promises persecution of one sort or another.

The gospel always, and by necessity, messes with idols,[18] with the things or people we have made into gods, with the things or people upon whom we have placed the trust we can only place on the living God. The gospel thus subverts the way of life built on idols. Thus welcoming and living the kingdom of God almost always brings some sort of persecution. If we understand this, stand under this, we will not back off, but will go on to bear kingdom life.

Soil three (Mt 13:22). Here Jesus explains why it is so hard to act on what we hear the Preacher say. There is something all around us that chokes the word of the kingdom. "And the one on whom seed was sown among the thorns, this is the one who hears the word, and the worry of the world and the deceitfulness of wealth choke the word, and it becomes unfruitful." This is one of the reasons why, for all the preaching that takes place in the Western world at the beginning of the twenty-first century, this world seems so out of touch with the gospel of the kingdom. Many Western Christians hear, but are not standing under. Because all around is "the worry of the world," says Jesus, literally "the worry of the age." And all around is, says Jesus, "the deceitfulness of riches." Note carefully: the problem is not the age, and it is not riches. The problem is "the worry" of the age and the "deceitfulness" of riches.

"The worry of the age." Note the definite article: *the* worry. Jesus seems to have something specific in mind. I think he is saying that the fundamental mark of the age—first and twenty-first—is worry, anxiety. Why? Because the age, having excluded the living God from

---

[17]Arias, *Announcing the Reign of God,* p. 460.
[18]See Bob Goudzwaard, *Idols of Our Time,* trans. Mark Vander Vennen (Downers Grove, Ill.: InterVarsity Press, 1984); just as relevant now as when he wrote it.

its public life, rests on very insecure foundations. Oh, the age does not think of it this way. It thinks its foundations are quite secure: "We are the masters of the ship." Why then, for all the bravado, does the age worry so much? Because the human spirit implicitly knows that the foundations cannot hold.

To be more blunt, when the age does not build upon the living God, the age builds on idols. The choice is either-or: the living God or lifeless idols. Any age built on idols will be marked by profound worry. For the human spirit implicitly knows idols cannot, in the final analysis, hold it all together. If the foundation is shaky, the superstructure cannot but wobble. And the wobble sets up a constant state of anxiety. As Isaiah saw and preached, societies without the living God as the center are terribly anxious, expending huge amounts of energy propping up their inadequate gods. Isaiah speaks of people seeking a craftsman "to prepare an idol that will not totter" (Is 40:20). He speaks of the need to fasten an idol with nails so that it will not totter (Is 41:7). Isaiah speaks of societies "carrying" their gods instead of being carried by the living God (Is 46:1-7).

Through the image of the third soil, Jesus is saying that we may want to follow him with reckless abandon—who would not want to live such a free life? But because we eat and drink and breathe "the age," we too get caught up in the worry of the age, and the gospel gets choked. We too get caught up in the driving questions of the age, "What shall we eat? What shall we drink? What shall we wear?" (see Mt 6:31). And the fruit of the kingdom does not emerge as it ought.

"The deceitfulness of riches," Jesus also says. We do not need any help to understand this. Riches trick us. Riches get us to think that they themselves are the sources of our wholeness. Riches get us to think that they themselves are our security against the uncertainties of the unknown future. And we are slowly dulled away from the things of the kingdom. Moses warned the people of Israel about this:

> When the LORD your God brings you into the land which He swore to your fathers, Abraham, Isaac and Jacob, to give you, great and splendid cities which you did not build, and houses full of all good things which you did not fill, and hewn cisterns which you did not dig, vineyards and

olive trees which you did not plant, and you eat and are satisfied, then watch yourself, that you do not forget the LORD who brought you from the land of Egypt, out of the house of slavery. (Deut 6:10-13)

The very riches God provides can deceive us away from God. They can lull us into thinking that the riches will make us whole and secure.

I will long remember a 1998 television commercial for an SUV. A mother and her son are driving in the vehicle on a country road in the midst of a violent storm. The wind is blowing, rain is pouring down, trees are falling across the road. But inside the SUV everything is perfectly calm. Soothing music from the CD player wafts through the car, around the leather seats. The child in the back seat strokes his dog. The mother calls back, "How's the dog?" And the narrator intones, "A little security in an insecure world." I wanted to shout, "Give me a break!" I have driven on a country road in a violent storm, in the Philippines, during a typhoon. Yes, it was warm inside the van I was driving. But it was hardly secure. The wind threatened to blow the van off the road.

Storms break the illusion created by the deceitfulness of riches. It is instructive to read a range of the sermons preached the Sunday after the horrible events of September 11, 2001, that day America watched the collapse of the World Trade Center towers in New York City. To what were preachers pointing people? What were they calling people to do? It was John Piper, pastor of Bethlehem Baptist Church in Minneapolis, Minnesota, who I think put everything into perspective. Here is how he opened his sermon in that frightening setting:

How shall I strengthen your hope this morning?

Shall I try to strengthen your hope politically, and comfort you that America is durable and will come together in great bipartisan unity and prove that the democratic system is strong and unshakable?

Shall I try to strengthen your hope militarily, and comfort you that American military might is unsurpassed and can turn back any destructive force against the nation?

Shall I try to strengthen your hope financially, and comfort you that when the market opens on Monday there will be stability and long-term growth to preserve the value of your investments?

Shall I try to strengthen your hope geographically, and comfort you that you live in the Upper-Midwest, far from the major political and military and financial targets that enemies might choose?

Shall I try to strengthen your hope psychologically, and send you to the web page titled "Self-Care and Self-Help Following Disasters" so that you can read there that "individuals with strong coping skills . . . maintain a view of self as competent . . . and avoid regretting past decisions"?

Should I try to strengthen your hope *eschatologically* by comforting you that you won't be on the earth anyway when the blazing fireball comes near your town?

The answer to those six questions is very easy for me: NO. I will not try to strengthen your hope in those six ways. And the reason I won't is also very simple: none of them is true.

The American political system is not imperishable.

The American military cannot protect us from every destructive force.

The financial future is not certain and you may lose your investments.

The Midwest is not safe from the next kind of terrorism, which may be more pervasive and more deadly.

The psychological efforts to feel competent and avoid regret are not healing, but fatal.

And eschatological scenarios that promise escape from suffering under God's end-time providence didn't work for the Christians in the World Trade Center last Tuesday, and they won't work for you either.

Piper goes on to then preach Romans 8:35-39, bringing us to our only comfort in life and in death.[19]

In the third soil Jesus warns us—hearers and preachers—of the tremendous influence of "the worry of the age" and "the deceitfulness of riches." The worry and deceitfulness neutralize us. And, says Dale

---

[19]John Piper, "A Service of Sorrow, Self-Humbling, and Steady Hope in Our Savior and King, Jesus Christ," Desiring God Ministries website (September 2001), <www.desiringgod.org/ResourceLibrary/Sermons/ByDate/2001/65_A_Service_of_Sorrow_SelfHumbling_and_Steady_Hope_in_Our_Savior_and_King_Jesus_Christ/>.

Bruner, the "neutralized believer is as much an unbeliever as a complete pagan, even though he stays right in the church."[20] Soil three calls us— hearers and preachers—to understand this and then stand under the word, which alone overcomes the worry and deceit.

So, finally, soil four (Mt 13:23). "And the one on whom seed was sown on the good soil, this is the [one] who hears the word and *stands under* it; who indeed bears fruit and brings forth, some a hundredfold, some sixty, and some thirty" (NASB modified). First-century farmers were not ready for this ending. Thirtyfold would have been wonderful enough; fiftyfold, extravagant; a hundredfold, extravagant beyond imagining. Brad Young calls the ending "a dynamic shock" because "such an abundant harvest would be more like an unattainable dream than common experience for most of the farmers listening to the story."[21]

Notice "who indeed bears fruit." We could render it "who automatically bears fruit." (See the parable in Mk 4:26-29.) For the real shock is not the amount of fruit, but that the word creates the fruit. The fourth soil simply stands under the word and thus becomes living, contagious evidence that a divine revolution is under way.

All four soils hear. All four soils hear Jesus' gospel, "Heaven is invading earth!" Soil one hears, but does not act on what it hears. Soil two hears and acts, but when trouble comes because of the word, backs off. Soil three hears and acts, but is too much caught up in the age and its worries and riches, and the plant dies away. Soil four hears, receives the word and consciously, intentionally stands under it.

Is Jesus telling us that when we preach, only one out of four hearers is going to truly hear? Or does Jesus' parable help us see what needs to happen for the kingdom to be more fully realized in our hearts, thus helping all hearers fully hear?

As I spend time with Matthew 13, I begin to realize that the soils want to hear and bear kingdom fruit; they are calling out to us preachers for some help. Imagine with me each of the soils speaking to us who preach.

---

[20]Bruner, *Churchbook*, p. 493.
[21]Brad H. Young, *The Parables: Jewish Tradition and Christian Interpretation* (Peabody, Mass.: Hendrickson, 1998), p. 258.

The hardened heart calls out, "Tell me to open my heart, if only a crack, and stand under every word Jesus speaks to me, if only for a moment." The shallow heart calls out, "Tell me to embrace the fact that following Jesus will bring me into trouble, and that I am to stand under Jesus when it comes." The cluttered heart calls out to the preacher, "Tell me to realize that the age is built on idols, that idolatry is ubiquitous and so subtle, and that I need to stand under Jesus so he can break the spell of the anxiety rooted in the lie." And the receptive heart calls out to the preacher, "Tell me to simply let Jesus be the kind of king he is, and tell me to simply stand under his word and let his word do what only his word can do."

So the apostle Paul can write to the new believers in Thessalonica, to new believers under great pressure, "We also constantly thank God that when you received the word of God which you heard from us, you accepted it not as the word of [human beings], but for what it really is, the word of God, which also performs its work in you who believe" (1 Thess 2:13). When any one stands under God's word, something happens. Not because of the condition of the person's heart, but because of the life-giving power of the word. The word itself (or, himself) softens hardened hearts, deepens shallow hearts, integrates cluttered hearts and flourishes in receptive hearts.[22]

In Matthew 13, Jesus is saying, "John (the Baptist) and all my other preachers of my gospel: My preaching is not failing. It's just that the human heart is more complex than you and other preachers know. There is so much in the way. But do not despair. The kingdom has come, is coming and will come." "Blessed is the one who keeps from stumbling over Me" (Mt 11:6, my paraphrase). Or, as Peter said to Jesus, after he asked if the twelve were also going to walk away with the crowds who were scandalized by his preaching, "Lord, to whom [else] shall we go?

---

[22]Here I should do an exposition of Isaiah 6:9-10, which Jesus quotes in Matthew 13:14; Mark 4:12; Luke 8:10; John 12:40 and which Paul quotes in Acts 28:26. But I am still working through these texts. Yes, it seems that the preaching of the word can serve to deaden and deafen the heart, suggesting that the listener plays an important, vital role in the word bearing fruit. The texts suggest preaching can play a role in God's judicial hardening of the heart. At this point I encourage preachers to put their weight on the awakening, softening, opening power of the word. We preach and leave it to God to do what he wills with the hearers.

You have words of eternal life" (Jn 6:68), words that are life (Jn 6:63).

In his essay "The Case for Expository Preaching," Earl Palmer, then pastor of First Presbyterian Church, Berkeley, California, wrote what I have heard him say many times since: "If I can just get people to consider the text, the text will do its own convincing."[23] Give the Word a chance—however small a chance—and it will win us (in whatever condition of the heart) into the life it alone can give.

---

[23]Earl Palmer, "The Case for Expository Preaching," *Theology, News and Notes*, December 1985, p. 9.

3

WHERE DOES IT HAPPEN?

A Paradigm for Expository Preaching

"WERE NOT OUR HEARTS BURNING WITHIN US while He was speaking to us on the road, while He was opening the Scriptures to us?" (Lk 24:32). They ask the question after their eyes are "opened" (Lk 24:31). They ask the question after they realize that it was the risen Jesus himself who had been walking with them on the road from Jerusalem to Emmaus, and that it was he himself who had taken them through the Bible, "beginning with Moses and with all the prophets," explaining to them from the Bible the events of Holy Week (Lk 24:27).

Therein lies the glory of preaching. Whenever preachers take a text of the Bible and try to faithfully "open" it, they are participating in the risen Lord's own opening of the text. In the preaching moment, the risen Jesus himself (through the person and ministry of the Holy Spirit) takes a text of Scripture in hand and opens it in such a way that confused and dejected men and women find their hearts "burning within." Jesus is at once the one who is preached and the one who is preaching.

In this chapter I am asking and seeking to answer the question, where does it happen? The miracle of preaching, where does it happen? In what mode does human speaking of human words become the speaking of words that are the word of God? And the answer I want to commend to all who preach is in *expository preaching*. It is the only place

I know where I can stand and have any confidence that what I say is what the living God is saying. It is the only place I know where we mere humans can dare to say or think, "Thus says the Lord."[1]

Yes, there is a role for sermons other than expository ones. So-called topical preaching, for example, does sometimes participate in God's transformation of people's lives. But the communicator runs two risks in preaching topically. On the one hand, topical preaching leaves too much to the preacher's ability to come up with the content of the sermon. And on the other, topical preaching can give an impression about the Bible that is not accurate. The preacher has to rummage through all kinds of different verses and try to make some coherent sense of them; too much is left to the preacher's ability to pull a message together. Such an approach suggests the Bible is a collection of sayings about various topics, a depository of principles to live by, rather than what it is, the story of the living God creating and redeeming a people for himself, for a world truly filled with the knowledge of his glory.

If a preacher senses the need to speak topically (due to some major event in the common life of the people, some major issue facing the whole church, etc.), I would encourage him or her to clearly ground the information about the topic in one major text and try to use other texts only if they are clearly in sync with the major text. That is, one would want to send the listener away not with "This is what the Bible says about this topic," but "Here is a passage, representative of the whole Bible, that says this about this topic." Should a preacher sense the need to do a series of sermons on a topic, it is, in my mind, best to carefully ground each of the separate sermons in one major text. Take, for example, a five part series on "Relationships in the Family of God." One might want to address topics such as forgiveness, blessing, submission, edification and love. Each of the themes should emerge from one major text, e.g., forgiveness from Matthew 18:21-35, or blessing from Luke 6:27-36, rather than simply stringing together lots of verses on forgiving. I urge this safeguard for topical preaching because, from my

---

[1]See James Daane, *Preaching with Confidence* (Grand Rapids: Eerdmans, 1980).

perspective, there is no assurance that the miracle of Ezekiel 37 will take place in any other place than the opening of a particular text of Scripture. Besides, the old adage is so true, "They that go deepest, go widest." Take people deep into one text on forgiveness, and they are more empowered to forgive than if you list, with brief comment, tens of texts on forgiveness.

There are other modes of preaching God has used and is using: narrative preaching, reflection preaching (as I call it—a kind of public *lectio divina*, etc.). I have received such modes and experimented with them myself. Still I argue that the safest, surest place to stand is in expository preaching.

What then is expository preaching?

Before I try to spell out what I mean by the term and what, therefore, I am advocating, consider some of the definitions proposed by some very effective preachers.

John R. W. Stott, in his book on preaching, *Between Two Worlds*, writes,

> Whether it (the text) is long or short, our responsibility as expositors is to open it up in such a way that it *speaks its message clearly*, plainly, accurately, relevantly, without addition, subtraction or falsification. In expository preaching, the biblical text is neither a conventional introduction to a sermon on a largely different theme, nor a convenient peg on which to hang a ragbag of miscellaneous thoughts, but *a master which dictates and controls what is said*.[2]

Note the two italicized phrases; both take us to the heart issue of preaching: Whose message are we speaking? And who is determining what is being said?

Thus, Haddon Robinson, in his widely issued *Biblical Preaching*, goes on to say,

> Expository preaching at its core is *more a philosophy than a method*. Whether or not a man [or woman] can be called an expositor starts with his [or her] purpose and with his [or her] honest answer to the question:

---

[2]John R. W. Stott, *Between Two Worlds: The Art of Preaching in the Twentieth Century* (Grand Rapids: Eerdmans, 1982), p. 26, emphasis added.

> Do you, as a preacher, endeavor to *bend your thoughts to* the Scriptures,
> or do you use the Scripture to support your thought?[3]

Again, note the two italicized phrases. Both get at the fundamental
motives involved in the whole process of crafting and preaching: am I
truly willing to let go of my understanding of God and God's ways in
the world and "bend" to his words?

Therefore, Sidney Greidanus, in his book *The Modern Preacher and
the Ancient Text*, to which I will turn in chapter five of this book, argues
that we come to the central issue when we ask, "By whose authority do
preachers preach? Whose word do they bring?"[4] His answer is worth
printing here in full:

> If preachers preach their own word, the congregation may listen po-
> litely but has every right to disregard the sermon as just another per-
> son's opinion. If contemporary preachers preach with authority, how-
> ever, the congregation can no longer dismiss their sermons as merely
> personal opinions [and I would add, the congregation would not even
> think in those ways] but must respond to them as authoritative mes-
> sages. The only proper authority for preaching is divine authority—
> the authority of God's heralds, his ambassadors, his agents. Heralds
> and ambassadors, we have seen, do not speak their own word but that
> of the sender. Contemporary preachers, similarly, if they wish to speak
> with divine authority, must speak not their own word but that of the
> Sender.[5]

Is this not the case with the Preacher himself, Jesus of Nazareth? "I
only do and say what I see My Father do and hear My Father say" (Jn
5:19-30 my paraphrase). The Word made flesh submits all his speaking to the word of the One who sent him. This suggests to me that the
most basic motive in preaching is not to win the hearer (as crucial as
that is) but to please the Sender. The Sender is the master, and to his
Word we bend all our thinking and speaking. *So help us Lord!* Donald

---

[3]Haddon Robinson, *Biblical Preaching: The Development and Delivery of Expository Messages*
(Grand Rapids: Baker, 1980), p. 20. Italics mine.
[4]Sidney Greidanus, *The Modern Preacher and the Ancient Text: Interpreting and Preaching Biblical
Literature* (Grand Rapids: Eerdmans, 1988), p. 12.
[5]Ibid.

Coggan spoke of "the magnificent tyranny of the Gospel": Christian preachers have "a boundary set" for them; when they enter the pulpit they are not an entirely "free" men or women.[6] Oh, to be so captive.

Bryan Chapell, in his helpful book *Christ-Centered Preaching: Redeeming the Expository Sermon*, gives us a complete definition of what I am after.[7] The italics in the following are his:

> An expository sermon takes its topic, main points and subpoints from the text. In an expository message the preacher makes a commitment to explain what this text means. . . . A sermon is not expository simply because it addresses a subject in the Bible. Neither does quoting numerous Scripture references in a sermon make a preacher an expositor. [That, by the way, is the risk of topical preaching.]
>
> A sermon that explores any biblical concept is in the broadest sense 'expository' but the *technical definition of an expository sermon requires that it expound Scripture by deriving from a specific text main points and subpoints that disclose the thought of the author, cover the scope of the passage, and are applied to the lives of the listeners.*[8]

Note the four verbs in the last sentence: expound, derive, cover and apply. All are governed by the one specific biblical passage at hand.

Consider two more definitions. Earl Palmer, whom I cited at the end of the last chapter, says that expository preaching is "the task of enabling a text to make its own point within the whole witness of the Gospel of Jesus Christ, and to affirm that message with persuasion and urgency in the language of the people of today."[9] This is the heartbeat of Jesus' parables in Matthew 13.

Lesslie Newbigin, in his profound theological commentary on the Gospel of John, written in dialogue with the worldviews of India of the twentieth century and not speaking to preaching as such, rounds out all the definitions: "My task is to make clear to myself and (if possible) to others the word which is spoken in the Gospel in such a way that it

---

[6]Donald Coggan, *Stewards of Grace* (London: Hodder & Stoughton, 1958), pp. 46, 48.
[7]Bryan Chapell, *Christ-Centered Preaching: Redeeming the Expository Sermon* (Grand Rapids: Baker, 1994).
[8]Ibid., p. 128, emphasis in original.
[9]Earl Palmer, "The Case for Expository Preaching," *Theology, News and Notes*, December 1985, p. 11.

may be heard in the language of this culture of which I am a part with all its power to *question* that culture."[10] Note the importance of oneself understanding the word first and the importance of connecting with the culture, but also *questioning* it. I will speak to this more fully in chapter ten.

I want to suggest some nuance for these definitions, hoping to move our understanding of expository preaching forward.

I begin with this presupposition: expository preaching is not about getting a message out of the text; it is about inviting people into the text so that the text can do what only the text can do.

Consider two pictures, the first depicting what most of us preachers have thought we are doing in expository preaching, the second depicting what I think we are doing, or are called to do.

Picture one. The congregation sends the preacher into the text (see figure 3.1). The preacher emerges from the text with a message that is then downloaded onto the congregation (see figure 3.2).

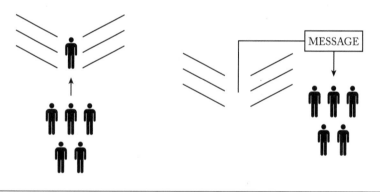

Figure 3.1   Figure 3.2

Picture two. The congregation sends the preacher into the text (see figure 3.3). The preacher, after a season of prayerful study, then invites congregation to join him or her in the text, engaging the text together (see figure 3.4).

---

[10]Lesslie Newbigin, *The Light Has Come: An Exposition of the Fourth Gospel* (Grand Rapids: Eerdmans, 1982), p. ix. Italics mine.

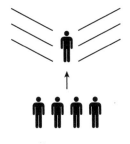
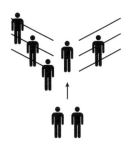

| Figure 3.3 | Figure 3.4 |

As one of my students, Scott Scruggs, put it in an essay for one of my preaching courses, "The text is the location of the close encounter with the Living God and the preacher's task is to walk his or her congregation into that reality."[11] The preacher's role is not that of an expert but that of a guide (as at an art exposition, or as the leader of a expedition), pointing to, calling attention to the essential aspects of the reality about which the text is speaking. As the preacher does this, something happens: the preacher and congregation begin to participate in what the risen Jesus, through the Spirit, is doing in and with the text.

What is God doing? That is the question we need to ask. What is the Lord of the text doing in and with and through the text?

As I read the Book, I conclude that God is doing at least five things with any text. An expository sermon on any text will, in one way or another, be participating in these five works. The five works are: encounter, news, worldview, obedience of faith and enablement. In any text, the Holy Spirit is

engendering an encounter with the Jesus of the text
in which he speaks news, good news
which causes a shift in worldview,
calling for a new step of the obedience of faith
(which he himself enables us to take).

Encounter. In and through every text of Scripture, the Spirit of God

---

[11]Scottt Scruggs, course paper for my course Advanced Preaching: The Christ Event, Regent College, Vancouver, B.C., 2004.

is engendering an encounter with God in Jesus Christ. That is, every text is, at its essence, about Jesus. Jesus himself tells us this throughout his earthly ministry. For example, in his intense interaction with the religious leaders around his audacious Sabbath-day claims ("My Father is working until now, and I Myself am working" [Jn 5:17]), Jesus says, "You search the Scriptures because you think that in them you have eternal life; it is these that testify about Me; and you are unwilling to come to Me so that you may have life" (Jn 5:39-40). Luke records Jesus making the same point on the first Easter Sunday on the road to Emmaus: "Then beginning with Moses and with all the prophets, He [Jesus] explained to them the things concerning Himself in all the Scriptures" (Lk 24:27). Nearly every time I read that passage I wish one of the two disciples walking with Jesus had taken notes that day. Notice that the verse says "in all the Scriptures." Jesus is saying that Scripture is about him. In order that we get the point, Luke records Jesus' own words about this: "These are My words which I spoke to you while I was still with you, that all things which are written about Me in the Law of Moses and the Prophets and the Psalms must be fulfilled" (Lk 24:44). "Then," says Luke, the risen Jesus "opened their minds to understand the Scriptures" (Lk 24:45), to understand that the Scriptures are about him. He is the essential message of the Scriptures.

Do you believe this? It is a crucial conviction for preaching that participates in God's transforming work in the world. The Holy Spirit has "breathed" (2 Tim 3:16 NIV) the text to bring about an encounter with the Jesus of the text.

E. Stanley Jones said about any biblical text, "Everyday I go to these words and say to them: 'Hast thou seen Him whom my soul loves?' And these words take me by the hand and lead me beyond the words to Him who is the Word."[12] I do not think we are ready to preach a text until we have been led through the text (I prefer *through* to *beyond*) to the Lord of the text. We are not yet really ready to participate with the Spirit's preaching of the text until the Spirit has engendered the encounter.

Does this mean then that every sermon is about Jesus? Well, yes. As

---

[12]E. Stanley Jones, *The Word Made Flesh* (Nashville: Abingdon, 1963), p. 7.

James S. Stewart emphasized, "Your task is not to send people away from church saying, 'That was a lovely sermon' or 'What an eloquent speech!' The one question is: 'Did they, or did they not, meet God today?'"[13] By "God" he meant the God we know in Jesus and as Jesus. John Piper puts it even more engagingly: preaching is an "expository exultation over the glories of God" in the Christ of the text, "designed to lure God's people from the fleeting pleasures of sin into the sacrificial path of obedient satisfaction with God."[14]

Does this mean that every sermon is about Jesus even if the text is not explicitly about him? Well, yes. Jesus the Word (Jn 1:1) meets us in every text. The Word, the *Logos*, is the living God's self-expression. "In the beginning was the Self-Expression, and the Self-Expression was with God, and the Self-Expression was God." How can it be otherwise? Only God can express God; only God can reveal God; only God can make God known. All God's making-God-known is the Word. The Word is there any time God is there. Every time God expresses God, the Word is there. The Word is there in every revelatory text. Which means, preachers do not need to "bring Jesus into the text"; they simply need to point to the way in which he is there in the text. "It is these that testify about Me" (Jn 5:39).

So, the first and foremost discipline for preaching is staying in the text until we meet the Lord of the text. Everything hangs on this. The transforming power of any text lies right here, in the encounter. "But we all, with unveiled face, beholding as in a mirror the glory of the Lord, are being transformed into the same image from glory to glory, just as from the Lord, the Spirit" (2 Cor 3:18). The photocopy is made by intense exposure to the original. We are to stay in the text until by exposure to the original, we are ready to speak of the Lord of the text.

By the way, this discipline is what will also enhance any worship acts leading to or flowing from the preaching event. The whole of the service can focus on and relish in the character of the Lord revealed and

---

[13]James S. Stewart, *Heralds of God* (1946; reprint, Vancouver, B.C.: Regent College Publishing, 2001), p. 31.
[14]John Piper, *The Supremacy of God in Preaching* (Grand Rapids: Baker, 1990), p. 39.

lived in the text. Any music, for instance, can sing about who God in Jesus is for us in today's text.

N. T. Wright says it well when he remarks that "preaching is meant to be an occasion when, so to speak, God happens; when that strange and yet familiar moment comes upon us, and we know we have been addressed, healed, confronted and kindled by the one who made us and loves us."[15]

News. In and through any text the risen Jesus, through the Holy Spirit, is announcing news. Good news. Gospel. Sometimes a text does this explicitly, sometimes implicitly. But always the text has news for us. Not simply opinion, not simply advice, not simply perspective, not simply exhortation to live differently. The text announces news.

News about God in Jesus as Jesus. News about what God has done, is doing and will do in Jesus. News about what God has done, is doing and will do that we cannot do. News about what God has done, is doing and will do that we need not do. A sermon, therefore, is faithful to a text if it is grounded in and filled with the news of the text.

Why, for all the "preaching" (the quotation marks are my gentle way of wondering if all preaching is in fact preaching) that goes on in North America at the beginning of the third millennium, is North American culture so un-Christian, even anti-Christian? Why isn't all the "preaching" having a greater effect on the culture? If I may be so bold to propose an answer, it is because too much of the "preaching" is good advice and not good news. Good advice without good news changes no one. Good advice without good news is either stifling legalism or oppressive moralism or powerless self-help. When in the mid-1970s Ian Pitt-Watson moved from Scotland to the United States to teach preaching at Fuller Theological Seminary in Pasadena, California, he spent the first half-year or so visiting as many congregations as possible to get a feel for the preaching of Southern California. He said he could summarize all the preaching he heard in one phrase: "It is good to be good, and nice to be nice." He said he rarely heard news about what God has done, is doing and will do in Jesus.

---

[15]In Donald Coggan, *A New Day for Preaching: The Sacrament of the Word,* rev. ed. (London: SPCK, 1996), p. 2.

People of any era in any part of the world are dying for news of what God does, news that makes a difference in their everyday lives. Every text has such news. Preachers are to stay in the text until captured by the news; any advice will flow from and be undergirded with and empowered by the news.

This is one of the secrets of the apostle Paul's preaching. All his good advice is grounded in good news. Or, to put it a bit differently, all his imperatives are grounded in indicatives: he always precedes any "now do" with "now is." This is seen most artfully and, I think, prototypically, in the letter to the Ephesians. The first half of the letter is almost totally indicative, holding before us the massive work of grace God has done, is doing and will do in Jesus: "Blessed be the God and Father of our Lord Jesus Christ, who has blessed us with every spiritual blessing in the heavenly places in Christ" (Eph 1:3). Chapters 1–3 celebrate the lavish, extravagant, all-encompassing, world-transforming, redeeming, reconciling news of the Trinity. Only then does Paul begin to move toward advice: "Therefore I, the prisoner of the Lord, implore you to walk in a manner worthy of the calling with which you have been called" (Eph 4:1). The series of "therefore(s)" in chapters 4–6 only make sense and actually work in light of what God did, is doing and will do, according to chapters 1–3.

This is why every sermon is a gospel sermon. What else are we going to preach? Every sermon must be full of gospel, or gospel living simply will not happen. Exhortation is grounded in and empowered by the kerygma, the message of the gospel.

As already mentioned, James S. Stewart is considered by most historians of preaching to be the greatest English-speaking preacher of the twentieth century.[16] In his *Heralds of God*, written in 1946, Stewart tells of the experience of one of the greatest preachers of the nineteenth century, Henry Ward Beecher. When Beecher began his ministry he was disappointed in the results: he saw so little of what preaching was suppose to accomplish. Then one day he thought: "There was a reason why, when the apostles preached, they succeeded, and I will find it out

---

[16]Whether he was the greatest "expository preacher" is debatable. See Timothy Warner's review of Stewart's *Walking with God*, forthcoming in *Bibliotheca Sacra*.

if it is to be found out."[17] Stewart calls us to do the same thing, "Search for the secret of the first generation of preachers of the Word."[18] What was their message, which consumed them "like a flame, and through them kindled the world?"[19]

Stewart, following Beecher, first observes what it was not. It was not a theory or an idea; it was not something they had deduced from observation or arrived at by imagination. "It was neither an argument with paganism, not a panegyric on brotherhood; neither ethical exhortation, nor religious education; neither mystical experience, nor spiritual uplift. It was not even a reproduction of the Sermon on the Mount."[20] That last sentence still jolts me as I think of what E. Stanley Jones said in the first third of the twentieth century pertaining to every century: the greatest need of the church is for "a blood transfusion" from the Sermon on the Mount in order to "renew radiant health within it that it may throw off these parasites and arise to serve and save the world."[21] But the preaching of the first preachers, though including the exhortation and edification of Jesus' great Sermon, was so different. In Stewart's words, "It was the announcement of certain concrete facts of history, the heralding of real, objective events."[22] "It was the proclamation of the mighty acts of God."[23] In particular, early Christian preaching declared the mighty acts of Christ dying for our sins and Christ being raised from the dead. And because of those acts the kingdom of God breaks into the world with power.

Listen to Stewart "herald" the news for us himself:

From the realm of the invisible beyond, the once far-off divine event had suddenly projected itself into history. What had formerly been pure eschatology was there before their eyes: the supernatural made visible, the Word made flesh. No longer were they dreaming of the kingdom age: they were living in it. It had arrived. This was the essential cri-

---

[17]Stewart, *Heralds,* p. 62.

[18]Ibid.

[19]Ibid.

[20]Ibid.

[21]E. Stanley Jones, *The Christ of the Mount: A Living Exposition of Jesus' Words as the Only Practical Way of Life* (Nashville: Abingdon, 1931), p. 22.

[22]Stewart, *Heralds,* p. 63.

[23]Ibid.

sis of the hour. . . . It was the stupendous tidings, dwarfing all other facts whatever, that the sovereign Power of the universe had left history asunder, traveling in the greatness of His strength, mighty to save. . . . [It was not] a summary of the ways men [and women] ought to act in an ideal society, but an account of the way in which God has acted in history decisively and for ever. . . . Nothing could be more marrow-less and stultified and futile than the preaching which is for ever exhorting 'Thus and thus you must act,' and neglecting the one thing which essentially makes Christianity: 'Thus has God acted, once and for all.'[24]

Marianne Meye Thompson makes the point best: "First and foremost, the gospel is God's action, God's story, God's saving initiative toward the world which he has created. It bears repeating: *the gospel is God's story. To preach the gospel, then, means sentences in which God is the subject of active verbs.*"[25] We need to stay in the text until we are captured by God's verbs, verbs with God as subject.

Worldview. What God does (and says) in the text changes the way we understand the world. Indeed, what God does (and says) changes the world even if we do not understand what changes.

In and through every biblical text the risen Jesus, through the Holy Spirit, is effecting a shift in worldview, giving us a new set of glasses through which to navigate our way through life. Every author of every text is writing out of a particular frame of reference and is, naturally, engaging the frames of reference of his reading or listening audiences, seeking to bring them into the author's way of understanding God and the world. Every text lives out Paul's desire and charge in Romans: "Do not be conformed to this world [or age], but be transformed by the renewing of your mind" (Rom 12:2); or, as J. B. Phillips rendered it, "Do not let the world around you squeeze you into its own mould, but let God re-mould your minds from within."[26] God does this remolding through Spirit-breathed texts, text after text after text, until we finally live in the world fully centered in Jesus Christ.

---

[24]Ibid., pp. 64-66. Passion for the gospel rises in me every time I read these pages.
[25]Marianne Meye Thompson, "Just Preach the Gospel," *Theology, News and Notes*, Winter 2007, p. 10. Italics hers.
[26]J. B. Phillips, *The New Testament in Modern English* (London: Geoffrey Bles, 1960).

The priest-psychologist John Powell helps us in his book *Fully Human, Fully Alive: A New Life Through a New Vision.*[27] I often quote his words when I want to help people understand the concept of worldview: "True and full living is based upon three components like the legs of a tripod. The three are intra-personal dynamics, inter-personal relationships and a frame of reference."[28] By *frame of reference* he means what others mean by *worldview*. He goes on to rightly observe, "Your vision of reality is not mine and conversely, mine is not yours. Both of our visions are limited and inadequate, but not to the same extent. We have both misinterpreted and distorted reality, but in different ways. The main point is that it is the dimensions and clarity of this vision that determines the dimensions of our world and the quality of our lives."[29] Thus, says Powell, "If we are to mature, to grow, to live [fully human, fully alive] there must be a change in the basic vision."[30] In every scriptural text the Spirit of God is causing a worldview shift, a change in our vision of reality.

Richard Bauckham, in his brilliant work on the book of Revelation, observes how the imagery of that portion of Scripture works to change our worldviews. What he says of the last book of the Bible is true of all the books. He speaks of the capacity of Revelation's visual imagery "to create a symbolic world which its readers can enter and thereby have their perception of the world in which they live transformed."[31] Bauckham reminds us of how the readers of the Revelation of Jesus Christ (which is the full title of the last book of the Bible) were constantly confronted with spectacular images "of the Roman vision of the world," intended to impress people with "Roman imperial power and the splendour of pagan religion."[32] Then Bauckham, not speaking directly to preaching, expresses the goal of texts and the preaching of texts: "In this context, Revelation provides a set of Christian prophetic counter-

---

[27]John Joseph Powell, *Fully Human, Fully Alive: A New Life Through a New Vision* (Nils, Ill.: Argus Communications, 1976), p. 10.
[28]Ibid.
[29]Ibid.
[30]Ibid.
[31]Richard Bauckham, *The Theology of the Book of Revelation* (Cambridge: Cambridge University Press, 1993), p. 17.
[32]Ibid.

images which impress on its readers a different vision of the world."[33] Different indeed! The imagery of the book consequently "effects a kind of purging of the Christian imagination, refurbishing it with alternative visions of how the world is and will be."[34] Through text after text after text, the risen Jesus changes the way we understand reality, until one day we actually live in his different reality.

James Sire defined worldview as "a set of presuppositions (or assumptions) which we hold (consciously or subconsciously) about the make up of the world."[35] N. T. Wright calls worldviews "the lens" through which a people, a society looks at their world, "the grid upon which are plotted the multiple experiences of life."[36] He suggests that worldviews can be understood in terms of four features: "characteristic stories; fundamental symbols; habitual praxis; and a set of questions and answers."[37]

Every human being, every human culture, every author, filmmaker, artist, doctor, scientist, teacher, homemaker, parent or politician is operating out of a particular worldview. We all automatically live out our deeply held assumptions. And every text is engaging those assumptions, either reinforcing them or calling them into question.

More concretely, every worldview is asking and trying to answer the following nine questions. My compilation below is inspired by those proposed by Sire and Wright. When preachers stand up with a text in hand, the listeners are asking—most of the time unconsciously, but sometimes quite intentionally,

1. What is prime reality? What is the "really real"?
2. Who or what are we? What does it mean to be a human being?
3. Is there such a thing as "morality," right and wrong? If so, what is its basis; how does one know the good and the bad?
4. What is the meaning of history? Or, is there any meaning?
5. What is wrong with us? Something is off—what is it?

---

[33]Ibid.

[34]Ibid. See my *Discipleship on the Edge: An Expository Journey Through the Book of Revelation* (Vancouver, B.C.: Regent College Publishing, 2004), thirty sermons in which I attempt to let the text of the Revelation change the way we understand reality.

[35]James Sire, *The Universe Next Door* (Downers Grove, Ill.: InterVarsity Press, 1976), p. 18.

[36]N. T. Wright, *Jesus and the Victory of God* (Minneapolis: Fortress, 1997), p. 138.

[37]Ibid.

6. Is there a solution; can things be fixed? By whom? How? How quickly?

7. Is there a God? If so, can this God be known? And is this God involved in the world, especially relative to human suffering?

8. What happens to a human being at death? (Asked more frequently than most preachers are aware and therefore needs to be spoken to more frequently than we do.)

9. What time is it? "There is an appointed time for everything. And there is a time for every event under heaven" (Eccles 3:1). Where are we in the flow of history?

The gospel speaks to all these questions, one text at a time, over a lifetime, slowly shaping a new metanarrative in our minds and hearts.

A number of years ago now (1997), I was at a coffee shop reading the newspaper, and I came across an article titled "'Star Wars' Our Public Religion."[38] The author, Orson Scott Card, was wrestling with why millions of people were lining up at movie theatres for the rerelease of the Star Wars trilogy. Mr. Card argued that it had little to do with cinematography: the special effects that dazzled people in 1977 were old hat in 1997. And he argued that it had little to do with nostalgia or entertainment or art. Card argued that it had to do with the fact that humans are incurably religious.

Here is how he put it: "We Americans, despite all appearances, have not abandoned religion. We've merely changed its name." Noting that American universities have for decades nurtured a disdain for Christianity, Card went on to say, "But abandoning a particular religion doesn't erase the innate human need for some religion, for a Deep Story"—is that not a great term for the gospel?—"that gives meaning to suffering and makes sense of the randomness of life. Hardly anybody can answer the easy Bible questions on Jeopardy anymore, but almost everybody can tell you about Obi-Wan Kenobi, Darth Vader, Yoda, and the Force." Card asserts that "Star Wars is the scripture of our public religion."[39]

In the article, Card goes on to show how much of life in America

---

[38]Orson Scott Card, "'Star Wars' Our Public Religion," *USA Today*, March 17, 1997, p. 13A.
[39]Ibid.

in 1997 could be explained in terms of Star Wars as "the established religion." Though one might question such a grand claim, he was on to something fundamental. "George Lucas [creator of Star Wars] did not create the moral world view we live in now, but he provided what all new religions must have: a scripture that makes the moral world view clear and compelling, carrying it vividly into the hearts of believers. Star Wars is religious literature."[40]

On those terms, is not most literature and art and science religion?

I both agree and disagree with Orson Card. I disagree that Star Wars was in 1997 the established religion of the day. More accurately, Star Wars was one of many "Deep Stories" trying to make sense of life in America at that time. Star Wars was big. But so was Star Trek. And Dionetics. And Scientology. And, of course, "The American Dream." But I fully agree with Card's more basic point: human beings have an innate need for some sort of religion, for some sort of Deep Story. We simply cannot live without some sort of metanarrative to help make sense of our personal narratives. Every culture in every era tells and retells its vision of reality in stories that give direction for daily living, form boundaries in which to do business, shape the dynamics of relationships and speak into the huge question of death.

That Easter, I opened my Easter Sunday sermon saying, "I want to retell the Deep Story shaped by what the apostle Paul writes in 1 Corinthians 15. I want to retell the Deep Story that emerges from what happened that morning, when Mary Magdalene, having first mistaken him for the cemetery gardener, met Jesus of Nazareth, risen from the grave." Every text is, in one way or another, about God's Deep Story and speaks to the Deep Stories by which people live.

I began preaching during the height of interest in the thinking of Rudolf Bultmann. Bultmann, sincerely wrestling with how the gospel could make sense in the then "modern" world, argued in his 1961 essay "The New Testament and Mythology" that preaching simply had to "demythologize" the gospel. Preaching had no choice but to strip Jesus and his gospel of all the "mythological" trappings in which the Bible preaches

---

[40]Ibid.

him. Bultmann wrote, "We can no longer believe in a three-storied universe which the creeds took for granted"—above the earth, on the earth and below the earth, as Philippians 2:10 says.[41] "No one who is old enough to think for himself supposes that God lives in a local heaven. There is no longer any heaven in the traditional sense of the word. And if this is so, the story of Christ's ascension into heaven is done away with. We can no longer look for the return of the Son of Man on the clouds of heaven or hope that the faithful meet him in the air" (see 1 Thess 4:17).[42]

Many Christian scholars and preachers agreed with Bultmann and said so publicly. Many other Christian scholars and preachers disagreed and said so publicly, but went on to live their lives as though they agreed with Bultmann; that is, heaven made no practical, measurable difference in their discipleship and ministry. I was one of them. I emerged from the interaction with Bultmann's worldview saying I believed in the biblical worldview, but in practice I lived the modern worldview. I was a closet demythologizer, able (I thought) to, for instance, explain the whole notion of the demonic in terms of human evil and human pathology. Then I had a number of experiences that could only be explained in terms of the biblical worldview of heavenly beings, both good and evil, at work in the world—the world I thought I understood as an "enlightened" university graduate with a degree in physics and theoretical mathematics.

I have come now to realize that the task of preaching is not to demythologize the gospel, but to remythologize the world with the gospel. I think that is the task of the Spirit-breathed texts we are called to preach. I am here using the language of Andrew T. Lincoln, in his scholarly work on the heavenly dimension in Ephesians.[43] Lincoln responds to the Bultmannian challenge by arguing that the church does not need to demythologize its theology and cosmology. Rather the church needs to remythologize it all. Our hermeneutics, even, need to be remythologized.[44] "It is not a question of whether modern people

---

[41]Rudolf Bultmann, "The New Testament and Mythology," in *Kerygma and Myth*, ed. H. W. Bartsch (London: SPCK, 1972), p. 4.

[42]Ibid.

[43]Andrew T. Lincoln, *Paradise Not and Not Yet: Studies in the Role of the Heavenly Dimensions in Paul's Thought with Special Reference to His Eschatology* (Grand Rapids: Eerdemans, 1981).

[44]Ibid., p. 4

will interpret their lives by symbols or myths but rather the question is which symbols or myths they will accept or choose. Will it be those rooted in the biblical perspective or those originating in some other world-views?"[45]

Through text after text, sermon after sermon, the risen Jesus, by the Holy Spirit, causes a shift in worldview. He causes a shift out of any frame of reference with the self or humanity at the center to a frame of reference with the risen and ascended Jesus at the center. He causes a shift to a Christocentric vision of the cosmos, "wherein Christ is the ontological, epistemological, and soteriological focus of all human thought and experience."[46] Oh, Lord, may it so be.[47]

Obedience of faith. Such a shift in vision naturally calls for a new way of life. As the apostle Paul says in both the beginning and end of his great epistle to the Romans, the gospel brings about "the obedience of faith" (Rom 1:5; 16:26), faith that obeys, and obedience emerging from faith. Having been ushered into an alternative reading of reality, indeed, into an alternative reality, one cannot but now live in a new way. Every text, in one way or another, calls us to a new step in the obedience of faith. As my friend Dick Whedinhelft puts it: "We cannot help but live out our worldview because we believe our worldview and cannot help but live out what we believe."[48]

I want to develop this a bit further. As I read the Book, the living God has given humanity only one command. Every other command is but a particular expression or specification of the one command. It is the command God spoke in the beginning in the garden: "From any tree of the garden you may eat freely; but from the tree of the knowledge of good and evil you shall not eat, for in the day that you eat from it you will surely die" (Gen 2:16-17). Note that the forbidden plant is the tree of the knowledge of good and evil. Whenever we preach this text we need to make sure to say the whole mouthful. It

---

[45]Ibid., p. 5.
[46]Michael P. Knowles, "'Christ in You, the Hope of Glory': Discipleship in Colossians," in *Patterns of Discipleship in the New Testament*, ed. Richard N. Longenecker (Grand Rapids: Eerdmans, 1996), p. 180.
[47]I will speak to this further in chapter ten, "Standing in the Mystery."
[48]In conversation.

is not "the tree of knowledge," as though God does not want humanity to learn, as though God is threatened by us wanting to know as
much as we can. It is not "the tree of good and evil," as though God
places before us the either-or of good and evil, as though God would
even put evil before us and tell us not to choose it. It is the tree of
the knowledge of good and evil. The whole phrase is a Hebrew idiom with a very specific meaning. Daniel P. Fuller has demonstrated
that this idiom is used in the Old Testament for a particular kind
of knowledge, to which any one who wants to truly live will not aspire. In his unpublished lecture notes, Fuller looks at every use of this
phrase: God has such knowledge (Gen 3:22), angels have it (2 Sam
14:17), and Solomon prayed for it (1 Kings 3:9); but children do not
yet have it (Deut 1:39; Is 7:15), and senile people have lost it (2 Sam
19:35).[49] Fuller then concludes, "The expression 'to know good and
evil' signified the possession of that maturity which frees one from
being dependent on someone else for guidance on how to act wisely.
Minors and senile people obviously do not have this maturity. But
Solomon and others who had to act in a leadership capacity could
have it [to a degree]." The command to not eat of the tree of the
knowledge of good and evil "would thus mean that Adam and Eve
were not to aspire to the maturity possessed by God himself whereby
they might consider themselves to be free from dependence upon him
and able to achieve the harmony they now enjoyed by taking matters
entirely into their own hands."[50]

We can therefore paraphrase God's one command this way: "Adam,
I have made you a glorious creature, the most glorious of all my works.
I have given you life, my life, life with me, a life that does not decay or
disintegrate or deteriorate or die. You can enjoy this life by trusting me,
by obeying just one command: do not try to live independently of me. I
have made you to thrive as you remain in dependence upon me for life,
for power, for wisdom. That is, you be you and let me be me; you be the
creature, I will be the Creator. In the day that you try to be me, that is,
when you try to go it alone, without me, you will die. I will not kill you;

---

[49]From his course on hermeneutics, Fuller Theological Seminary, 1970.
[50]Daniel P. Fuller, "Unity of the Bible," syllabus, Fuller Theological Seminary, 1969, pp. viii-3.

I will not need to kill you; you will have chosen death. Only one command: trust me by staying dependent on me. And you will live!"

Every command from that time on is but another way of saying "Trust me." Take the Ten Commandments, for example. What is the first line of the Law? Most people will say, "You shall have no other gods before Me" (Ex 20:3). It is not the first line. The first line is, "I am Yahweh your God, who brought you out of the house of slavery" (Ex 20:2 NASB modified). Before speaking any of the commandments God announces a relationship God already established and a freedom God already won. "I am Yahweh your God." It is the language of covenant. It means, "I have chosen to be God to you; I have chosen to give you myself; I have chosen to place all that I am, all that characterizes me as God, at your disposal." Then come the commands, the implication being, "Here now is what it means to live in this relationship I have already established, in this freedom I have already won for you; trust me to be who I am, and you will need no other gods."

Martin Luther had a vivid way of defining faith. He said that faith does not mean just mentally assenting to the gospel truths, but faith means "throwing yourself on God." Every text of Scripture, understood in its context, calls us to throw ourselves on God. No text, understood in its context, ever calls us to throw ourselves on ourselves. Every text calls us to trust God by obeying God and to obey God by trusting God. The task of preaching is to show how any specific exhortation is but another specific way of saying, "Throw yourself on God."

Consider the following illustration, which was inspired by the teaching of Daniel Fuller, and which I often use.

You are not feeling well. So you go to the doctor.

She checks you out. Because she is such a competent doctor, she immediately diagnoses the problem and prescribes the cure. "Here," she says, "take two of these pills a day, do not eat any candy bars, eat three kinds of vegetables everyday and walk a mile a day."

You say, "Okay, sounds reasonable and good to me."

On your way out of the office you turn to the receptionist and say to him, "That doctor is the greatest. She is so good. She makes me feel cared for. I am glad I found her."

You go home. The next day you take only one of the two pills. You sneak a bite of a Snickers bar, you eat only two of the three vegetables and you walk only a half mile. "This will do," you say. "Besides, I know myself better than the doctor does."

You continue in this vein the rest of the week.

At the end of the week you return to the doctor's office.

"Good morning," she says.

"Good morning," you reply.

"How are you feeling?"

"Not so well."

"Oh, dear. I am surprised. What I prescribed usually helps. Did you do what I said to do?"

"Sort of."

"Sort of? What does that mean?"

"Well, you know, sort of."

"Did you take the two pills each day?"

"Sort of."

"Sort of?"

"Yes, I took one each day."

"One?"

"Yeah, one."

"Oh, I said to take two."

"Yeah, I know."

"Well, did you knock off the candy bars?"

"Sort of."

"Sort of?"

"Yeah, I snuck a bite of Snickers each day."

"I said no bites."

"Yeah, I know."

"Tell me Darrell, do you want to get well?"

"Of course!"

"I wonder . . . Did you eat the three kinds of vegetables?"

"Well . . ."

"Don't tell me. Sort of."

"Right. I only ate two kinds."

"Did you walk a mile?"

". . . No . . . only a half mile."

Then she says, "Do you trust me?"

"Oh, yes . . . of course . . . you are the best."

"Yes, I heard you tell my receptionist that. If I am the best, why don't you trust me?"

"I do trust you!"

"No, you do not."

"How can you say that?"

"Because you did not do what I said to do."

That is the "obedience of faith." Every "do" of every text is but another way of saying, "Trust me." Texts change lives, and preaching texts changes lives, because every text calls for a new step of trusting God by doing what God tells us to do.

Enablement. In and through every text, the risen Jesus, through the Holy Spirit, is enabling us to do what we are called to do. Given everything we have explored in this chapter, are we surprised by this? If the Word made flesh is speaking in the sermon—which he is doing if the sermon is faithful to the text—then what he says will happen. Again, his word not only informs; it performs, it transforms. The Spirit who breathes the text breathes his power into us to live the text. (I will develop this further in chapter seven on implication and application.)

Expository preaching is the place, the venue, where the miracle of divine transformation takes place. For in expository preaching the preacher is participating with what the risen Jesus, through the Holy Spirit, is doing in and with and through a text. He is

engendering an encounter with the Lord of the text

in which the Lord announces news, good news

which causes a shift in worldview,

calling for a new step of trusting obedience;

enabling us to do it, to actually live in the new reality opened up to us by the opening of the text.

4

HOW DOES IT HAPPEN?

Verbs of Participation

UP TO THIS POINT I HAVE BEEN USING the verb *preach* in a generic sense. I am, however, aware that it is not the only verb the Bible uses for the preaching moment, and moreover, that the wonderfully diverse church of Jesus Christ uses it in many diverse ways. In this chapter, I want to now try to give more precision to the word and activity called preaching.

I am often asked if I think there is a difference between preaching and teaching. Different people mean different things by both of the words. In his insightful book *The Four Voices of Preaching*, Robert Stephen Reid recalls a story Walter Wangerin Jr. shared after preaching one Sunday morning. The "matriarch" of the congregation brought up this question of preaching and teaching.

> Now Miz Lillian was holding my hand in hers, which was work hard-ened, her little finger fixed forever straight, unable to bend. "When you teach," she said, instructing me, "I learn something for the day. I can take it home and, God willing, I can do it. But when you preach—" She lowered her voice and probed me the deeper with her eyes—"God is here. And sometimes he's smiling," she said, "and sometimes he's frowning surely."[1]

---

[1]Walter Wangerin Jr., *Miz Lil and the Chronicles of Grace* (San Francisco: Harper and Row, 1988), p. 37, quoted in Robert Stephen Reid, *The Four Voices of Preaching: Connecting Purpose and Identity behind the Pulpit* (Grand Rapids: Brazos, 2006), p. 15.

She is a wise woman. She recognizes that the same preacher operates in different "verbs of communicating" and these different verbs have different rhetorical styles and different outcomes for the listener.

Now, most of the time when I am asked if I think there is a difference between preaching and teaching, or if a sermon should be evangelistic, exhortative or numerous other possibilities, the person is implicitly wondering if there is a traditionally appropriate verb for what preaching is doing, or ought to do, during the Lord's Day worship service. This is especially the case when the asker grew up in the church during the heyday of Christendom (that now-collapsed arrangement when the Christian faith largely ruled the day).[2] In the Christendom model the Sunday sermon was for "preaching," and the Sunday school class or midweek class was for "teaching." Which meant that in the sermon preachers did not need to do much "teaching," for preachers could assume most people knew the grand narrative of the Bible and most of the stories within it. Preachers could, for instance, say at the beginning of their sermon, "It has been a three-days-in-the-belly-of-the-whale kind of week," and nearly everyone would know the allusion in the comment. Try that in the first decade of the third millennium and you'll see faces that say, "Huh, what is that all about?" Under the Christendom arrangement the Sunday sermon tended toward what I would call "oration,"[3] the sermon having hardly any teaching component because, again, preachers could assume a whole wealth of biblical literacy. Not now. From my perspective there is now no way preachers can communicate the gospel without doing a significant amount of teaching. And doing a lot of other things conveyed by other verbs.

I have been using the phrases "preaching moment" and "preaching event." Let me now use a more expanded phrase, "communicating-the-gospel moment," and suggest that in it a host of verbs operate. As Gerhard Friedrich points out in his article on heralding in *The Theological*

---

[2]Stanley Hauerwas and William H. Willimon, *Resident Aliens: Life in Christian Colony* (Nashville: Abingdon, 1989).
[3]O. C. Edwards, *A History of Preaching* (Nashville: Abingdon, 2004); Richard Lischer, *The Company of Preachers: Wisdom on Preaching, Augustine to the Present* (Grand Rapids: Eerdmans, 2002); David Dunn-Wilson, *A Mirror for the Church: Preaching in the First Five Centuries* (Grand Rapids: Eerdmans, 2005).

Dictionary of the New Testament, whereas we in our time tend to use only the word *preach,* the New Testament "is more dynamic and varied in its modes of expression."[4] He adds, "But our almost exclusive use of 'preach' for all is a sign, not merely of poverty of vocabulary, but the loss of something which was a living reality in primitive Christianity."[5] I agree and would argue that this variety of modes of communication is unavoidable given the huge scope of the gospel and given the dynamics of the communicating moment,[6] not to mention the varied styles of preachers.

The main verbs of participating in the divine transformation of the world I want to explore in this chapter are: evangelize, herald, teach, exhort, prophesy, confess and witness.

Before we do so, consider table 4.1, which identifies four different possible contexts in which the verbs of communicating the gospel might operate.[7]

Table 4.1

I. • In an intentionally sacred space • Some gospel knowledge	III. • Not in an intentionally sacred space • Some gospel knowledge
II. • In an intentionally sacred space • No gospel knowledge	IV. • Not in an intentionally sacred space • No gospel knowledge

Quadrant I represents the traditional preaching context: in a church building, or a building being used as a church, with at least the core of the assembled group familiar with the gospel. Quadrant II represents events like weddings and memorial services, or special outreach events put on by a congregation, where the majority of those gathered in the

---

[4]Gerhard Friedrich, "κῆρυξ, κτλ.," in *Theological Dictionary of the New Testament,* ed. Gerhard Kittel and Gerhard Friedrich (Grand Rapids: Eerdmans, 1964-1976), 3:703.

[5]Ibid.

[6]I commend to you two books that were published as I was in the process of writing. Each develops the concerns I have in this chapter in different ways and I think each helps fill in the whole picture. The first, already referenced, by Robert Stephen Reid, who looks at the "communicating moment" from his wealth of study in communication theory. *The Four Voices of Preaching.* The other author, who comes at the issues as a seasoned observer and teacher of preaching, is Kenton Anderson, *Choosing to Preach: A Comprehensive Introduction to Sermon Options and Structures* (Grand Rapids: Zondervan, 2006). I will come back to both resources.

[7]I offer my thanks to someone I cannot recall, whose diagram I am modifying here.

space have no, or very little, knowledge of Jesus and his gospel, but expect some reference to him and it. Quadrant III represents a gathering of people in, say, a city park or a large civic auditorium, again, with at least the core of those assembled familiar with the gospel and wanting the rest in the crowd to know the gospel. (I had the privilege of preaching for the Hollywood Bowl Easter Sunrise Service in 1999 and for three Easter Sundays in a row in the Orpheum Theatre of downtown Vancouver, the event sponsored by First Baptist Church of Vancouver—what a joy!). Quadrant IV represents community events not sponsored by any Christian organization as such, like a civic meeting, or a citywide meeting to celebrate or mourn; very few attendees would have any working knowledge of the gospel and would not be expecting any reference to Jesus and his good news. (I love to speak in such spaces!)

Now, it would seem that certain verbs of communicating the gospel belong to specific quadrants: i.e., evangelize in IV, witness in III, exhort and teach in I, herald in II and IV. To a degree this works: each quadrant calls for the communicator to speak in one or two of the various modes. But I want to suggest that all the verbs we will explore in this chapter operate well in any quadrant. And I want to argue that all the verbs are definitely operating in quadrant I. I also want to argue, therefore, that the preacher need not fret about speaking in only one "appropriate" verb, as though only one verb belongs in the pulpit.

In this book I am focusing on quadrant I. But I would argue that the source of what is said in the other three quadrants is the same: a specific text of Scripture, whether the hearers know this or not. I think they should know it, but the "glory of preaching" can happen without holding up a Bible and reading a text. It's just that the message is the message of a text. Texts are the only source of messages that can work the miracle of Ezekiel 37—in any quadrant. Let us now explore the seven verbs one at a time. Each of the verbs is involved in communicating the gospel.

Evangelize (euangelizō). It simply means, "to announce good news." Angels did it: "I am Gabriel, who stands in the presence of God, and I have been sent to speak to you and to bring you this good news" (Lk 1:19); on Christmas Eve, the lead angel of the heavenly hosts says, "Do not be afraid; for behold, I bring you good news of great joy, which will be for all the people" (Lk 2:10). John the Baptist did it: "So with many other exhortations he preached the gospel to the people" (Lk 3:18). Jesus did it: In his Nazareth sermon he declares, quoting Isaiah, "THE SPIRIT OF THE LORD IS UPON ME, / BECAUSE HE ANOINTED ME TO PREACH THE GOSPEL TO THE POOR" (Lk 4:18); "I must preach the kingdom of God to the other cities also, for I was sent for this purpose" (Lk 4:43); "Soon afterwards, He began going around from one city and village to another, proclaiming and preaching the kingdom of God" (Lk 8:1). Jesus sent his first disciples to do it: "Departing, they began going throughout the villages, preaching the gospel and healing everywhere" (Lk 9:6). The early church did it: "Therefore, those who had been scattered went about preaching the word" (Acts 8:4), literally, "good-news-ing the word"; the Samaritans "believed Philip preaching the good news about the kingdom of God and the name of Jesus Christ" (Acts 8:12); "When he had seen the vision, immediately we sought to go into Macedonia, concluding that God had called us to preach the gospel to them" (Acts 16:10). As you can see, angels, John the Baptist, Jesus, his disciples and messengers, went from village to village, city to city, nation to nation, announcing good news.

The New Testament uses the word *euangelion,* transliterated in English as *evangel,* the root of the words *evangelize* and *evangelical.* Or, better yet, (to make up some terms) *good-news-ize* and *good-news-ical.* To be "evangelical" is to be evangelistic, to be gripped by good news and to want the world to hear and receive good news.

It is a secular word, *euangelion,* used by the Caesars on the advent of their ascent to rulership. The *euangelion* of Caesar Augustus, for instance, was that since he as a "son of god" had now come, the world was entering a new age. It was Augustus, in fact, "who first borrowed the Greek word 'gospel' or 'good news' and applied it as a label for a new world order represented by his reign."[8] The emperor sends his messengers, his evangelists, throughout the empire with his evangel. And so too the great Emperor Jesus: He sends his messengers, his evangelists,

---

[8]Philip Yancey, *The Jesus I Never Knew* (Grand Rapids: Zondervan, 1995), p. 33.

throughout the whole world with his evangel.

Three other concepts consistently attend the use of the verb *evangelize:* joy, victory and altered reality.

Joy. "I bring you good news of great joy" (Lk 2:10). Joy is the dominant emotion of the one declaring the good news, and it is the dominant emotion of those who hear the good news. This tells me that joylessness among a people is the result of not enough hearing of the good news. "Joy reigns when this word is proclaimed."[9] Why?

Victory. In the secular world as well as in the Old Testament, the *evangel* was the announcement of a victory, a victory over enemies. "A messenger comes from the place of battle and declares victory over enemies or the death of an opponent."[10] The verb was consistently used for the proclamation of news of victory. "The messenger appears, raises his right hand in greeting and calls out with a loud voice: *Chaire . . . nikomen.*"[11] "Rejoice . . . we have the victory!" So Mark tells us that Jesus came from the desert where he had faced the temptations of the great enemy of God. And Mark then writes, "Jesus came into Galilee, preaching the gospel of God" (Mk 1:14). Caesar has his gospel; so does the living God. Mark continues with the content of God's gospel, "The time is fulfilled, and the kingdom of God is at hand; repent and believe in the gospel" (Mk 1:15). Jesus comes into Galilee from a place of battle, where he has won a victory. In Mark's mind Jesus won the victory over the evil one in the desert. Jesus emerges from the desert as victor, and as the great evangelist he comes into Galilee to announce good news: "Rejoice . . . I have the victory."

Altered reality. The victory and the announcement of it alter the whole situation. When the Roman messenger rides into town to announce Caesar's evangel, life for the village is altered: Caesar is now lord in the place, and Caesar's way will now be the way people are to live. Jesus comes into Galilee announcing God's evangel: Jesus is now lord in the place, and Jesus' way will now be the way people are to live.

---

[9]Gerhard Friedrich, "εὐαγγελίζομαι, κτλ.," in *Theological Dictionary of the New Testament*, ed. Gerhard Kittel and Gerhard Friedrich (Grand Rapids: Eerdmans, 1964-1976), 2:720.
[10]Ibid., 2:707.
[11]Ibid., 2:722.

When Caesar Augustus was born as a "son of god," his birth was hailed as the beginning of a new age; the birth of a new ruler means "a new era dawns for the whole world."[12] God's evangel is all about the birth of a new ruler, the "Son of God," who has come and won the victory over all that stands in God's way, thus forever altering the way the world goes together. This altering of reality is at the heart of the verb *evangelize*. Because the victory has been won, life can now be lived in a new way. In the movie *The Matrix: Revolutions*, after the war with the machines has ended, a young man comes running with the news, "War is over! War is over!" That is what evangel and evangelizing is all about.

The prophet Isaiah longed for that day when Yahweh would win the victory, ascend to his throne, reign unrivaled as Sovereign, and usher in a new day. That day is today. "How lovely on the mountains / Are the feet of him who brings good news, / Who announces peace / And brings good news of happiness, / Who announces salvation / And says to Zion, 'Your God reigns!'" (Is 52:7). The apostle Paul quotes this text in the part of his letter to the Romans where he is speaking about preaching, but in place of "him" (singular) he puts "them" (plural), for now many more are given the privilege of running across mountains into villages with the gospel of God.

E. Stanley Jones, a Methodist missionary to India, China and Japan in the middle of the twentieth century, whom many Indian Christians call the greatest missionary since the apostle Paul, embodies the spirit of the verb *evangelize* better than anyone I know. He writes, "The early Christians did not say in dismay, 'Look what the world has come to,' but in delight, 'Look what has come to the world.'"[13] The early Christians looked out on a world as challenging, as frightening, as confusing, as overwhelmingly broken as ours, and they did not say in dismay, "Look what the world has come to." "What the world has come to" is not the content of biblical preaching; how bad things are, how immoral things are, how chaotic things are. That is not the note sounded in biblical preaching. Rather, the note of evangelical preaching—in the face of all that we see in the world—is, "Look what has come to the world."

---

[12]Ibid., 2:725.
[13]E. Stanley Jones, *Abundant Living* (Nashville: Abingdon, 1942), p. 183.

The true King has come, the one and only Son of God has come and won the victory. Jones continues: "They saw not merely the ruin, but the Resources for the reconstruction of that ruin. They saw not merely that sin did abound, but that grace did much more abound."[14] This is God's evangel.

So, to do this verb of participating is to stand up in front of a group of people, Bible in hand (or Word in heart), and announce radically transforming news, news about a new order of things, a new era for the world, news that calls us to get in sync with this new order.

Lord, please release the power of this verb in our preaching!

Herald (kēryssō). This is the word most regularly translated as "preach" in the New Testament, also often translated as "proclaim." It means to openly declare a new public reality. John the Baptist did it: "Now in those days John the Baptist came, preaching in the wilderness of Judea" (Mt 3:1). Jesus did it: "From that time Jesus began to preach" (Mt 4:17); "Jesus was going throughout all Galilee, teaching in their synagogues and proclaiming the gospel of the kingdom, and healing" (Mt 4:23); "He has sent me to proclaim release to the captives . . . to proclaim the favorable year of the Lord" (Lk 4:18-19); "He kept on preaching in the synagogues of Judea" (Lk 4:44). Jesus sent others to do it: "and He sent them out to proclaim the kingdom of God and to perform healing" (Lk 9:2). The early church did it: "Philip went down to the city of Samaria and began proclaiming Christ to them" (Acts 8:5); "And He ordered us to preach to the people, and solemnly to testify that this is the One who has been appointed by God as Judge of the living and the dead" (Acts 10:42); "but we preach Christ crucified" (1 Cor 1:23); "preach the word" (2 Tim 4:2).

The verb *kēryssō* gets its essential meaning from the noun *kēryx.* The *kēryx,* or herald, was a messenger sent by and authorized by the emperor to speak a message on the emperor's behalf. The message is a public message, one meant to be heard in the public arena.[15] The herald arrives in the village or city, goes to the city square and, holding the regal scroll in hand, cries out, "Hear ye, hear ye," and reads the royal

[14]Ibid.
[15]Lesslie Newbigin, *Truth to Tell: The Gospel as Public Truth* (Grand Rapids: Eerdmans, 1991).

edict. The *kēryx* is not proclaiming his own word, his own discoveries, his own insights, his own opinions on the nature of life in the empire; he is proclaiming the word of another—nothing more and nothing less. The word *kērygma* refers to the content of that which is proclaimed in the public square.

According to Gerhard Friedrich, the critical fact about *kēryssō*, "heralding," is its "eventness." This verb involves declaring an event—God's entering into the world in Jesus Christ. But doing the verb *kēryssō* is also an event itself; the kerygma happens in the act of heralding. "The decisive thing is the action of proclamation itself: the divine intervention takes place through the proclamation. Through it the kingdom of God actually comes."[16] Thus, when in his Nazareth sermon Jesus says he has been sent and anointed by the Spirit to "proclaim release to the captives . . . to proclaim the favorable year of the Lord," he can go on to say, "Today this Scripture has been fulfilled in your hearing" (Lk 4:21). Of course, *kēryssō*, "heralding," makes happen what it proclaims. "Todayness" is what this verb accomplishes. When the "herald" stands in the city square and proclaims the emperor's edict, what is proclaimed becomes the new reality right then and there, "today." "When heralds proclaimed the year of Jubilee throughout the land with the sound of the trumpet, the year began, the prison doors were opened and debts were remitted. The preaching of Jesus is the blast of the trumpet. Its result is that the Word proclaimed became a reality."[17]

And the only appropriate response is not understanding, but faith. Understanding will come in due time. The message demands a decision on the part of the hearer. And faith is the only logical decision: enter into and learn to live the new reality created by the message.

Again, the message is a public message. It is "meant to ring out on the streets and from the roof-tops."[18] I learned this when preparing a series of sermons on the book of Daniel. I learned that chapters 1 and 8–12 are written in Hebrew. But chapters 2–7 are written in Aramaic, the lingua franca of the day. In chapters 2–7, Daniel records a series of

---

[16]Ibid., p. 704.
[17]Ibid., pp. 706-7.
[18]Ibid., p. 709.

visions given to secular rulers of the day, Nebuchadnezzar and Belshaz-zar in particular. His visions illuminate the nature and coming of the kingdom of God. Why write these in Aramaic? Why not in Hebrew? Because the visions were intended to be heard not only in the syna-gogue but also, primarily, in the halls of government. The visions were public news for the public realm. The gospel is meant for the public square and has public implications for the good of all.

Because of this aspect of heralding, a number of scholars argue that this verb does not factor into our understanding of what preachers are doing on a Sunday morning in a church building. Craig Evans, for ex-ample, after surveying the meaning and use of the verb *kērysso* writes: "It is the thesis of this study that a preacher, as one who preaches the gospel to those who are ignorant of it, and a parish minister, as one who shepherds the flock, are not one and the same."[19] Evans, working with 2 Timothy 4:2, acknowledges that "on occasion" as a minister, Timo-thy "must herald the (authentic) gospel."[20] But, to conclude "that the primary aspect of the pastor's ministry and the primary function of the assembled congregation is to hear a sermon is to misconstrue the NT concept of the preacher or herald."[21] He goes on to observe that none of the church fathers uses the term *kēryx* for the parish pastor: in the New Testament only Paul (1 Tim 2:7; 2 Tim 1:11) and Noah (2 Pet 2:5) are called by this title.[22] "It is never used in the sense of 'preaching' to a local congregation."[23] Other scholars have done similar lexical studies and made similar conclusions relative to the work of the parish pastor.

What are we to make of such studies? Do they indicate that pastors should not attempt to herald the gospel in our day? One one hand, such studies are technically right: this verb of participating is not regularly used of the work of what we normally call preaching. But on the other hand, its sparse usage need not preclude heralding as a legitimate activ-

---

[19]Craig A. Evans, "'Preacher' and 'Preaching': Some Lexical Observations," *JETS* 24, no. 4 (1981): 315.

[20]Ibid., p. 318.

[21]Ibid.

[22]Ibid.

[23]Ibid., p. 319. Not quite so, as Luke uses this verb three times of Jesus preaching in a synagogue (Lk 4:18, 19, 44).

ity for a pastor. I maintain that *kēryssō* should have its place among the other preaching verbs. The verb *sing* in the Epistles describes what goes on in congregational worship, but probably does not, for example, ever refer to a group of people who, having met on Thursday night to rehearse a piece of music, then sing it for those assembled. This does not mean that what the New Testament envisages by the verb "sing" cannot be lived out through a choir on the Lord's Day. (As long as it does not take the place of the congregation also singing.) That the activities of a parish minister do not include the verb *herald*—in the New Testament or in the church fathers—does not mean the parish minister should not do it, or that the congregation does not need it. As I read the ecclesiastical landscape, most churches are starving for this verb to operate.

Heralding needs to be done in the Lord's Day worship for at least three reasons. First, the gathering of people on Sunday morning is a public event; anyone is welcome. We never know who will be there and who will be in need of the heralding ministry. Working with the insights of J. T. Bakker, Jacob Firet puts it so well when he writes: "There is no watertight division between the missionary situation on the one hand and that of preaching in the Christian community on the other. Should *kerygma* and *homilia* become parallel but isolated entities, that could lead to a church that meets behind closed doors."[24] Second, we believers are a forgetful lot (an understatement). We need to be reminded again and again of the essential content of the kerygma. We need a herald to sound the trumpet every time we meet for worship. Third, we are always in a new situation since the last time we gathered for worship and, therefore, we always need a fresh word, a fresh kerygmatic word. Quoting Jacob Firet again,

> One could say that the *kerygma* belongs especially in the church because never before has it been "now," because the person who hears it has never been this person before and her situation has never been the situation of this moment. The entire word of God gathers itself together in the *kerygma* and focuses on the unique present. However it was yesterday, however it will be tomorrow—"this is the day of salvation."

---

[24]Jacob Firet, *Dynamics in Pastoring* (Grand Rapids: Eerdmans, 1986), p. 49.

"Today, if you hear his voice, harden not your hearts."

"See, I have set before you this day life and good, death and evil" (Deut. 30:15).

Here salvation stands perpendicularly upon the situation of this person and the *mebasser* [*messenger* in Hebrew] cries out: "Behold your God!" Isaiah 40:9).[25]

So, to do this verb of participating is to stand up before a group of people, Bible in hand (this time all the more crucial, as a kind of "hear ye, hear ye" scroll) and declare news, public news that has public implications for the public realm.

Oh Lord, release the power of this verb into our preaching!

Teach (didaskō). This verb means to develop the implications of the gospel, of the kergyma, both in terms of content and behavior. Jesus did it: "Jesus was going throughout all Galilee, teaching in their synagogues" (Mt 4:23); "He opened His mouth He began to teach them" (Mt 5:2), and out comes his Sermon on the Mount; After the Sermon, "the crowds were amazed at His teaching; for He was teaching them as one having authority" (Mt 7:28-29); "He began to teach again by the sea. . . . And He was teaching them many things in parables" (Mk 4:1-2). Jesus sends his disciples to make disciples (students or learners) of all the nations, "teaching them to observe all that I commanded you" (Mt 28:20). The early church did it: "they entered into the temple about daybreak and began to teach" (Acts 5:21); "And for an entire year they met with the church and taught considerable numbers" (Acts 11:26); "And he settled there a year and six months, teaching the word of God among them" (Acts 18:11); "And we proclaim Him, admonishing every one and teaching every one with all wisdom, that we may present every one complete [mature] in Christ" (Col 1:28 NASB modified).

The verb conveys a concern to educate the whole person "in the deepest sense."[26] To teach is to help men and women understand the coming and nature of the kingdom of God, and specifically to help

---

[25]Ibid., p. 50.

[26]Karl Heinrich Rengstorf, "διδάσκω," in *Theological Dictionary of the New Testament*, ed. Gerhard Kittel and Gerhard Friedrich (Grand Rapids: Eerdmans, 1964-1976), 2:137.

men and women understand and live relationships ordered under the will of God—divine-human relationships as well as human-human relationships.[27] Although exercising this verb of communicating the gospel does involve spelling out doctrine (thus the phrase, "sound doctrine" in the Pastoral Epistles), the real burden is ethical. "Teaching them to do, to obey." Teaching has not achieved its end until those who learn the doctrine actually begin to live in light of the doctrine. Indeed, for the teacher the truth is not truth until it is lived. Through faithful, systematic unpacking of the gospel, teaching brings about maturing disciples, people who are beginning to live like Jesus, the master teacher himself.

So, to do this verb of participating is to stand, Bible in hand (and likely many of the tools used to better understand the Bible) and spell out what the new reality announced and preached looks like in everyday living.

Oh Lord, release the power of this verb in our preaching!

Exhorting (parakaleō). Like the noun Jesus uses for the Holy Spirit, Paraclete, this verb has a wide range of meanings. It is, therefore, too narrow to render it as "exhort." Literally, it is "to call alongside," *para-* meaning alongside, as in paralegal or paramedical; and *kaleō* meaning called. And *parakaleō* can refer to being called alongside to do many different things. So the verb is variously translated "to call to," "to beseech," "to exhort," "to convict," "to comfort," "to admonish," "to console." It means, in the words of the familiar saying, "to comfort the afflicted and to afflict the comfortable." John the Baptist did it: "with many other exhortations he preached the gospel to the people" (Lk 3:18)—and what exhortations they were! Although the verb is not used of Jesus' earthly ministry, he was doing it all the time. And the early church did it: Peter, in the context of the first Christian sermon, "with many other words he solemnly testified and kept on exhorting them, saying, 'Be saved from this perverse generation!'" (Acts 2:40); Barnabas, after witnessing firsthand the work the Spirit was doing among the Gentiles in Antioch (what he called "the grace of God") "rejoiced and

---

[27]Ibid.

began to encourage them all with resolute heart to remain true to the Lord" (Acts 11:23); "Judas and Silas, also being prophets themselves, encouraged and strengthened the brethren with a lengthy message" (Acts 15:32). Paul uses this verb many times: "I urge you therefore," "I beseech you therefore" (Rom 12:1, translations mine); "Now I exhort you" (1 Cor 1:10); "Therefore I exhort you, be imitators of me" (1 Cor 4:16); "I . . . urge you to walk in a manner worthy of the calling to which you have been called" (Eph 4:1 ESV); "preach the word; be ready in season and out of season; reprove, rebuke, exhort, with great patience and instruction" (2 Tim 4:2). (Notice how many times a number of verbs of communicating are used in the same sentence?) And then, in Hebrews, the quintessential sermon of the New Testament, called "this word of exhortation" (Heb 13:22), the preacher says, "And I urge you" (Heb 13:19), "I urge you" (Heb 13:22); "but encourage one another day after day" (Heb 3:13).

We could express the energy of this verb as "wooing proclamation for salvation" in all its dimensions.[28] A wooing that especially participates in the wooing done by God. "We are ambassadors for Christ, *as though God were making an appeal through us*" (2 Cor 5:20, emphasis added). That Pauline text also demonstrates the driving force of this verb: appealing to live in what already is. Nowhere in New Testament preaching is there a call to exhort a person to act in order to make salvation real; everywhere the preaching exhorts people to enter into and live the salvation already made real. The imperative of exhortation always and consistently emerges from the indicative of the evangel and kerygma. Because God has already acted and moved toward us in Jesus Christ, we are being wooed—sometimes being grabbed by the collar—to now live what is. "The exhortation is distinguished from a mere moral appeal by this reference back to the work of salvation as its presupposition and basis."[29] To *exhort* then, is to do whatever we can—comfort, convict, convince—to help others do whatever they can to take the next step in discipleship, by grace.

---

[28]Otto Schmitz, "παρακαλέω, κτλ.," in *Theological Dictionary of the New Testament*, ed. Gerhard Kittel and Gerhard Friedrich (Grand Rapids: Eerdmans, 1964-1976), 5:795.
[29]Ibid.

So, to do this verb of participating is to stand up, or at times kneel down beside, a group of people, Bible in hand, and speak a word that moves troubled, discouraged, embattled, sputtering disciples to the next stage in the obedience of faith.

Oh Lord, release the power of this verb in our preaching!

Prophesy (prophēteuō). The verb means to speak a word directly imparted to the speaker by God. As the Old Testament prophets put it, "The word of the LORD came upon me" (e.g., Jer 1:4, 11, 13); they were not speaking something they deduced from observing the world around them, or developed after a long season of study and thinking. "The word came to me," that is, "from outside me and my intellectual processing." It means, in the words of Canon Michael Green, "speaking a particular word from God to a particular people at a particular time in a particular place."[30] Zacharias, father of John the Baptist, did it: "And his father Zacharias was filled with the Holy Spirit, and prophesied, saying" (Lk 1:67), and out came his hymn now called "The Benedictus," Latin for "Blessed be" (Lk 1:68-79); Caiaphas the high priest did it: "Now he did not say this on his own initiative, but being high priest that year, he prophesied that Jesus was going to die for the nation" (Jn 11:51). The gospel writers do not use the verb to describe Jesus' speaking, but the people who heard him thought in terms of his having prophesied: the Samaritan woman at the well, after Jesus named her past without any previous conversation with her, says, "Sir, I perceive that You are a prophet" (Jn 4:19); after raising the dead son of the widow of Nain, the people were "gripped" by fear, and began to glorify God, "saying, 'A great prophet has arisen among us!' and, 'God has visited His people'" (Lk 7:16); after hearing Jesus teach at the Feast of Tabernacles, many in the crowd say, "This certainly is the Prophet" (Jn 7:40), speaking of the promised prophet like Moses (Deut 18:15). When Jesus spoke, people experienced "prophetic speech." The early church did it in fulfillment of prophecy: "YOUR SONS AND YOUR DAUGHTERS SHALL PROPHESY" (Acts 2:17), "and they began speaking in tongues and prophesying" (Acts 19:6); Philip had four virgin daugh-

---

[30]Michael Green, *I Believe in the Holy Spirit* (Grand Rapids: Eerdmans, 1977), pp. 168-74.

ters "who prophesied" (Acts 21:9 NIV). The apostle Paul was eager that disciples prophesy: "Pursue love, yet desire earnestly spiritual gifts, but especially that you may prophesy" (1 Cor 14:1); "Therefore . . . desire earnestly to prophesy" (1 Cor 14:39).

Exercising this verb is not at the control of the speaker. One cannot announce, "At 4:00 p.m. this afternoon, I will prophesy." "The word came to me"; a word one has not figured out ahead of time. Oh, one may have been thinking about the issues involved for some time, maybe even reading widely and praying earnestly. But "the word" that comes, when prophesying, is "from above," "outside ourselves." Which means that we cannot make a one-to-one correspondence between what we ordinarily do in preaching and what happens in prophesying.[31]

As I observe this verb at work in Scripture and history and my own experience, three other inseparable concepts stand out: direct, from beyond and "in your face."

Direct. This mode of communicating involves insight given directly by the Holy Spirit; there is no other way the speaker could have known what is being said. During his trial before the religious authorities, soldiers who were holding Jesus mocked him and beat him. Since he was blindfolded, Jesus by all appearances did not know who was inflicting the pain. One of the soldiers inadvertently shows us what *prophesy* involves: he says to Jesus, "Prophesy, who is the one who hit You?" (Lk 22:64). That is, "Tell us what is going on that you cannot deduce using unaided human means of knowing." Preachers regularly have people come up to them after a sermon saying, "You have been living in my house, haven't you? You were speaking directly to me today, weren't you?" When that happens to me I say to myself, "I was not even thinking about this person!" and then say to him or her, "Yes, God was speaking directly to you. God loves you that much!"

---

[31]The dynamics and questions around this verb are many and complex. Consult the following range of perspectives: Walter Brueggemann, *The Prophetic Imagination* (Minneapolis: Fortress Press, 2001); Jack Deere, *Surprised by the Power of the Spirit* (Grand Rapids: Zondervan, 1993); Wayne Grudem, *The Gift of Prophecy* (Wheaton, Ill.: Crossway, 2000); David Hill, *New Testament Prophecy* (Atlanta: John Knox Press, 1979), and *Prophecy Past and Present* (East Sussex, U.K.: Highland Books, 1989); Ben Witherington III, *Jesus the Seer* (Peabody, Mass.: Hendrickson, 1999).

From beyond. What is spoken in exercising this verb goes beyond what the speaker is consciously thinking. Caiphas, "high priest that year," whom I cited earlier, says of Jesus to the ruling council, "You know nothing at all, nor do you take into account that it is expedient for you that one man die for the people, and that the whole nation not perish" (Jn 11:49-50). In that moment, Caiphas thinks only in terms of political expediency: if the Romans kill this one man they will be satisfied and leave the rest of the people alone. But also in that moment, unknown to himself, he is speaking beyond what he is thinking. He is preaching the gospel! As John says, "Now he did not say this on his own initiative, but being high priest that year, he prophesied that Jesus was going to die for the nation, and not for the nation only" (Jn 11:51-52). So many times preachers say more than they know. Sometimes we get to hear what that is, sometimes we never know. But it happens. For the living God loves his people and knows that they do not live by bread alone "BUT ON EVERY WORD THAT PROCEEDS OUT OF THE MOUTH OF GOD" (Mt 4:4, quoting Deut 8:3).

In your face. This verb of communication has an "in-your-face-ness" to it. We see this in the prophet Nathan. God calls Nathan to speak to King David, who is hiding in the secrecy of his affair with Bathsheba. After he tells the king a parable, and after the king is furious about the injustice in the story, Nathan looks at David and says, "You are the man!" (2 Sam 12:7). This "in-your-face-ness" is what the woman at the well experienced when Jesus spoke of her painful past and conflicted present (Jn 4:16-19). It is what the apostle Paul says is supposed to happen when this verb of participating is exercised: "But if all prophesy, and an unbeliever or an ungifted man enters, he is convicted by all, he is called to account by all; the secrets of his heart are disclosed; and he will fall on his face and worship God, declaring that God is certainly among you" (1 Cor 14:24-25). As Miz Lill said to Walter Wangerin, "When you preach"—she does not know the exact term to use—"God is here." This is awesome to witness. How many times do preachers hear someone say after the sermon, "God spoke to me today, and I will never be the same"?[32]

---

[32]To this dynamic of preaching we need to be intentionally attentive and guard space in the worship services for people to appropriately respond. To the preacher God says, "Be still, I am doing something you did not plan. Give me room to work."

You can see then why I say that we preachers do not have control over the prophesying aspect of participating in divine transformation of the world. All we can do is pray that God would speak directly, beyond our knowledge and face-to-face with people when we speak.

So, to do this verb of participating is to stand, Bible in hand, before a group of people, and while evangelizing or heralding or teaching, expect the risen and ascended Jesus to speak in ways we had not planned or imagined.

Oh Lord, release the power of this verb in our preaching!

Confessing (homologeō). It means "to agree in statement," "to say the same thing."[33] *Homo:* the same; *logeō:* to say or speak. John the Baptist did it: "he confessed, and did not deny, but confessed, 'I am not the Christ'" (Jn 1:20). Jesus says he will do it on "that day," to those who said, "Lord, Lord," but did not act on their words: "I will declare to them, 'I never knew you'" (Mt 7:22-23); "Therefore everyone who shall confess Me before others, I will also confess before My Father who is in heaven" (Mt 10:32 NASB modified). The early church did it and calls us to do it: "If you confess with your mouth Jesus as Lord, and believe in your heart that God raised him from the dead, you shall be saved" (Rom 10:9); "If we confess our sins, He is faithful and righteous to forgive us our sins and to cleanse us from all unrighteousness" (1 Jn 1:9); "Every spirit that confesses that Jesus Christ has come in the flesh is from God" (1 Jn 4:2); "Whoever confesses that Jesus is the Son of God," God abides in that person and that person in God (1 Jn 4:15); "you made the good confession in the presence of many witnesses" (1 Tim 6:12). One day the whole universe "will confess *[exhomologeō]* that Jesus Christ is Lord, to the glory of God the Father" (Phil 2:10-11). To confess is to "make solemn statements of faith."[34]

The New Testament envisions six different settings in which this verb operates.[35] The first happens when one is making a confession

---

[33]Otto Michel, "ὁμολογέω," in *Theological Dictionary of the New Testament*, ed. Gerhard Kittel and Gerhard Friedrich (Grand Rapids: Eerdmans, 1964-1976), 5:199-219.

[34]Ibid., 5:209.

[35]Oscar Cullman, *The Earliest Christian Confessions*, trans. J. K. S. Reid (London: Lutterworth Press, 1949), pp. 18-34. Cullman names five of these, which correspond to the first five I am listing.

of faith in the believing community, at one's baptism, for instance, or at one's commissioning for ministry. The second happens when one is making a statement of faith along with other believers in a worship service, as many of us do using the Apostles' or Nicene Creed. The third happens in a court setting, in a more hostile environment, when one is asked to declare what one believes. The fourth happens in a polemical context, when one needs to state what one believes so that the dialogue can move forward. The fifth happens in spiritual warfare, when struggling with the demonic ("in the name of Jesus Christ"). And the sixth happens "on that day," when all are called to account.

David Lose, of Luther Seminary in Saint Paul, Minnesota, suggests that we in the opening years of the third millennium are in a context wherein preaching now requires operating in the mode of this verb.[36] In a postmodern world, with its suspicion of all faith claims (and with its insistence that there isn't one single metanarrative) and with its suspicion about words (especially religious words) we need to embrace the long tradition of confessing Jesus Christ in the communicating-of-the-gospel moment. Lose writes: "I propose that preaching that seeks to be both faithful to the Christian tradition and responsive to our pluralistic, postmodern context is best understood as the public practice of confessing Jesus Christ."[37] He is encouraging preachers to reclaim this centuries-old practice "that rests not on empirical proof but on a living confession of faith" and "leads not to certainty but to conviction, and lives not in the domain of knowledge but rather in the realm of faithful assertion."[38]

After surveying the use of the verb in Scripture and tradition, Lose then suggests "the sermonic language" inherent to "confessing."[39] He suggests four adjectives for this mode of communicating: *ultimate, urgent, relational* and *vulnerable.*[40] I think he is actually developing the

---

[36]David Lose, *Confessing Jesus Christ: Preaching in a Postmodern World* (Grand Rapids: Eerdmans, 2003).

[37]Ibid., p. 3. In the book he italicizes this sentence.

[38]Ibid., pp. 145-88. He carefully explains what he means by all this, especially in the chapter "Confession and the Biblical Canon."

[39]Ibid., p. 220.

[40]Ibid., p. 221.

spirit in which one confesses in our time. *Ultimate:* preaching is serious business because we are confessing ultimate truth. Jesus is Lord, and in his death and resurrection God has acted for the redemption of the whole cosmos. "Preaching that shies away from making such claims denies the gospel."[41] A Christian sermon not only has moments of declaration of ultimate truth, but "the sermon's center of gravity is located in them."[42] *Urgent:* the ones spoken to have to respond in some way. "When someone confesses 'I love you,' only one kind of response will do, a confession of similar character: either 'I love you, too,' or 'I don't love you,' but certainly not, 'that's interesting,' 'the poets have many interesting things to say about love,' or, to echo Pilate, 'What is love?'"[43] *Relational:* confession is person-to-person language, language that cares about how the hearer is responding because we want the hearer to know what we know, to see what we see, to hear what we hear, to feel what we feel. *Vulnerable:* "while the language of confession asserts a new reality, it does not claim to be able to prove it," (as in the opening chapter of this book).[44] Preachers step out before others and state the truth as clearly and boldly as possible, and then they step back, so to speak, realizing how helpless they are to "make it real" for the hearers.

So, to do this verb of participating is to rise, Bible in hand, and "take a stand." "Here I stand, I can say nothing else, nothing more." And confessing means to trust the truth itself (himself) to win the hearts and minds of hearers.

Oh Lord, release the power of this verb in our preaching!

Witnessing (*martyreō*). The meaning of this verb is shaped by the related noun, *martys,* "witness," meaning "one who remembers, who has knowledge of something by recollection, and who can thus tell about it."[45] The word is used primarily of a witness in a court setting, where it denotes persons who can and do "speak from personal experience"

---

[41]Ibid., p. 222.
[42]Ibid.
[43]Ibid., p. 224.
[44]Ibid., p. 228.
[45]H. Strathmann, "μάρτυς, κτλ.," in *Theological Dictionary of the New Testament,* ed. Gerhard Kittel and Gerhard Friedrich (Grand Rapids: Eerdmans, 1964-1976), 4:475.

about events in which they themselves were involved, either as specta-
tors or recipients of the action.[46] It is one of John's favorite words, used
by him more than by any other biblical author. John the Baptist did it:
"John bore witness of Him" (Jn 1:15 NKJV); "And John bore witness" (Jn
1:32 NKJV); "And I have seen, and have borne witness" (Jn 1:34 ASV);
In all cases John's witness was to Jesus as the preexistent one, Messiah,
Lamb of God, Son of God and baptizer in and with the Holy Spirit.
Jesus did it: "Truly, truly, I say to you, we speak that which we know,
and bear witness of that which we have seen" (Jn 3:11 ASV modified); "I
am One who bears witness of Myself" (Jn 8:18 NKJV); "For this cause I
was born, and for this cause I have come into the world, that I should
bear witness to the truth" (Jn 18:37 NKJV). The Father bears witness:
"And the Father who sent Me, He has borne witness of Me" (Jn 5:37
ASV); "And the Father who sent Me bears witness of Me" (Jn 8:18 NKJV).
The Spirit, the Paraclete, does it: "The Spirit of truth, who proceeds
from the Father, He will bear witness of Me" (Jn 15:26 ASV modified).
Jesus says his disciples will do it: "And you [the first band of believers]
also will bear witness" (Jn 15:27 NKJV); "you [the whole church] will
receive power when the Holy Spirit has come upon you; and you shall
be witnesses to me" in all the world (Acts 1:8).[47] And the "classic" text
on this verb: "That which was from the beginning, that which we have
heard, that which we have seen with our eyes, that which we beheld,
and our hands have handled, concerning the Word of Life (and the life
was manifested, and we have seen and bear witness, and proclaim to
you, the eternal life, which was with the Father, and was manifested
unto us)" (1 Jn 1:1-2 ASV).

Would you agree that whether we use the actual term or not, this
verb is at the heart of any authentic communication of the gospel?
Granted, the one speaking the truth of the gospel need not actually
believe what is being said; the truth itself (himself) speaks for itself
(himself). But, the communication moment is all the more transforma-

---

[46]Ibid., 4:476.
[47]Note: When preaching this text it is crucial to put the emphasis where Jesus does. That is,
he does not command us to "be witnesses." Rather, he makes a promise: "the Holy Spirit will
come upon you." Being a witness is the result of Jesus doing something for us and to us and
in us!

tive if the speaker believes the words being spoken. All preaching that impacts others involves authentic witnessing.[48] Thomas Long puts it so well: "The court has access to the truth only through the witness. It seeks the truth, but it must look for it in the testimony of the witness. The very life of the witness, then, is bound up into the testimony. The witness cannot claim to be removed, objectively pointing to the evidence. What the witness believes to be true is part of the evidence."[49] Richard Bauckham, building on the work of the Swedish New Testament scholar, Samuel Byrskog,[50] rightly argues that "the ideal witness" is not "the dispassionate observer but the one who, as a participant" has been close to the events and "whose direct experience" enables him or her to understand and interpret what they have seen or heard.[51] Speaking of the eyewitnesses whose testimonies are recorded for us in the four Gospels, Bauckham says, "Involvement was not an obstacle to a correct understanding of what they perceived as historical truth. It was rather the essential means to a correct understanding of what had really happened."[52] So too with the recorded preaching of the first eyewitnesses. Passionate involvement of the preacher with the truth is not an obstacle to the hearers believing the message; it is part of the means the Spirit uses to validate the truth. The witness is so involved in the truth that should the hearers despise the truth of the message, "the witness may suffer, or even be killed, as a result of the testimony. It is no coincidence that the New Testament word for 'witness' is martyr."[53] That is often the cost of faithful preaching.

When this happens we are to rejoice, for we are participating in the witness of the "faithful witness" (Rev 1:5; see also Rev 19:11), who "testified the good confession before Pontius Pilate" (1 Tim 6:13).

So, to do this verb of participating is to stand up, Bible in hand (unless it has been stripped from us), in some cases hand on Bible, and sim-

---

[48]Thomas Long, *The Witness of Preaching* (Philadelphia: Westminster, 1989).

[49]Ibid., p. 44.

[50]Samuel Byrskog, *Story as History—History as Story*, repr. ed. (Leiden: Brill, 2002).

[51]Richard Bauckham, *Jesus and the Eyewitnesses: The Gospels as Eyewitness Testimony* (Grand Rapids: Eerdmans, 2006), p. 9.

[52]Ibid.

[53]Long, *Witness*, p. 44.

ply tell what we ourselves have seen and heard and touched concerning
the gospel, and with the woman at the well say something like, "Come,
see a man who told me all the things that I have done; this is not the
Christ, is it?" (Jn 4:29). William Temple, when serving as archbishop
of Canterbury, has been quoted as saying, "It is quite futile . . . saying
to people, 'Go to the cross.' We must be able to say, 'Come to the cross.'
And there are only two voices which can issue that invitation with effect. One is the voice of the Sinless Redeemer, with which we cannot
speak; the other is the voice of the fogiven sinner, who knows himself
forgiven. That is our part."[54]

Oh Lord, release the power of this verb in our preaching!

What a many-verbed wonder is the preaching moment: Announcing
the joyful news of God's victory over all that threatens life, a victory
that forever alters our situation; heralding God's great public "now,"
news that makes a claim on public life; developing the full implications
of the news for everyday life; coming alongside people to help them
move on in faith toward maturity; speaking, unconsciously for the most
part, words directly from God, words beyond what we ourselves are
thinking in the moment, words that "get in the face"; confessing the
truth with urgency and in vulnerability; witnessing to what we ourselves have experienced of God's incredibly good, good news.[55]

The following brief statements summarizes the passion inherent in
each verb and the intended outcome of each.

- Evangelize: the passion is joy; the hoped-for outcome is to "receive
  Jesus" and enter into his new world order.

- Herald: the passion is truth; the hoped-for outcome is to "hear Jesus"
  and trust this new reading of reality.

- Teach: the passion is understanding; the hoped-for outcome is to
  "obey Jesus" and do what he tells us to do.

- Exhort: the passion is freedom; the hoped-for outcome is to "follow
  Jesus" and walk with him into a new way of living.

---

[54]Quoted in John R. W. Stott, *The Preacher's Portrait: Some New Testament Word Studies* (London: Tyndale Press, 1961), p. 66.
[55]See Firet, *Dynamics*, pp. 82-83 for a more academic way of rendering this.

- Prophesy: the passion is revelation; the hoped-for outcome is to "see Jesus" and live a new life in light of him.

- Confess: the passion is "no choice but to speak"; the hoped-for outcome is to "join Jesus" and see if you too find in him a rock on which to stand.

- Witness: the passion is life; the hoped-for outcome is to "live Jesus too" and see if he does not do for you what he has done for me.

So what do we do with this expansive understanding of the "communicating moment"?

God speaks through all these verbs, or more precisely, God speaks in all of these verbal ways. God therefore transforms human lives through all these ways of communicating the gospel. All these verbs are, to one degree or another, at work in most "communicating moments." But one verb will likely dominate and move the sermon. Using Robert Reid's analogy regarding "voices of preaching," all the verbs "may be along for the ride, but only one . . . should be behind the wheel."[56] That one verb arises from what the preacher's goals for listeners. And ideally, that verb should be "behind the wheel" of the text being preached. That which moves the sermon ought to be that which moves the text. Or, the voice of the sermon ought to be the voice of the text. By *voice* I mean here "burden," "trajectory," "drumbeat," "desired outcome." Yes, preachers have their own personal bents they bring to the task (from exegesis to homiletics[57]), the congregational dynamics are bent in certain ways, as is the surrounding culture, but the preacher's job is to conform to the bent of the text. So if the text teaches, the sermon is a teaching sermon; if the text confesses, the sermon is a confessing sermon. Again, the preacher cannot escape her or his own gifting or wiring; but the preacher, under the authority of

---

[56]Reid, *Four Voices*, p. 32. Reid is using the term "voice" to refer to the preacher's way of approaching the preaching task. He uses terms like "particular cultural consciousness," "a person's personal center of gravity in matters of truth," "assumptions about the nature of language appeals and the nature of authority appeals" (p. 22). He then suggests four "archetypical voices," each with a different desired outcome for the hearer: the teaching voice, "*explain* a meaning"; the encouraging voice, "*facilitate* an encounter"; the sage voice, "*explore* insight"; and testifying voice, "*engage* congregational identity" (pp. 23-24).

[57]To be more fully developed in the next chapter, "Moving from Text to Sermon."

the text, is to communicate in the verbal bent of the text.[58]

So, we enact the verb (or verbs) that the text requires. We enact the verb (or verbs) that our hearts, when moved by the text, desire. We do not fret about what it is called. We simply join the living God in communicating his gospel.[59]

---

[58]To be more fully developed in chapter eight, "The Person of Preacher."

[59]For further reading I commend to you John R. W. Stott's *The Preacher's Portrait: Some New Testament Word Studies* (Grand Rapids: Eerdmans, 1961), where he explores a number of these verbs and their noun forms in greater detail.

PART TWO

HUMAN MECHANICS

OF PARTICIPATING

5

MOVING FROM TEXT TO SERMON

Inhabiting the Text

WE NOW MOVE FROM "THEORETICAL foundations for participating" to what I am calling "human mechanics of participating." In other words, we move from a philosophy of preaching to a practice of preaching.

Why the word *mechanics?* Why not *technique*, or *labor*, or the more fancy *praxis?* Why *mechanics?* Not because the process of preaching, from text to sermon, is mechanical—it is anything but! Not because one can simply follow a series of steps and magically produce a sermon. I have chosen the word because it reminds us that although we are participating in the work of the living, triune God, we humans do have work to do, hard work. I am avoiding the word *technique* because of its affinity with *technology*, with all its potential for manipulation. I am avoiding the word *labor* because it conveys, at least to me, a weightiness God does not want us to carry.

There are possibly two better words. The first is *liturgy*, from the Greek *leitourgia*, which has the meaning of both work and worship. The "liturgy of participating" would convey the great truth that it is in worship that we know God most intimately and hear God most clearly. Preaching that transforms emerges out of a heart and mind at worship. The second word is *dance*. Robert Reid speaks of "the homiletical dance that makes up the human and divine dimensions of preaching."[1] What

---

[1]Robert Stephen Reid, *The Four Voices of Preaching: Connecting Purpose and Identity Behind the Pulpit* (Grand Rapids: Brazos, 2006), p. 29.

I develop in this chapter could also be thought of as "dance steps in participating." Indeed, dance conveys the joy and energy and work of the relationship into which the living God draws us in Jesus.[2]

But I will use the word *mechanics*, for though there are times when we are working through the process of text to sermon and our spirits are worshipping, and though there are times through the process when our feet want to dance, most of the time we simply have to keep at it, doing the hard and steady work of study, interpreting, crafting, recrafting, practicing and praying.

What I am attempting to do in the following pages is to get inside the process preachers go through as they prepare to preach an expository sermon. In what follows I am also trying to get inside my own mind and heart, and identify some of what happens as the Holy Spirit enables me to move into a text, be captured by the text (or, more accurately, by the divine person behind the text) and then move from the text into a sermon. I am in no way suggesting that this is the only way one goes about the task. You will notice that I have learned from many others, who, though using different vocabulary, seem to follow something like the process I develop here. You will also notice that at points I differ from a number of the textbooks currently used in preaching courses.

Lesslie Newbigin's statement in his theological commentary on the Gospel of John (previously quoted in chapter three) expresses well a goal that should guide any process of sermon preparation. The mission statesman writes, "My task is to make clear to myself and (if possible) to others the word which is spoken in the Gospel in such a way that it may be heard in the language of this culture of which I am a part with all its power to question that culture."[3]

First I offer a word of encouragement before we launch into our discussion of process. Ian Pitt-Watson, a first-rank preacher, reminds us that sermons are more "born" than they are "constructed."[4] He encour-

---

[2]See C. Baxter Kruger, *The Great Dance* (Jackson, Miss.: Perichoresis Press, 2000).

[3]Lesslie Newbigin, *The Light Has Come: An Exposition of the Fourth Gospel* (Grand Rapids: Eerdmans, 1982), p. ix.

[4]Ian Pitt-Watson, *A Primer for Preachers* (Grand Rapids: Baker, 1986), p. 10.

ages us to think of the crafting of a sermon in terms of the formation of a baby—it is born, not "constructed" as are buildings or airplanes. This is true of any work of human creativity. More often than not, as one does the hard work of preparation, the sermon simply happens, emerging in front of us as we live in the biblical text.[5] Maybe this is why for centuries the word *deliver* has been used for preaching? While the verb *deliver* also gives the sense of conveying tradition ("I received from the Lord that which I also delivered to you," 1 Cor 11:23; see also 1 Cor 15:3), the same verb also comes from the realm of baby-making. In sermon-making we go through the same stages: conception, gestation (often very uncomfortable: "What possessed me to do this?"), birth (hopefully on the day it is supposed to be delivered!) and then postpartum blues (an unfortunate but necessary grief).[6]

Pitt-Watson, working with this baby-vs.-building image, suggests that a sermon looks and feels and works a lot like a human being.[7] A sermon has

- a heart (the theme and purpose statement)

- a skeleton (its main points, conceptual structure)

- a backbone (a natural harmony)

- joints (smooth transitions)

- lifeblood (emotion, passion, conviction)

- flesh (illustrations, everyday examples)

- muscle (application that requires and enables action)

- Spirit (the breath and breathing of the living God) (my addition)

All this reminds us that, regardless of the process we go through, the sermon comes to life not only because of the process but also because of the way the Spirit of God works with the preacher. What emerges at the end of the process is usually different than what we expected, different than what we set out to create. That is just fine. We are, after all,

---

[5]Ibid.
[6]A must-read essay is Charles Haddon Spurgeon, "The Minister's Fainting Fits," in *Lectures to My Students* (Grand Rapids: Zondervan, 1972), pp. 154-65.
[7]Pitt-Watson, *A Primer for Preachers*, p. 10.

dealing not only with a text, but also with a living person who meets us in the text.

Getting started. Our first task is to select the text. It should be one that is manageable for a single sermon. The selection process is a function of a number of different possibilities. They include

1. the preacher's sense of the leading of the Holy Spirit

2. the preacher being assigned the text

3. the text assigned by the lectionary (if that is part of one's tradition)

4. the next text in a series of sermons on a book of the Bible

5. the call of unusual circumstances (a special event in the life of the congregation, city or world; a natural disaster, such as a hurricane or earthquake; a tragic event, such as a terrorist attack or automobile accident involving students of the local high school)

The third and fourth possibilities put us preachers on firmer ground; we are less likely to be preaching our best Christianized thoughts or preaching only out of what is happening in our own lives.

Once the text is selected, the next first task, if task is the word for it, is to pray. Every time. Something like this: "O living God, will you now in your mercy and grace open this text to me. And then will you open my mind and heart to see and hear what you have opened. This I pray in Jesus' name, and for the greater fame of his name." This prayer is informed by a text we have already come to appreciate: Luke 24, the stories of Jesus meeting two dejected disciples on the road to Emmaus on the afternoon of the first Easter, and of Jesus later meeting with all the other disciples in Jerusalem on the first Easter Sunday evening. Luke speaks of a double opening. He says, "Then He [Jesus] opened their minds to understand the Scriptures" (Lk 24:45). But before that, Jesus had opened the Scriptures to them (Lk 24:27, 32). We pray for both. We pray with the apostle Paul for "a spirit of wisdom and of revelation in the knowledge of Him . . . that the eyes of your heart may be enlightened" (Eph 1:17-18). God must open the text to us and then open us to what is opened. And for this double miracle we pray.

Having selected the text and prayed, it is good to do two simple things. First, read the text out loud four or five times. As we vocalize the words, our ears hear, our minds automatically become attuned to different nuances of meaning and our minds be begin to ask questions of the text. Second, read the text in a number of different translations (at least four). Again, our minds will automatically go to work noticing the differences in rendering and will naturally begin to ask, "What accounts for these?" These two simple actions get us well on our way.

The overall process. There are four basic steps to the overall process. Not that we take them one at a time, for they often overlap. They are

- devotional—opening our minds and hearts to what God is saying to us, the preachers, in the text.

- exegetical—the word comes from *exēgeomai*, "to lead out," "to show the way." This is the process of learning what the author of the text was saying to his first readers/listeners in their historical, cultural setting.

- hermeneutical—Hermes was the god who served as messenger/herald of the other gods. This is the process of discovering the message—what the text now says to our historical, cultural setting.

- homiletical—the word comes from *homologeō*, to confess, to "say the same thing," to "consort with." This is the process of finding ways to package what the text is saying to our setting in ways that connect with our setting.

Again, it is not that we do one, then two, then three, then four in a nice, neat order. Often the homiletical form can emerge early in the exegetical phase; often the devotional impact comes in the hermeneutical phase. Yet it is helpful to lay out, if you will, the logistical mechanics for the process.

Think of the following pages as me walking with you through a recipe for a gourmet meal: it may feel tedious, even boring at times, but hopefully you will anticipate all the delicious aromas of the only food that satisfies the human heart and mind.

Before reading any further, I invite you to now stop and select a text you would like to preach. Then take some time to go through the above preliminary aspects of the process. Pray for the Spirit's illuminating work, read it aloud, read it in a number of different versions. Then keep the text in mind as we walk through the following aspects of the process. Doing so will help ground the theoretical discussion in practical application.

THE DEVOTIONAL STEP

First, we want to hear what God speaks to us before we ask what God wants us to say. And we will better understand what the text is saying to us if we go "all the way back," so to speak, and ask, "Why has the Holy Spirit even bothered to breathe this text?" The answer to this is what we developed in chapter three: encounter, news, worldview shift, obedience of faith, enablement.

Encounter. What about the nature and character of God (Father, Son and Holy Spirit) is manifested in this text? Are there other texts of Scripture that come to mind which manifest the same character or attributes? Are there texts that come to mind which manifest a "But, on the other hand," or a "Yes, but there is this other side of God too"? What song comes to mind as you read this text? What stories from literature, film or your own life point to what is being revealed here?

News. What is the news of the text? To what dimension of our fallen condition does the text speak? Bryan Chapell works with the idea of the "FCF," the "Fallen Condition Focus . . . the mutual human condition that contemporary believers share with those to and for whom the text was written that requires the grace of the passage."[8] What news does the text have for this condition? Do any other texts of Scripture that declare the same news come to mind? Are there texts that come to mind which declare, "But, on the other hand"? To what condition of your life does this text speak? What song comes to mind as you read the text? What stories from literature or film or your experience point to the news announced here?

You can see that already the steps are overlapping; it is hard to do "devotions" without thinking about the whole world.

---

[8]Bryan Chapell, *Christ-Centered Preaching: Redeeming the Expository Sermon* (Grand Rapids: Baker, 1994), p. 42.

Worldview shift. What dimension of your worldview is being challenged here? What dimensions of the text's worldview are hard for you to embrace? What difference would it make if you were to adopt the worldview of this text? Are there other texts of Scripture calling us to this worldview? Are there texts that seem to say, "But on the other hand"? What song comes to mind as you think about this? Can you think of a story from literature or film or your experience that points to this alternative reading of reality?

Obedience of faith. What are the discipleship implications? What is the text calling you to do? What are the explicit calls and what are the implicit calls? Is there a promise to claim? Is there a command to obey? Is there a great truth to affirm? Are there other biblical texts calling for the same action? Are there texts that say, "But on the other hand"? How is this command to "do" related to the character of God revealed in the text? Can you see how this response is but another dimension of trust? What difference would it make if you actually obeyed and did what the text compels?

Enablement. Does the text give you any help in how to obey this command to "do"? Explicitly, actually calling you to trust Jesus? Or is the call implicit? Does any other biblical text come to mind wherein we are definitively promised the enablement of the Holy Spirit to do what is required?

This devotional step is important for a number of reasons, chief among them being to allow the text to get a hold on us before we try to get a hold on it. I like how a Jewish scholar, Michael Fishbane, expressed his process of seeking to understand any piece of literature. He writes, "Everything depends on how we read; on how we enter the magic circle of a text's meanings; on how we smuggle ourselves into its words, and allow the texture of a text to weave its web around us."[9]

THE EXEGETICAL STEP

This is the least "creative" step of the process. Here we simply have

---

[9]I do not remember where I saw this exact wording, but see Michael Fishbane, *Text and Texture: Close Readings of Selected Biblical Texts* (New York: Schocken Books, 1979) wherein he develops this idea in greater detail.

to set aside as best we can what we think the text is saying and try as hard as we can to let the text speak for itself. William Willimon, in his book on the preaching of Karl Barth, urges us that "the only way to understand the text is a willingness to stand within the all-embracing interpretive world of the texts and the Lord of the texts."[10] Willimon says that Barth argues that "the reader or hearer must realize that this story is a real description of the real world, and the central character of this story is busy helping one to discover one's place within this real world."[11] This is what exegesis helps us do.

There are two critical initial steps in exegesis. Number one: do not immediately consult the commentaries. You will later on, but not now. Why? Because you and I want to come to the commentaries out of our own serious reading of the text. If we begin with someone else's reading we never really hear the text for ourselves. Resist the temptation to speed up the process and simply pull a commentary from the shelf.

Number two: try to memorize the text.[12] Memorization engages the mind in the kinds of issues involved in exegesis. We will, for example, unconsciously recite a present tense when the text uses the past; or we will use a finite verb when the text uses a participle; or we will say "in" when the text uses "into," or "by" when the text uses "through," etc. Memorizing the text kicks the mind into exegetical high gear. And we save a lot of time.

We then do the work of word studies. It takes time. But it must be done.

When investigating the text's verbs, watch for tense, voice and mood. Take, for example, Galatians 5:16. The NRSV renders it, "Live by the Spirit, I say, and do not gratify the desires of the flesh." Two commands. The NASB renders it, "walk by the Spirit, and you will not carry out the desire of the flesh." One command, one promise. Which is it? Before we can preach the text we have to do some work.[13] Another

---

[10]William H. Willimon, *Conversations with Barth on Preaching* (Nashville: Abingdon, 2006), p. 32.

[11]Ibid.

[12]I got this idea from Jeannette Scholer in 1999 when she served as coordinator of academic programs at Fuller Theological Seminary.

[13]It is the NASB: "will not carry out," a promise. In Greek it is *ou mē* + the aorist subjunctive, the

example comes from Ephesians 5:21. Most versions render it "and be subject." Paul, however, uses a present participle, the fifth in a row (the others being "speaking," "singing," "making melody," "giving thanks"). Why translate what appears to be the end of a series of participles as an imperative? The present participle is used to express the consequences of an action. "Be filled with the Spirit," says Paul (Eph 5:18), and the result will be the series of actions, i.e., a series of actions that can only be done when filled with the Spirit. What is Paul's point? Only by the power of the Spirit can human beings live in submission to one another.

Other parts of speech require our attention as well:

- Nouns. Watch for number, case and gender. Do the words mean just one thing, or is there a range of meaning? Which is the author using here?

- Adjectives. Watch for number, case and gender. Look carefully at which adjective is modifying which noun.

- Adverbs. How are they modifying the time, tone and intensity of the action?

- Prepositions. These are little words with huge implications. Pay close attention to them.

Galatians 4:4-7 provides one example of prepositions carrying theological weight. In this text, Paul declares that in the fullness of time, "God sent forth His Son, born of a woman." In each clause the preposition is *ek,* meaning "out of," more exactly, "out of the center of."[14] The prepositions proclaim the mystery of Jesus' identity: out of the center of a woman and out of the center of the living God, and consequently, fully human, fully divine. One could write a book on the New Testament use of prepositions, especially those used relative to Jesus and his relationship with us ("in Christ," "with Christ," "through Christ," "for

---

most emphatic way to express a negative possibility. I cannot understand why RSV (and then NRSV) mistranslate the verse. We are talking about two very different forms of spiritual life!

[14]See Bruce Metzger, "Table II. Geometric Arrangement of the Greek Prepositions," in *Lexical Aids for Students of New Testament Greek* (Theological Books Agency, 1973); and William D. Mounce, *Basics of Biblical Greek* (Grand Rapids: Zondervan, 1993), p. 80.

Christ," "Christ in you," "Christ for us," etc.).[15] Watch how the different translations you consulted handle these matters. Before we can faithfully preach the text we need to have some idea of why the versions have chosen the renderings they have—astute listeners will ask us afterward!

Perhaps a more substantive example will serve us well at this point. Take a look at the second half of the best known of Jesus' parables, the parable of the prodigal son in Luke 15. (Actually, it should be called the parable of the two prodigal sons.) In Luke 15:25-32, Jesus tells how the older of the two sons reacts to the surprising, scandalous love of the father for the younger son. The older son insults his father by not going into the party, a party the father has thrown out of the joy of receiving his child home. Jesus says, "He became angry and was not willing to go in" (Lk 15:28). The older son, in that culture, is shaming his father. And how does the father respond to this shaming action? Jesus says, "And his father came out [of the house] and entreated him" (Lk 15:28 asv). Entreat. Not punish. Not argue. Not harangue. Let Kenneth Bailey fill out the point Jesus is making.

> The Greek word for "call" is *kaleō*. Many different shades of meaning can be given to the word by prefixing prepositions to it. For example:
>   *en-kaleō:* "call against" or "accuse";
>   *eis-kaleō:* "call in" or "invite";
>   *epi-kaleō:* "call by name";
>   *pro-kaleō:* "provoke" or "challenge"
>   *pros-kaleō:* "summon" or "call to oneself" as an officer would summon
>   an orderly, or a master a servant;
>   *syn-kaleō:* "call together";
>   *para-kaleō:* "appeal to" or "entreat" or "try to conciliate."
> Luke knows this family of words well and uses it more than any other New Testament writer. In v. 26 the older son "summons" *(pros-kaleō)* the youth to demand information. Here in v. 28 we fully expect the father to likewise "summon" *(pros-kaleō)* his older son, to demand an explanation for his public rudeness. Or perhaps he will "challenge" him *(pro-kaleō)* or even "accuse" him *(en-kaleō).* Rather, in direct contrast

---

[15]I hope one day to write a book titled *Prepositional Theology!*

to the son who summons an inferior to demand an explanation, the father goes out to "entreat" *(para-kaleō)*, to "appeal to," to "try to conciliate." Robertson, in his monumental grammar, gives us the key to the two prepositions used here with the same word. He says that *para* merely means "beside" or "alongside" (cf. our "parallel"), and *pros* suggests "facing one another." So the son "summons" the youth to stand facing him as an inferior should. But the father tries to "entreat" his son. He calls on him to "stand alongside" his father, to look at the world from the father's perspective.[16]

Isn't that good? Bailey models paying close attention to the words the biblical author has chosen. (And he models exegesis in the service of proclamation.)

Having done word studies, we move on to understand how the author of the text is taking all these verbs and nouns and adverbs and prepositions to say something to his original audience and, through the Spirit, to us. Here we now want to grasp the point the author is making.

Actually, our minds have already begun to move in this direction. For the human mind craves order: our minds, under most circumstances, the exception proving the rule, are seemingly hard-wired to make sense of things. Is this not one of the implications of being made in the image of the God of the Bible, the God who speaks into chaos and brings into being order (Genesis 1)? So, in one sense we never really have to shift into exegesis; we are always exegeting everything in life.

More specifically, we want to seek out the main point of the section we are preaching. This main point will be what the sermon is all about. There may be a cluster of points, but we want to seek out the "big idea" integrating all the points. The assumption here is that the author of the document (Isaiah, John, Paul, Peter or Jude, et. al.) really wants to communicate to those he cares about and is using language with a high degree of intentionality and not simply throwing out thoughts and ideas randomly. I know that a number of philosophers argue that we cannot trust human language to convey any real meaning, that authors them-

---

[16]Kenneth Bailey, *The Cross and the Prodigal*, rev. ed. (Downers Grove, Ill.: InterVarsity Press, 2005), p. 83-84.

selves do not really know what they are saying, and that hearers take what they hear and give the words their own meaning. That may be so in some cases. But I think most human beings use words because they want to say something that has very specific meaning, and that most listeners want to understand what the words they hear were intended to mean. Yes, it can be messy: the word we choose turning out not to be the one we should have used, the other person understanding the word we chose differently than we intend, etc. But still, given the dynamic nature of language and the messiness of communication, most people intend to say what they mean and mean what they say.

At this point in the process, the genre of the text we are preaching is going to determine how we proceed in exegesis, especially in determining the main point. Different literary forms or genres call for different exegetical procedures. In what follows, I can only give basic hints for working with the various genres of the Bible. One of the most complete developments on this is Sidney Greidanus's *The Modern Preacher and the Ancient Text: Interpreting and Preaching Biblical Literature.*[17] To that work you can turn for more complete guidance.

In the following paragraphs I pass on to you some things I am learning about the exegesis of various genres. At this point you may want to only read the section on the genre of the text you have chosen to preach; you can consult the other sections when you are preaching another genre. Again, if this seems tedious recall the potentially delicious results of following a detailed recipe.

Hints for getting inside epistle texts. We begin by asking a question such as, "What was going on in the lives of those for whom the text was originally penned?" This, of course, means we need to be reading the whole epistle in which our single text is found. G. Campbell Morgan, one of the foremost preachers of the early twentieth century, never preached out of a biblical book unless he had read it forty or fifty times![18] Having done so he could then flow with the author's think-

---

[17]Sidney Greidanus, *The Modern Preacher and the Ancient Text: Interpreting and Preaching Biblical Literature* (Grand Rapids: Eerdmans, 1988).

[18]Jill Morgan, *Man of the Word: The Life of G. Campbell Morgan* (1951; reprint, Grand Rapids: Baker, 1972); G. Campbell Morgan, *The Ministry of the Word: The James Sprunt Lectures, Union Theological Seminary* (New York: Fleming H. Revell, 1919); and *Preaching* (London: Marshall,

ing; he could see the movements within the text, for he knew how the author entered the text and how the author exited the text. So, "What was going on in the lives of the original readers?" Was there a conflict that needed to be resolved? A tragedy that called for comfort? Was there some oversight or neglect in some aspect of discipleship? Was there a wrong idea that needed to be corrected? Or was it that the proclamation of good news was needed? (My assumption, of course, is that people always need to hear good news.)

We then get more specific and ask other kinds of questions. What are the finite verbs? In particular, are there any imperatives? Daniel Fuller argues that imperatives are always a good clue to the passion of the author. If there are imperatives, are there any participles? Past tense participles usually give us the reason for the imperatives; present participles usually give us what results from obeying the imperative. Who or what are the subjects of the finite verbs? We want to be clear about who is doing what. Are there any modifying clauses? How are they related to the action of the finite verb(s)? Take care to notice any prepositional clauses. Why one preposition and not another? Are there any adverbial clauses?

Again, we should assume that the author is using language and grammatical constructions intentionally for one thing and not another. Paying attention to all this is what it means to bend your mind to the text.

Having engaged the above questions, can we now see how everything in the text relates to the main point? If not, go back through the questions. Can we see how the main point is related to the text's context in the larger letter? Can we see how it is related to both the text that precedes and the text that follows? We know we have found the main point when we can account for everything else in the text in light of it.

A personal note: I sentence diagram every epistle text I preach. (I have sentence diagrammed nearly every New Testament letter.) This enables me to see how the passage goes together around the main point.[19] *For* or *because* give the ground or support of the main point;

Morgan and Scott, 1937).

[19]I learned this from Daniel Fuller at Fuller, 1969-1972, and am profoundly grateful to him. His

therefore or *so* give the results or consequences of the main point; *when*, *before* or *after* give temporal indications of what is happening; *but* or *nevertheless* help us see a point "on the other hand"; *and* and *furthermore* show us that more is going on; *as* or *in this way* give further explanation; *like* illustrates the main point; and *if. . .* , *then* shows the conditions and promises of the main point. One could accomplish the same end by drawing a picture of a house, for example, showing how all the pieces go together to make a whole; or a picture of a flower pot, the pot being the main point, the legs beneath it the supports or reasons, the plant being the consequences, the leaves the specific fruit that emerges in our lives when we live the main point.

If at this point things are not clear, set the work aside, go for a walk, run an errand, take a nap or listen to the news. Just let your mind percolate all the data without the pressure of having to come to any firm conclusion. This, by the way, is why we do not want to begin the preparation process on Saturday evening! Exegesis takes time—build it into the schedule earlier in the week. I will say a lot more about this in chapter nine, "The Life of the Preacher."

Hints for getting inside Old Testament narrative texts. On the one hand, simply retelling the story is not yet preaching.[20] On the other hand, a didactic analysis of the story reshapes the form of the text, unintentionally distorting the message of the text.[21] We avoid these two extremes by treating the story as a story and by seeing it as part of the Grand Story. Also, in some way, it intersects and shapes our own stories.

But the author is not just telling a story for the sake of entertainment. The author is not just relaying mere facts for historical record. The author is giving a discourse, an artfully crafted representation and interpretation of the facts.[22] And the author does this by employing

---

work has been further developed by Thomas Schreiner, *Interpreting the Pauline Epitles* (Grand Rapids: Baker, 1990). See especially the chapter "Tracing the Argument."

[20]Graeme Goldsworthy, *Preaching the Whole Bible as Christian Scripture* (Grand Rapids: Eerdmans, 2000). "Preaching involves a transferring of the point of the passage to today's hearers" (p. 150).

[21]Greidanus, *Modern Preacher*, p. 147.

[22]M. A. Powell, *What Is Narrative Criticism?* (Minneapolis: Fortress, 1990), p. 23.

rhetorical devices, usually geared for the ear, devices by which the author is intentionally leading his readers/hearers into his understanding of the facts. Such devices include the following:[23]

- Lead words or key words, often repeated in the text: "game" in Genesis 25-27, "son" in Genesis 22 (ten times); repeated phrases or sentences: "the account of the descendants of," "your son, your only son" (Genesis 22: 2, 12, 16)

- Contrast: "lifted up his eyes" (Genesis 13:10, 14; in this passage Lot lifts his eyes to see the fertile land Abraham lifts his eyes to see the Lord)

- Comparison: "took," "ate," "gave" (Genesis 3:6); "listened to the voice of," "took," "gave" (Genesis 16:2-3—a repeat of the fall?)

- Cause and effect: "deceive" (Genesis 27:18-24; 29:25; 37:32-33; 38:14, 25)

- Literary patterns: parallelisms: simple, complex, chiastic[24]; inclusion: beginning and ending with the same language and imagery, to frame the unit, to emphasize by repetition, to set up a dramatic revelatory moment (see, for example, Genesis 32, where the author keeps speaking of Jacob's fear in seeing Esau's face, but surprisingly, Jacob ends up seeing the face of God)

- Scene description: Genesis 28:10-11 (setting sun, entering testing); Genesis 32:31 (rising sun, heading home)[25]

We pay attention to all these kinds of "cues" so that we hear what the author wants us to hear and not just what we think the story is about.

We can also ask questions such as Where does the story fit into the ongoing story being developed in the book? This is crucial to ask of every text in the Abraham and Sarah story. Where does the story fit in

---

[23]These and more are more fully explained by Bruce Waltke in *Genesis* (Grand Rapids: Zondervan, 2001), pp. 31-43.

[24]See David Dorsey, *The Literary Structure of the Old Testament A Commentary on Genesis—Malachi* (Grand Rapids: Baker, 1999), pp. 1-46.

[25]If you want to see how all this exegetical work pays off in preaching read Bruce Waltke's sermon, "Reflections on Retirement from the Life of Isaac," in *CRUX* 32, no. 4 (1996): 4-14.

the larger metanarrative of the grand Story?

A crucial question can keep us from making wrong deductions about less-than-clear stories. Where else in the Bible is the story told or interpreted or applied? (Example: Genesis 15 in Romans 4, Hebrews 11 and James 2.) What about the character of God is being revealed/manifested here? Are the characters being held before us as models to follow, or are they simply illustrating the way it is in a fallen world under mercy? What about divine-human interaction is being opened up here? (The answer will lead to the "do" of the sermon.) And are there texts in the gospels where the Word made flesh reveals what the Word who was in the beginning with God and is God reveals in the Old Testament text? Bringing such a text into a sermon on an Old Testament story is not "bringing Jesus in," for as I argued before, he is already there. (Here, of course, we have moved into the hermeneutical step. The steps, after all, overlap.)

One of the practical issues we will need to keep in mind throughout our exegetical work is how much of what we learn we will actually take into the sermon. How much background material should we incorporate? Two rules of thumb: lean is best, and use only as much as is needed to enable the listeners to actually follow the story line.[26] Although a teaching component may be necessary for opening a narrative text, we do not want to bog people down in a lot of detail.

Hints for getting inside prophetic texts. The most challenging work here involves trying to understand the historical context in which the prophets are speaking. Prophetic preaching, prophesying, is more forth-telling than it is foretelling, although often in the forth-telling (declaring God's word for that particular context), foretelling is taking place (see 1 Pet 1:11-12). Thus, perhaps more than any other place, knowing what is being said to the original hearers/readers is absolutely essential for accurately discerning what is being said to us in our time and place. As Elizabeth Achtemier put it, "The prophets are not [usually]

---

[26]A master at finding the balance is J. Barrie Shepherd. See, for example, his *Encounters: Poetic Meditations on the Old Testament* (New York: Pilgrim Press, 1983). See also Steven D. Mathewson, *The Art of Preaching Old Testament Narrative* (Grand Rapids: Baker Academic, 2002).

preaching 'eternal truths.' They are announcing reactions of Yahweh to specific situations in Israel."[27] Thankfully we have available to us many resources to help us do the historical study.[28]

Thus we find in all the Prophetic literature deliberate reference to specific persons, times and places. "In the year of King Uzziah's death I saw the Lord" (Is 6:1). What do we know about this king? And what is so important about the year he died? "The words of Amos, who was among the sheepherders from Tekoa, which he envisioned in visions concerning Israel in the days of Uzziah king of Judah, and in the days of Jeroboam son of Joash, king of Israel, two years before the earthquake" (Amos 1:1). What do we know about these people? What is significant about the earthquake? When did it happen? Jeremiah locates everything he writes with specific rulers at specific times: "The words of Jeremiah the son of Hilkiah, of the priests who were in Anathoth in the land of Benjamin, to whom the word of the LORD came in the days of Josiah the son of Amon, king of Judah, in the thirteenth year of his reign. It came also in the days of Jehoiakim the son of Josiah, the king of Judah, until the end of the eleventh year of Zedekiah the son of Josiah, king of Judah, . . . until the exile of Jerusalem in the fifth month" (Jer 1:1-3; see also, e.g., Jer 3:6; 21:1; 25:1; 28:1; 32:1; 33:1; 34:1; 35:1; 36:1; 40:1).

So, in order to rightly preach this genre we need to honor the consistent particularity of the texts. Prophesying, as we saw in chapter four, is, in the words of Michael Green, speaking "a particular word to a particular people at a particular time for a particular purpose."[29] Yes, that word ends up speaking beyond the particulars; but we will not understand that

[27]Elizabeth Achtemier, *The Old Testament and The Proclamation of the Gospel* (Philadelphia: Westminster Press, 1973), p 139. My qualification added.

[28]Some of the best are *The Anchor Bible Dictionary*, ed. D. N. Freedman, 5 vols. (New York: Doubleday, 1992); *Dictionary of Biblical Imagery*, ed. Leland Ryken, James C. Wilhoit and Tremper Longman III (Downers Grove, Ill.: InterVarsity Press, 1998); D. E. Gowan, *Theology of the Prophetic Books: The Death and Resurrection of Israel* (Louisville, Ky.: Westminster John Knox, 1998); Victor H. Matthews, *Social World of the Hebrew Prophets* (Peabody, Mass.: Hendrickson, 2001); Iain Provan, V. Philips Long and Tremper Longman III, *A Biblical History of Israel* (Louisville, Ky.: Westminster John Knox, 2003); William Sanford LaSor, David Allan Hubbard and Frederic W. Bush, *Old Testament Survey: The Message, Form, and Background of the Old Testament*, 2nd ed. (Grand Rapids: Eedrdmans, 1996).

[29]Michael Green, *I Believe in the Holy Spirit* (Grand Rapids: Eerdmans, 1977), p. 169.

word unless we first understand it in its particular context.[30]

We also need to keep before us the fundamental intent of the prophetic, encounter with the living God. Amos's "Prepare to meet your God!" (Amos 4:12) is the heartbeat of all the prophets. And we need to keep before us the fundamental intent of the encounter, to reveal the nature and character of the living God and, in the process, reveal the fundamental nature and character of the people. "Prophecy is essentially a ministry of disclosure, a stripping bare. Prophets tear the masks away and show the true face of the people behind them."[31] Thus the reaction of the woman at the well to Jesus: "Sir, I perceive that You are a prophet" (Jn 4:19). Jesus had done what prophets do, disclosed the reality behind the façade. So we ask of any prophetic text, what does this reveal about the living God? And, what does this reveal about human beings?

As we work with any specific prophetic text, we need to also keep before us the larger message of the prophets as a whole. Although their word is consistently particular, they all share the same burden. First, prophetic texts respond to the glory of God; they are captured by, enthralled with, arrested by, dazzled by the living and holy God. Second, prophetic texts deal with the mišpāṭ of God, the justice of God, the way the living and holy God structured the universe and the judgment of God upon his people. Third, they all share the weighty burden of realizing that "the end has come" (Amos 8:2). Sin is now having its full consequences. Fourth, they all know the reason for the judgment: Israel has violated the covenant with Yahweh, ignoring and disobeying the good commandments of the good God; Israel has chosen to rely on material wealth and military power, forming alliances with those who have nothing to do with Yahweh and his will in the world; Israel has turned from the living God to other, false nongods; Israel is a harlot (Hosea, Jeremiah, Ezekiel) and a rebellious child (Hosea, Jeremiah). Just as, according to Deuteronomy 21:18-21, harlots and rebellious sons are to be put to death, Jerusalem is to be destroyed and the temple lev-

---

[30]A preacher who does this so well is Mardi Dolfo-Smith of Tenth Ave. Alliance Church in Vancouver, B.C., <www.tenth.ca>.

[31]Hans Walter Wolff, *Confrontation with Prophets* (Philadelphia: Fortress, 1983), p. 35.

eled. They are all clear about the nature of the judgment; it will come "in kind" upon the people. "I shall bring your ways upon you" (Ezekiel 7:4 NASB modified); "I shall bring their conduct upon their heads" (Ezekiel 9:10 NASB modified). Fifth, they all know the finality of the judgment: sin has so distorted and destroyed God's people that the only thing to do is start over. And sixth, all prophetic texts declare the good news: God, by a sovereign act of mercy and grace, will bring about a new work, a radically new work, centered in one person (the servant of Isaiah 42–53), affecting not only Israel but the whole world, indeed, the whole cosmos. Each particular prophetic word emerges from this larger burden.

All this suggests that we cannot preach one text of one prophet without reading not only the whole of that prophet's work but also all the work of all the prophets (or representative sections at least). Perhaps this is why we do not hear that much preaching from this genre—it takes a lot of work! But when we truly do the work, our minds and hearts come alive with the passion for the glory of God and God's full re-creation of life. I echo what Barry G. Webb says in the introduction to his commentary on Isaiah about the fruit of his laboring in that prophet:

> I have soared into the heavens and seen the glory of God, and with new eyes I have seen this world and my own place in it. The view has been breathtaking. I am not less mortal or sinful than before. My awareness of these things has been sharpened, not diminished; but I am surer now than ever before that they are no obstacles to my communion with God or to the full realization of what he has purposed for me.[32]

People of our day, of any day, are dying for the same kind of transforming vision.

Let me say one more word about working with the prophets. In the midst of their historical particularity, prophetic texts contain a word beyond, a word needing fuller outworking. Thus, we need also to keep in mind the "progressive fulfillment" nature of the prophetic. What

---

[32]Barry G. Webb, *The Message of Isaiah*, The Bible Speaks Today (Downers Grove, Ill.: Inter-Varsity Press, 1996), p. 12.

Joel sees and records in his work (Joel 2:28-32), for example, is not fully
realized until after the coming of Jesus and the outpouring of the Holy
Spirit on the day of Pentecost (Acts 2:15-21). William Sanford LaSor
helps us most when he speaks of the fulfilling of prophecy as "filling
up" the vision; God gradually "fills up" the text by "filling it full."[33] Or
we could say there is a trajectory to the prophecy, and God keeps moving it forward until we come to the trajectory's intended destination.
And that destination is, finally, Jesus Christ.

Hints for getting inside Gospel texts. Writing about the Gospel
according to John, George Beasley-Murray makes an apt observation for preaching Gospel texts: "Every item in it [John] calls out to
be preached, and that for a simple reason: every item in it has been
preached!"[34] What is true of John is equally true of Matthew, Mark
and Luke. Before it was gathered into this unique genre, into Gospels, the material in the four books was preached. "The proclamation of the earliest preachers became the material out of which the
Gospels were produced. . . . [They] are *the heritage bequeathed to humanity by the labours of preachers.*"[35] It was all "the embodiment of the
Kerygma."[36] Likewise, we see this in the sermon-speeches in Acts.
(See Acts 10:36-43, which is a good summary of the flow of the Gospel according to Mark.)[37]

---

[33]Lecture in Old Testament Theology, Fuller Theological Seminary, 1971.

[34]George Beasley-Murray, *Preaching the Gospel from the Gospels* (Peabody, Mass.: Hendrickson,
    1996), p. 27.

[35]Ibid., p. 9. Italics mine.

[36]Ibid.

[37]Resources for studying the sermons in Acts: F. F. Bruce, *The Speeches in the Acts of the Apos-
    tles* (London: Tyndale, 1941); Colin J. Hemer, "The Speeches and Miracles in Acts," in *The
    Book of Acts in the Setting of Hellenistic History* (Tübingen: J.C.B. Mohr [Paul Siebeck], 1989);
    W. Ward Gasque, "The Book of Acts and History," in *Unity and Diversity in New Testament
    Theology: Essays in honor of G. E. Ladd*, ed. Robert A. Guelich (Grand Rapids: Eerdmans,
    1978), pp. 54-72; Richard Longenecker, *The Acts of the Apostles: Introduction, Text and Ex-
    position*, Expositor's Bible Commentary, ed. Frank Gaebelein (Regency Reference Library,
    Zondervan, 1981) pp. 212-14, 229-31; Bruce W. Winter and Andrew D. Clarke, eds., *The Book
    of Acts in Its Ancient Literary Setting*, The Book of Acts in Its First-Century Setting 1 (Grand
    Rapids: Eerdmans, 1993). Ronald E. Osborn, *The Folly of God: The Rise of Christian Preaching*
    (St. Louis, Mo.: Chalice Press, 1999) argues that the speeches/sermons in Acts are the "big
    moments" because Luke understands the power of oratory/rhetoric: "Rather than narrating the
    advance of Christianity, he writes the triumph of the Word of God" (p. 788); John R. W. Stott,
    The Message of Acts: The Spirit, the Church and the World (Downers Grove, Ill.: InterVarsity
    Press, 1990), pp. 69-72, 79-81.

We want, all things being equal, to preach a single pericope, a single story or encounter. Or a set of closely interrelated units, such as Mark 4:35–5:43, where Mark shows Jesus' authority over the wide range of forces that threaten to undo us.

At this point it is good to pray something like, "Lord Jesus, this text is fundamentally about you [or your revelation of your Father]; will you please emerge from the text and meet me?" "Grab me" might be an even better way to pray. Martin Luther said: "The Bible is alive—it has hands and grabs hold of me, it has feet and runs after me."[38] Nowhere is this as true as in the four Gospels.

We then simply ask the "news reporter" questions: What? Who? When? Where? Why? How? This will likely necessitate some more historical research. We live in a time when there is no shortage of such material: books on Jesus and his time are legion. As it ought to be: "And there are also many other things which Jesus did, which if they were written in detail, I suppose that even the world itself would not contain the books that would be written" (Jn 21:25).

We then move on to ask why the author has included this particular pericope. He has at his disposal hundreds of such stories or teachings. Of all that was available to him, why did he choose to include this one? The Gospel writers are not just passing on facts; they are not just telling stories or relaying sayings. They are also theologians and preachers: they are making a statement about Jesus, a statement they believe to be relevant to the lives of their readers. So, what is the reason for this pericope? How does it relate to the ones preceding and following it?[39] How does this pericope relate to the overall burden of the particular Gospel? What does the text tell us about who Jesus is and what Jesus does for humanity? What does the text tell us about the nature of the divine-human relationship and the dynamics of discipleship?

Hints for getting inside apocalyptic texts. Richard Bauckham wrote that Revelation is "a work of immense learning, astonishingly meticu-

---

[38]Quoted by Philip Jenkins in *The New Faces of Christianity: Believing the Bible in the Global South* (Oxford: Oxford University Press, 2006), p. 18.

[39]Read G. Campbell Morgan's *Studies in the Four Gospels*, 4 vols. (Westwood, N.J.: Fleming H. Revell, 1927) to watch a preacher practice such attentiveness.

lous literary artistry, remarkable creative imagination, radical political critique, and profound theology."[40] After spending thirty years in the book, I agree. The same can be said of Daniel.

The definition of *apocalyptic* most often used is that articulated by J. J. Collins: "'Apocalypse' is a genre of revelatory literature with a narrative framework, in which a revelation is mediated by an otherworldly being to a human recipient, disclosing a transcendent reality which is both temporal, in so far as it envisages eschatological salvation, and spatial, in so far as it involves another, supernatural world."[41] Note especially the terms "temporal" and "spatial." Apocalyptic literature is speaking about both a temporal coming of God and the kingdom and a spatial coming of God and the kingdom. "Your kingdom come . . . on earth as it is in heaven," Jesus teaches us to pray. And apocalyptic literature helps us understand how this happens, how the future spills over into the present and how heaven invades the earth.

As we do our work in this genre, we need to keep before us the fundamental orientation of apocalyptic literature and, therefore, its fundamental pastoral purpose. Apocalyptic literature proclaims, "Things are not as they seem." Or, more accurately, "Things are not only as they seem." There is more to reality, more to the flow of history, more to the present historical moment than can be known with our unaided intellect, emotions or imaginations. And it is the purpose, the pastoral purpose, of the apocalyptic to open up that "more." An apocalyptic work accomplishes this in two ways. One, it sets the present moment, in all its ambiguity and uncertainty, in light of the unseen realities of the future: Jesus is coming and bringing with him a new heaven and a new earth. And two, and more germane to this genre, it sets the present moment, in all its ambiguity and uncertainty, in light of the unseen realities of the present. This genre, if you will, gives us a new set of glasses enabling us to see what we otherwise are unable to see—about the future, yes, but also (and primarily) about the present. "It is not that the here-and-now are left behind in an escape to heaven or the eschatological future, but that the here-and-now look quite different when

---

[40]Richard Bauckham, *The Climax of Prophecy* (New York: T & T Clark, 1993.), p. ix.
[41]J. J. Collins, "Introduction: Toward a Morphology of a Genre," *Semeia* 14 (1979): 9.

they are opened to the transcendent."[42] How desperately we need what this literature gives.

As we work with this genre, a number of aspects of the apocalyptic need to be kept in mind. (1) The imagery and symbolism are intended to reach beyond our intellect and emotions into the imagination. The content of texts is to be "felt" as much as understood. (2) The authors are describing the symbols, the images being given to them, not the reality the symbols symbolize "The descriptions are descriptions of the symbols, not the reality conveyed by the symbols."[43] For example, in Revelation 5:6, the risen and ascended Jesus is presented as a Lamb, "as if slain, having seven horns and seven eyes." Is that actually the form in which he presently exists? If he were to break through to us from behind the curtain of hiddenness, would he have seven heads and seven eyes? Of course not. John is describing the imagery through which the risen and ascended Jesus is choosing to present himself to us. In Revelation 12:14, the woman who gave birth to the Son who rules the world, who herself is a symbol of the people of God, is presented as being carried to a safe place on "the two wings of the great eagle." Some preachers, misunderstanding how the apocalyptic works, have suggested that what we find here is a huge U.S. Air Force jet carrying God's people away from imminent danger. Not so. John is simply relaying the symbol, not the reality. (3) The meaning of the symbols is found in the rest of the Bible. The "two wings of the great eagle" are found in Exodus 19:4 as a picture of God carrying his people out of Egypt, through the desert, into the Promised Land: "You yourselves have seen what I did . . . how I bore you on eagles' wings, and brought you to Myself." For the most part, the source of the imagery and symbolism is the rest of the Bible; look there first.[44] (4) We need to ask of the numbers used: are they statistics or symbols? They are symbols. Seven heads, seven eyes: symbols. One hundred forty-four thousand: symbol. One thousand: symbol. Of what? That is the work we have to do. (5) The "narrative"

---

[42]Richard Bauckham, *The Theology of the Book of Revelation* (Cambridge: Cambridge University Press, 1993), p. 8.

[43]Bruce Metzger, *Breaking the Code* (Nashville: Abingdon, 1993), p. 82.

[44]See especially the work of G. K. Beale, *The Book of Revelation*, New International Greek Testament Commentary (Grand Rapids: Eerdmans, 1999), pp. 77-99.

(as described by J. J. Collins) does not proceed chronologically. This is key for exegesis and thus for preaching. The scenes are not given in chronological order. The question to ask John, for instance, is not "what happens next?" but "what did you see next?"[45] The book of Revelation, for example, "does not unfold in a straightforward sequential way. Many times the action of the visions takes us back over territory we have already covered, introducing new information, changed perspectives and surprising twists of plot."[46] This has huge exegetical and then hermeneutical implications.[47]

As you can see, there is much more to say about each of the genres we briefly entertained. I have tried to demonstrate that each genre calls for a different, unique kind of exegetical work.[48]

Now, at this point in the process our minds are full (but, I trust, our hearts are "strangely warmed"). And we are wondering, How am I going to preach this? This is so good!

Please take some time now to do more specific exegesis on your text.

THE HERMENEUTICAL STEP

We now intentionally address the step into which we have naturally been pulled all along. We want to discern how the main point of the text speaks to our personal, communal, historical and cultural context.

Here are some questions we can ask: How is the main point related to the particular emphasis of your ecclesiastical tradition?[49] Does it undergird it? Does it counterpoint it? Does it question it? (At this point we are especially aware of how difficult it can be to bend our own agenda to the text's natural bent.) Try to come at the text from a perspective

---

[45]Michael Wilcox, *I Saw Heaven Opened* (Downers Grove, Ill.: InterVarsity Press, 1975).

[46]Paul Spilsbury, *The Throne, the Lamb and the Dragon* (Downers Grove, Ill.: InterVarsity Press, 2002), p. 50.

[47]See my *Discipleship on the Edge: An Expositional Journey Through the Book of Revelation* (Vancouver, B.C.: Regent College Publishing, 2004).

[48]See John Goldingay, *Models for Scripture* (Grand Rapids: Eerdmans, 1994) for a helpful look at the different "forms" of Scripture and the way they speak to us.

[49]Ronald Allen, *Interpreting the Gospel: An Introduction to Preaching* (St. Louis, Mo.: Chalice Press, 1998), pp. 153-76.

different than your own.[50] How does a male hear it? How does a female hear it? How does a married person hear it? A single person? A rich person? Middle class? How does a poor mother of three children hear it? Someone from North America? From Africa? From the People's Republic of China? From Brazil? How does a person living under a democratic form of government hear it? Someone under a dictatorship? (I learned to listen in this vein when we first moved to Manila in 1985.) How does the person whose life is going well hear it? Someone who has just experienced a family tragedy? Someone who manages a bank? Someone who plays professionally in a rock band? Not that we have to ask all these questions every time, nor do we have to actually articulate any answers in the sermon; it is just that asking such questions furthers our understanding in the hermeneutical part of the process.

Now try to state the main point of your text in a single sentence. I know this seems like we have moved out of the hermeneutic step into the homiletical, but we have not. Try to put the main point the author made for the people of his time in terms that people of our time can hear. This is hard work, but absolutely necessary if the sermon is going to "hang together." It may take three or four rewrites until something gels. State the big idea for those to whom it was originally written. Then state it for us.

Okay, now consult the commentaries. I think of this step as "meeting with the sisters and brothers," as clarifying and refining my thinking in concert with the church. We need the commentators to help us be as faithful as we can be. Not that the commentators have it right and we must bow to their insights; the fact is, even the best biblical scholar can miss something crucial in the text and thus move in a way slightly out of sync with the author of the text.

Ask the commentators (ideally at least three) the questions that have been brewing throughout the process. "So why do you think John uses the preposition 'into' and not 'in' when he speaks of believing Jesus?" "So why did Paul use a participle when we were set up for an imperative?" "In what sense is James using the word 'faith' in 'faith without

---

[50]So Thomas Long, *The Witness of Preaching* (Louisville, Ky.: Westminster John Knox Press, 1989), p. 166.

works is dead'?" "Why did Paul refer to 'Apphia our sister' in his letter to Philemon? What implication does this have, if any, to our understanding of the place of women in ministry?" You get the point. Where do I agree with the commentators? Where do I disagree? Why? Who is correct? Or is this an example of needing to humbly make the best choice I can under the circumstances? What else do the commentators see that I did not? What did I see that they did not?

Now restate the main point in light of the interaction with the fellowship of exegetes. Can we state it in language our hearers regularly use? This is why the same exegesis will result in different-sounding sermons in different contexts. How can I say it for twelfth-grade students? A seventh-grade student? A third-year university philosophy major? A man who operates the gigantic crane on the subway project near my house? A homemaker? The elderly? Someone in prison? (This has been a really good discipline for me lately, making me all the more aware of the millions of people living in bondage even in "free" North America.)

Remember the verb in the subtitle of this book: *participating*. It speaks to every aspect of preaching, even, or especially, to this process. Helmut Thielicke, one of the finest preachers of the twentieth century, encourages us at this point by reminding us that the Holy Spirit, who inspires the text we are preaching, is "the great Hermenuet."[51] Even as we do all this sometimes mechanical work, the Spirit is at work, and we are participating in a work beyond ourselves.

THE HOMILETICAL STEP

After all our devotional, exegetical and hermeneutical work, we are ready to move to the homiletical step. We have been doing some of this work all along the way, the preacher's mind and heart cannot help it, always thinking, *So what is the best way to say this to the people I know?*

How now do we package all that we believe we are supposed to preach?

---

[51]Helmut Thielicke, *Prolegomena: The Relation of Theology to Modern Thought Forms*, The Evangelical Faith, trans. Geoffrey W. Bromiley (Grand Rapids: Eerdmans, 1977), 1:130-33. Four additional Thielicke sermon series have been published, all by James Clarke & Co. of Cambridge, England, and translated by John W. Doberstein: *How the World Began: Sermons on the Creation Story; Life Can Begin Anew: Sermons on the Sermon on the Mount; Prayer That Spans the World: Sermons on the Lord's Prayer;* and *The Waiting Father: Sermons on the Parables of Jesus.*

Or, as my wife has taught me to think, how now do we serve up a home-cooked meal that is both delicious and nutritious? People are sick of (and sick from) fast food; they should not get more of it in preaching!

One of the practical issues is how to illustrate what we understand the text to be proclaiming. We begin by asking if the text itself contains any illustrations. Do the word studies help us? Once we've mined the primary text for illustrations, we continue. Are there stories in the rest of the Bible that illustrate the burden of the text? Are there stories in the history of the church that can help? Are there stories in the common life of the hearers? Note the order in which I asked the questions; it was deliberate. We look for illustrations from the inside out, not from the outside in. That is, we resist the temptation to immediately turn to the illustration collections in the latest book or Internet site. Too quickly using illustrations from the outside can skew the message in the direction of the illustration and not in the direction of the text. Any illustration has a trajectory to it: it begins at a specific point and is using specific language and imagery to move us to a specific end. Too quickly using an outside illustration runs the risk of then bending the trajectory of the text into the trajectory of the illustration. It is always best to begin from the inside, looking for illustrations first in the text itself, then in the Bible, then in church history, then in the common life of one's particular community and only then from outside these sources.

The master at this was Charles Haddon Spurgeon. He found nearly all his illustrations right in the text. One example will suffice, his teaching from Psalm 5:

> Give ear to my word, O Lord,
> Consider my groaning.
> Heed the sound of my cry for help, my King and my God,
> For to You I pray.
> In the morning, O Lord, You hear my voice;
> In the morning I will order my prayer to You and eagerly watch.
> (Ps 5:1-3)

Spurgeon, in his exegetical work, notices that "to You do I pray" (Ps 5:2) is literally, "I will direct my prayer unto You," and the verb David chooses is used of an archer. So he says, "I will put my prayer upon the bow, I will direct it towards heaven, and then when I have shot up my arrow, I will look up to see where it has gone."[52] Nearly everyone can relate to the imagery, and it comes right out of the text. Spurgeon also notes that the verb David uses in Psalm 5:3 is often used of an orderly laying out the wood and the pieces of the slain animal on the sacrificial altar and for the setting of the bread on the table in the tent. Therefore, "I will arrange my prayer before You." "I will lay it out upon the altar in the morning, just as the priest lays out the morning sacrifice."[53] Spurgeon gives a very practical way of thinking about daily prayer, the idea emerging out of the word studies.

Hopefully by this time in the process all the creative juices are flowing. If not, set all the work aside for a while. Go do something else. Our minds and hearts will keep processing things, and in a different frame of mind and heart, things will begin to gel. Again, this is why we cannot begin preparation on Saturday, or even on Friday, or on Tuesday. I will say more about this later.

Before we walk through some of the homiletical steps, we need to focus on two aspects of packaging the content in order to be heard. So let me delay moving to actual sermon construction to explore these at some length.

Before you turn the page to the next chapter, take some time to gather up your thinking thus far (insights and questions) on the text you have chosen to preach.

---

[52]Charles Haddon Spurgeon, *Psalm I to LXXXVII*, The Treasury of David (Nashville: Thomas Nelson), 1:46.

[53]Ibid.

6

MOVING INTO THE SERMON

Ordering for Orality

AS I SUGGESTED, THERE ARE TWO KEY issues for packaging what we discover in the devotional, exegetical, hermeneutical process. They are order and orality—a clear flow and rhetorical devices geared to the ear.

Martin Luther, in his typically bold way, reminds us that "faith is an acoustical affair."[1] He is, of course, only following the apostle Paul: "Faith comes from hearing, and hearing by the word of Christ" (Rom 10:17). Luther makes the point more graphic: "Stick your eyes in your ears."[2] The homiletical step is all about presenting the truth of the text for the ear. And, as I said, there are two key tasks: ordering the sermon for the ear and using rhetorical devices that enable the ear to hear.

Let's consider these one at a time.

ORDER

"Humans need and appreciate communication that is arranged and organized," writes David Dorsey in his extremely helpful study, *The Literary Structure of the Old Testament*.[3] Whether it is a book, a letter, a recipe, a news article (in print or on the Internet), a lecture or a sermon,

---

[1]Quoted by Richard Lischer, *A Theology of Preaching: The Dynamics of the Gospel* (Nashville: Abingdon, 1986), p. 70.
[2]Ibid.
[3]David A. Dorsey, *The Literary Structure of the Old Testament: A Commentary on Genesis-Malachi* (Grand Rapids: Baker, 1999), p. 15.

we need and appreciate an orderly presentation of the content. The human brain is hard-wired for order. A clear order to the sermon helps it move forward.

Bryan Chapell writes, "A well-planned sermon begins with a good outline—a logical path for the mind."[4] By the term *outline*, neither Chapell nor I necessarily mean a "one, two, three" structure. By *logical*, we do not mean linear only. Like other teachers of preaching, Chapell recognizes that ideas flow from one to the next in other kinds of ways: "As preachers mature they will discover that rhetorical 'moves,' homiletical 'plots,' concept-rich 'images,' thoughtful transitions, implied ideas, and other measures can often substitute for the formal statement of points in their outlines."[5] But always there remains the need, and desirability, for clear movement of thought. He goes on to say that "good outlines clarify the parts and progress of the sermon" for the preacher's mind and eye, but also, and primarily, for the listener's mind and ear.[6] He suggests the purposes and advantages of good outlines:

> Unity—"each feature relates to the one thing the sermon is about"
> Brevity—"pegs on which to hang much additional information"
> Harmony—"landmarks"
> Symmetry—the ear "expects" this
> Progression—the sense that we really are moving somewhere
> Distinction—each part is taking us forward
> Culmination—we are going to reach a destination[7]

There are, naturally, many different varieties of sermon outlines. Bishop William Quayle was right: "The dreary teaching that all sermons must be constructed after one pattern is as insane as to assert that all plants should look alike. Every species must be unlike. God is no delighter in monotony. He delights in variety. Every text has a distinct call to spread forth its own roots and lift up its own trunk and toss out

---

[4]Bryan Chapell, *Christ-Centered Preaching: Redeeming the Expository Sermon* (Grand Rapids: Baker, 1994). p. 150.
[5]Ibid., p. 151.
[6]Ibid.
[7]Ibid., pp. 133-34.

its own branches and wear its own foliage, and in due season bear its own fruit."[8] Thomas Long identifies at least eleven different forms, each of which I have used and found effective.[9]

1. If this . . . then this . . . and thus this.

2. This is true . . . in this way . . . and also in this way . . . and in this way too.

3. This is the problem . . . this is the response of the gospel . . . these are the implications.

4. This is the promise of the gospel . . . here is how we may live out that promise.

   (Indicative—imperative)

5. This is the historical situation . . . these are the meanings for us now. "Then . . . today." "Today . . . then . . . today."

6. Not this . . . or this . . . or this . . . or this . . . but this.

7. Here is the prevailing view . . . but here is the claim of the gospel.

8. This . . . but what about this? . . . well, then . . . yet, what about this?

9. Here is a story.

10. Here is a letter.[10]

11. This? . . . Or that? . . . Both this and that.[11]

And there is the "tried and true" form which most of us were encouraged to use at the beginning of our preaching ministry. Some, even after decades, still use it; it still delivers the goods in a clear, clean, accessible way:

---

[8]William A. Quayle, *The Pastor-Preacher* (Jennings and Graham, 1910), p. 375, speaking of the variety of forms the apostle Paul used in his preaching.

[9]Thomas Long, *The Witness of Preaching* (Louisville: Westminster John Knox, 1989).

[10]I find that if I am stuck and do not know how to move forward, I sit down and write a letter to either my grandmother (as if she were still here) or one of my children or one of my neighbors, and it is amazing how in relatively short order things begin to flow.

[11]Long, *Witness*, pp. 127-30.

Introduction—to the text to be read and expound ed
Reading of the text—giving as much attention to it as to the sermon
Introduction—to the main point, the homiletical idea
Elaboration—of the main point (ideally in the way the text does it)
Elaboration one
    Illustration one
Elaboration two
    Illustration two
Elaboration three
    Illustration three
Implication/Application (this may also take place under each of the
three elaborations)

Bryan Chapell modifies this traditional form by suggesting that the sermon be built around the basic movement, "Because God, we must."[12] Because God has acted, is acting, or will act in Jesus Christ (which every text is announcing), we must act (in some way consistent with the teaching of the text). So Chapell proposes the following.

Read the text
    Introduce the problem (the "Fallen Condition Focus")
    and God's response (the "Redemptive Focus")
Body of the sermon
    Because God . . .
        1. We must . . .
            Illustrate
        2. We must . . .
            Illustrate
        3. We must . . .
            Illustrate
Conclusion

I appreciate what Chapell is doing with this form; he wants to make sure that the sermon actually makes a difference in the listener's everyday life. God has done, is doing or will do something, and we cannot just go back to life as we knew it before we heard the news. But, and I will elaborate on this in the next chapter, not every text calls for a

---

[12]Chapell, *Christ-Centered*, p. xx.

"must." Some announce a "can"; others a "need not"; still others an "is." So the body of the sermon can also take the form

Because God . . .
   1. We can . . .
      Illustrate
   2. We can . . .
      Illustrate
   3. We can . . .
      Illustrate

Because God . . .
   1. We need not . . .
      Illustrate
   2. We need not . . .
      Illustrate
   3. We need not . . .
      Illustrate

Because God . . .
   1. There is . . .
      Illustrate
   2. There is . . .
      Illustrate
   3. There is . . .
      Illustrate

Because God . . .
   1. We are . . .
      Illustrate
   2. We are . . .
      Illustrate
   3. We are . . .
      Illustrate

Because God . . .
   1. We are . . .
      Illustrate

2. We can . . .
   Illustrate
3. We must . . .
   Illustrate

Some texts even leave us—and our actions—out of the picture; some texts are about God. Period. Consider Romans 3:21-26. In this case, the basic homiletical form would be

Because God . . .
   1. God . . .
      Illustrate
   2. God . . .
      Illustrate
   3. God . . .
      Illustrate

The simple "tried and true" format with its variations has a long and rich heritage. John R. W. Stott used it very effectively. James S. Stewart worked with it in every sermon of his I have read, simply varying the ways in which he phrased the subpoints. Charles Spurgeon worked with it. So did John Chrysostom. And so did Jesus of Nazareth, the Preacher.

Consider Jesus' "bread of life" sermon preached in the synagogue in Capernaum and recorded for us in John 6:32-58. Swedish New Testament scholar Pedar Borgen argues that the synagogue sermon of the first century followed a basic form:[13]

A text is read (usually from a cycle of readings)[14]
   It has a number of words or phrases: a, b, c

The preacher of the day restates the text in his own words: a', b', c'
The preacher then comments on or elaborates on each of these words or phrases one at a time.

---

[13]Pedar Borgen, *Bread from Heaven: An Exegetical Study of the Concept of Manna in the Gospel of John and the Writings of Philo*, SNT 10 (Leiden: Brill, 1965), p. 157.
[14]Aileen Guilding, *The Fourth Gospel and Jewish Worship: A Study of the Relation of St. John's Gospel to the Ancient Jewish Lectionary System* (Oxford: Clarendon, 1960).

a'
b'
c'

Sometimes other biblical texts are cited under these sections. The preacher then restates the text again, with other nuances. Jesus' "bread of life" sermon follows this basic pattern:

Jesus is given the text by the Passover crowd: Exodus 16:4, 15 (Jn 6:31)
  (This is one of the "prescribed" texts for Passover.)
  "Our fathers ate the manna in the wilderness; as it is written
  'He gave them bread out of heaven to eat.'"
    a: Bread
    b: Out of heaven
    c: Eat
Jesus restates the text in his own words.
  He makes it clear that the "he" who gave the bread is God, not Moses.
  And he says God not only "gave" but "gives."

  Then he gives his restatement: "For the bread of God is that which comes down out of heaven, and gives life to the world" (Jn 6:33).

Jesus then speaks to each of the three words of the text.
  a' Bread: "I am the bread of life" (Jn 6:35-40).
  b' Out of heaven: "I . . . came down out of heaven" (Jn 6:41-51).
    He quotes Isaiah 54:13 (also a reading for Passover), "THEY SHALL ALL BE TAUGHT OF GOD" (Jn 6:45).
  c' Eat: "Eat the flesh of the Son of Man" (Jn 6:52-57).

Jesus then restates his restatement of the text:
  "This is the bread which came down out of heaven;
  not as the fathers ate, and died, the one who eats this bread shall live forever" (Jn 6:58).

This simple structure helps me appreciate why John was able to remember it and write it down for us (he has probably given us only the core of what was likely a longer teaching). And this simple structure should encourage us preachers in our time to not feel we need to be any more sophisticated in our preaching. (Of course, we are not to feel constrained to such a form either.)

Here then is an expanded version of the basic, "tried and true" sermon outline.

1. *A brief introduction to the reading of the text.* (Those in the more liturgical traditions have it easy: "Our text for today is . . ." Nice. To the point.) The introduction is answering the question the listener is implicitly, sometimes explicitly, asking, "Why should I give this text my attention?" And the introduction is saying, "I know where we are living right now." We want, if at all possible, to use language and imagery congruent with the language and imagery of the text; we do not want to go against the language-imagery trajectory of the text.

2. *The reading of the text.* It should be read from the Bible itself, not from a piece of paper or off the screen where it has been projected; we want to communicate again and again, in every way possible, that we are people of the Book. It is helpful to practice reading the text so that it is heard clearly.

3. *Prayer for illumination and guidance.*

4. *Introduction to the main point of the sermon, which is the main point of the text.* Again, we want to use language and imagery congruent with the language and imagery of the text. (Thus if we are using a story here, we should phrase things in such a way that the hearers are led into the thought forms and thought world of the text.) We want to state the "big idea" as succinctly as possible—preferably, in ten to fifteen words—using active verbs.

5. *Development of the main theme.* Ideally this follows the way the text itself unfolds, the subpoints in words and images congruent with the main point. These can be elaborations, reasons, consequences, etc.

6. *Illustrating each of these subpoints.* Again, we want to watch the trajectory of the illustration so that we do not lead the hearer out of the text, but further into the text.

7. *Implication/application of the main theme.* This can take place, and usually naturally does, along the way. Any "go and do" of the sermon is determined by the "go and do" of the text. We need not feel in any way obligated to come up with something for the listener to do: let the text be the master here. If the text calls for rejoicing, then so does the

sermon; if the text calls for repentance, then so does the sermon; if the text simply calls for standing still and doing nothing, then so does the sermon. We want to make clear how any imperative is grounded in an indicative; how any good advice emerges, naturally, inherently, out of good news. We are not asking people to apply a truth; we are inviting people into a truth, to participate in the new reality shaped by the truth.[15] Ideally, we want to show how any "go and do" is but another way of saying, "Trust the God of this text." We want people to throw themselves on God, not on their own abilities.

Perhaps a number of working illustrations on order will help.

Take Isaiah 9:2-7, the great Christmas text. Imagine preaching it the Sunday after Christmas.

Introduction to the reading of the text.

What have we just celebrated? The question is important to ask because the culture, for the most part, is simply going to go back to business as usual, as though nothing of any real significance happened in the event we just celebrated. A child was born. Okay. What are the consequences? What difference does it make? In your life? In my life? In the life of this city? In the life of our world riddled with conflict, driven by fear, aching for direction and hope. What have we just celebrated?

I invite you, on this Sunday after Christmas, to listen to a text that gives us one of the most comprehensive answers to our question. It comes from the prophet Isaiah. That is, it comes from a time long before the events we just celebrated happened. You have seen and heard the words of the text many times, as they are printed on many Christmas greeting cards and sung in many Christmas carols. Because of the work of George Frideric Handel, the key line in the text has been immortalized in the music of the Western world: "For unto us a child born, unto us, a son is given." Even as I say the words many of you began to sing them in your head. "For unto us a child." "For unto us." "For." The key word is that little word, *for*. Because. "Because unto us a child is born."

Hear now the word of God. Isaiah 9:2-7.

Reading of the text.

Introduction to the body of the sermon.

---

[15]I will develop this more fully in chapter seven.

After the reading I would develop some of the historical background of the text. In particular I would help people feel the level of fear the people of Isaiah's day were experiencing. The then-greatest superpower of the world was at the borders of Judah. Judah was no match. Yet through Isaiah, God tells the people not to be afraid. Why? "For a child will be born to us." "Because a child will be given to us."

I would here help the listeners see that the "for" or "because" of Isaiah 9:6 is pointing back to what is promised in Isaiah 9:2-5. Leading up to the main point, to the homiletical theme: "Because the Child is born, everything changes; because the son is given, we have hope in the face of fear."

Body of the sermon.
Because the child is born:
   1. Light shines in the darkness (Is 9:2)
        Develop this
   2. Joy emerges in the gloom (Is 9:3)
        Develop this
   3. Freedom breaks through the oppression (Is 9:4)
        Develop this
   4. Peace overcomes strife (Is 9:5)

Transition.
Why can this happen?
Because of who the child is—the son with all the names!
   Wonderful
        Explain
   Counselor
        Explain
   Mighty God
        Explain
   Father of eternity
        Explain
   Prince of Peace
        Explain

Transition.
And who is this child?

Survey all the possibilities after Isaiah's prophetic word.

No one fit the bill.

Until that night when the midnight sky filled with angelic voices singing,

"Do not be afraid . . . unto you a Savior has been born."

Because Jesus Christ, the Child, the Son, has been born, given and "the government is on His shoulders" (Is 9:6):

1. We can know light in the darkness.
2. We can know joy in the gloom.
3. We can know freedom in the oppression.
4. We can know peace in the strife.

Application/implication.

Where do you need to give him "the government" today? When Wonderful Counselor Mighty God Father of Eternity Prince of Peace is given access and control, everything changes. Invite him into the darkness. Invite him into the gloom. Invite him into the oppression. Invite him into the strife.

"For unto us." "Because unto us." Everything can be different.

This text and its promises are so rich it might be good to develop a series of sermons. One could take one of the four consequences of "the child" being born and develop it more fully, showing how the names, the attributes, of Jesus make this possible.

One more example might help round out this emphasis on ordering for the ear.

Take Ephesians 5:15-21, an appropriate text for any Sunday, but especially after Pentecost, the celebration of the coming of the Holy Spirit.[16] Imagine we are doing a full series of expositions of Ephesians and come to Ephesians 5:15-21.

Introduction to the reading of the text.

We are currently making our way through one of the most powerful documents in human literature. Over the past weeks we have been making our way through a letter written from prison, yet strangely, a letter full of life! We are working through the letter the apostle Paul wrote

---

[16]The Christian church will have finally understood the fullness of the gospel of the triune God when Pentecost is as big an event as Christmas and Easter.

from prison to the believers of the first-century city of Ephesus. And I want you to know that I am thrilled with the reports of what this letter is doing in your lives. So many of you speak of feeling like you have "come alive," some for the first time, some experiencing a fresh awakening to the life and love of the triune God whom Paul celebrates in the letter.

Today we come to the part of the letter that explains why we are experiencing what we are experiencing. Our text today is Ephesians, chapter 5, beginning at verse 15 and going through verse 21. Right in the middle of the text, as the key to the text, and explaining why the letter is full of life, and why many of us are experiencing new life, is the exhortation, "Be filled with the Spirit."

Hear now the word of God.

Read the text.

Introduction to the main point, the "homiletical theme."
The text pulses with life. A life I want to live.

The text begins with "therefore." It is the sixth "therefore" we have encountered in our journey through the letter to the Ephesians. That is, it is the sixth major implication of being brought into the grace of God in Jesus Christ.

Review.
We have seen that the letter has two halves of almost equal length: chapters 1-3 and chapters 4-6. In chapters 1-3 Paul develops for us "the glory of God's grace." In chapters 4-6 Paul develops for us "the walk of God's grace." In the first half of the book Paul opens up for us the sheer wonder of what God in his grace has done for us, for the whole cosmos, in Jesus Christ. And then in the second half he opens up for us what a life captured by that glorious grace looks like in everyday life. The second half begins, "I, therefore, the prisoner of the Lord, entreat you to walk in a manner worthy of the calling with which you have been called" (Eph 4:1). Having opened up the grand vistas of grace, he then opens up how to walk in that grace.

Thus in the second half of the letter we meet this word "therefore." God has acted, therefore we act. God has called us into this expansive grace, therefore walk in it, walk in a manner consistent with it. Walk in the extravagant grace of God.

Now, you notice that in this text, following the "therefore," Paul gives, in rapid succession, six exhortations. You notice, I am sure, that he gives them in pairs, three pairs of two exhortations. And you notice, I am sure, that the pairs are in a "not, but" arrangement. Do not do this, but do this. Three times: not this, but this.

> Be careful how you walk,
> not as unwise, but as wise . . .
> Do not be foolish, but understand what the will of the Lord is.
> And do not get drunk with wine, . . .
> but be filled with the Holy Spirit. (Eph 5:15-18)

What I want to suggest to you today is that this series of exhortations all leads to the last. That is, the key exhortation is "Be filled." "Be filled with the Holy Spirit."

"Be careful how you walk, not as unwise, but as wise."

Okay, what does that mean?

"Do not be foolish, but understand what the will of the Lord is."

Okay, and what is that will?

"Do not get drunk with wine, but be filled." "Filled" is what you are trying to do by getting drunk. "Be filled with the Holy Spirit." Walking wisely, walking in the will of the Lord, is all about being filled, filled with the Spirit of God, filled with the third person of the Trinity, filled with the very life of God that filled and animated the Lord Jesus when he lived on this planet in our flesh and blood.

"Be filled." That is the main point of this text. "Be filled." Passive verb, implying that this is not something we can do. It is something that must be done for us. We cannot fill ourselves. Which is why Paul refers to drunkenness as "dissipation"—the filling from wine dissipates, vanishes. When we try to fill ourselves the filling dissipates. But not when God fills us. God does not dissipate. God does not vanish.

And when God fills us, look what happens! Paul tells us in this text that four things happen. He uses four participles, four "-ing" words. Actually five, but two of them go together.

(Readers, you see where I am going.)

So the body of the sermon would then look something like this.
What does it mean to "be filled with the Holy Spirit"?
How does it happen? (Do we have any part to play in this?)
When God fills us with the Holy Spirit

1. We find ourselves speaking to one another differently
   Explain, illustrate
2. We find ourselves singing and making melody to the Lord
   Explain, illustrate
3. We find ourselves giving thanks to God the Father
   Explain, illustrate
4. We find ourselves submitting to one another
   Explain, illustrate (this is the great miracle of grace!)

The application/implication.
(Clearly, I think, the "do" is to invite the filling. Because Paul puts it the way he does, it would be a violation of the text for the preacher to "come up with" a list of how-to's. The text leaves us totally dependent on God to do what only God can do.)

Order is the first key to "packaging" the sermon in order to be heard. The second key is orality. And it turns out that the first key is key to the second key. We are ordering the message for the ear; the order flows when it is geared to the ear.

ORALITY

At the beginning of the chapter I quoted David Dorsey: "Humans need and appreciate communication that is arranged and organized." He makes the claim in the context of his discussion of biblical literature having been written not to be read but to be heard, even when read. "The Bible was written for an oral culture; the text was heard before it was seen; it was intended to be read aloud."[17] This, by the way, is the best way to hear the message of the last book of the Bible, the Revelation of Jesus Christ: read it out loud. "Blessed is the one who reads and those who hear the words" (Rev 1:3). It takes about ninety minutes to read the book orally, but it is worth the time to hear what is hard to see.

Dorsey then addresses what is crucial for preaching. Since the Bible was written for an oral culture, "the text had to have a kind of 'oral typesetting.'"[18] The authors were compelled to use "structural signals that would be perceptible to the listening audience," signals geared

---

[17]Dorsey, *Literary Structure of the Old Testament*, p. 15.
[18]Ibid.

more for the ear than the eye.[19] Preachers are also so compelled. We have to write for the ear; we have to speak for the ear.[20]

Martin Luther again: "Faith is an acoustical affair." "Stick your eyes in your ears." And then even more boldly, "He who will not take hold with his ears but wants to look with his eyes is lost."[21] Luther is not disparaging seeing—not at all! How could he? What would life be without seeing? He is simply observing that we humans are wired in such a way that we finally see by hearing; we finally understand what we see when we hear what we see. In the end, it is the spoken word that enables us to really see what we are seeing.

Take the Lord's Supper for instance. Someone who knows nothing about it comes into a room and sees on a table a loaf of bread and a cup of wine. They may be taken by the smell of the bread, by light dancing through the wine. They see all these people gathered around this table, seemingly experiencing something related to the bread and the wine. The person sees a lot—but does not see . . . until the word is spoken. "This is my body given for you, . . . this cup is the New Covenant in my blood." When the Word is spoken what they see is now understandable. It is the audio that finally gives meaning to the visual. We are acoustically wired visual creatures.

Many say that we in the early part of the twenty-first century are a visual culture. They turn to the prominent role of television and film as justification. But the power of a film does not lie in its sights alone but also in its sounds. Take away the musical dimension, for instance, and see how many people will still enjoy films. Take away the audio dialogue and very few will watch. The sights are finally seen when they are heard; the sights finally have meaning when heard. I have observed preachers using film in their sermons, a legitimate thing to do. But I notice that the film clip only makes sense for the sermon because of

---

[19]Ibid.

[20]For a more sophisticated development of all this see G. H. Guthrie's work on the book of Hebrews, the most brilliantly crafted sermon in the Bible: *The Structure of Hebrews: A Text-Linguistic Analysis* (Dissertation, Southern Baptist Theological Seminary), pp. 16-34, 55-60. See also Tex Sample, *Ministry in an Oral Culture: Living with Will Rogers, Uncle Remus & Minnie Pearl* (Louisville, Ky.: Westminster John Knox, 1994).

[21]In Lischer, *Theology*, p. 70.

the dialogue. Yes, simply playing the audio dialogue without the visual would not be as meaningful. But playing the visual without the audio would have no meaning, or very little. (Interestingly, after writing the above sentences, I went downstairs for a break, picked up the entertainment section of the paper and read a review of one of the latest films. The reviewer describes the movie as "derivative, boring and utterly lacking in charm." And then comes this line: "reminding us that, even in a visual medium like film, if you have nothing to say to begin with, there's not much to see at the end.")[22]

Why is this the case? Because of the different ways sight and sound work. Walter Ong, in his now classic work *Orality & Literacy: The Technologizing of the Word*, writes: "Sight isolates, sound incorporates."[23] He is not disparaging sight. He is simply observing how sight and sound work. "Whereas sight situates the observer outside what he views, at a distance, sound pours into the hearer."[24] He is certainly describing how it works for me. "Sound pours into the hearer." From all around, even if the sound is coming from only one place. "Vision comes to a human being from one direction at a time: to look at a room or a landscape, I must move my eyes around from one part to another. When I hear, however, I gather sound simultaneously from every direction at once."[25] The sound envelops us, centering us. It is why we so enjoy high-fidelity surround sound. Ong writes, "You can immerse yourself in hearing, in sound. There is no way to immerse yourself similarly in sight."[26]

The sermon becomes a sermon when we hear it in the room or on the street. The sermon comes to life when what we have been visualizing (i.e., writing) becomes audible (i.e., speaking). Again, I am not disparaging writing: I have spent a long time writing this book! It is just that the written word does not finally accomplish its purpose until it is heard. Am I the only one whose lips move when I read? Am I the only one who hears something in my head as I read? I do not think so.

[22]Kamal Al-Solaylee, Review of "Angel-A," *The Globe and Mail*, Friday, June 8, 2007, p. 3.
[23]Walter Ong, *Orality & Literacy: The Technologizing of the Word* (New York: Routledge, 1982), p. 72.
[24]Ibid.
[25]Ibid.
[26]Ibid.

It is how we were created: we finally see by hearing.

It is how relationships work. We know each other with increasing completeness when we speak. Yes, we can deduce a lot about each other from our actions; for the most part we automatically live out who we truly are. But we do not really know who the other is unless and until the other speaks. Walter Ong speaks of speech coming from the interior of a person; a word "is the call of one interior through an exterior to another interior."[27] This is the wonder of the gospel: the living God chooses to speak, to communicate from the interior, telling us who he is inside.

There seems to be a "hierarchy of communication means."[28] And the hierarchy is part of what differentiates cultures, especially the Hebrew/Christian culture and the Greek culture, both of which those in the so-called Western world are heirs. Eugene Peterson, working from the insights of Walter Ong, observes, "The ancient Hebrews and the ancient Greeks differed in their primary sensory orientation: the Hebrews tended to think of understanding as a kind of hearing, whereas the Greeks thought of it as a kind of seeing."[29] Thus the Greeks practiced religion in highly visual ways: statues of gods and goddesses, impressively sculptured sacred spaces meant to impress and overwhelm, drama in literature enacting the divine-human and divine-divine encounter. "In Greek culture the divine was looked at and talked about."[30] The gods were external to the lives of average people and so were known visually.

The Hebrew/Christian culture, however, was shaped by audio events. Two events in particular: "The unseen God speaking his word to Moses and the people at Sinai, and the word becoming flesh in Jesus, the Christ."[31] Instead of focusing on images and statues with the Greeks,

---

[27]Walter Ong, *The Presence of the Word* (New Haven, Conn.: Yale University Press, 1967), p. 309.

[28]This phrase I owe to Ken Shigematsu, pastor of Tenth Avenue Alliance where my family worshiped during our first years in Vancouver; he used it in a conversation we had over lunch regarding the matter we are attending to in this chapter.

[29]Eugene Peterson, *Working the Angles: The Shape of Pastoral Integrity* (Grand Rapids: Eerdmans, 1987), p. 78.

[30]Ibid., p.79. (Peterson is building on the work of Northrop Frye.)

[31]Ibid.

the Hebrews, followed by the Christians, "listened to the one God. . . . When they met together they did not look at a statue or watch a play, they heard a command and answered with a prayer. The difference is radical and revolutionary."[32] And this difference is always in danger of being blurred.

When one looks at a statue one is in control of the event; one can linger as long as one has time to do so. But when one hears a word one is not in control of the event; one either receives what is said and acts on it, or the word moves on. In the one case the issue is whether I enjoy what I see; in the other the issue is whether I will live what I hear. Let Peterson spell out the implications for us:

> They [Hebrews and Christians] knew how easy it was for the ardor of obedient listening to be diluted into amused watching, and took measures to guard their aural concentration. They sensed that surrounding themselves with all those god-images reduced them to less than they knew themselves to be. Religion as entertainment is always more attractive, but is also less true. It is pretty poor stuff compared to the word.[33]

This is the major affirmation of Psalm 19, the psalm that celebrates God's self-revelation. David begins with God's self-revelation in what is seen: "The heavens are telling the glory of God; and their expanse is declaring the work of His hands" (Ps 19:1). But then David shifts to the Torah (inadequately translated simply as "law"). The word *Torah* is related to the verb meaning to throw, as in throwing a javelin. The idea is that in Torah God has "thrown" what he is thinking and what he knows, especially about the make-up of reality; God has "thrown out" to us the interior reality of God's self which can finally only be known by a word. In verse after verse David celebrates the life-giving power of the spoken word: restoring the soul, making wise the simple, bringing rejoicing to the heart and enlightening the eyes. David is in no way denigrating God's self-revelation in creation; he is simply recognizing the "hierarchy of communication means." The spoken word ranks highest because revelation by the word is the most unambiguous. Jacob

---

[32]Ibid.
[33]Ibid.

Firet can thus say, "God's servants are people who listen; God's people are a listening people. Our Christian religion is a religion of faith by hearing, the hearing of the word."[34]

How then do we preachers attend more carefully to orality so that our listeners might truly hear the Word? How can we develop our "eye-ear" coordination so we can play our part in God helping people to see by hearing?

A communicator who has thought long and hard about this is Robert Jacks. In two practical books, *Getting the Word Across: Speech Communication for Pastors and Lay Leaders*[35] and *Just Say the Word! Writing for the Ear*,[36] he shares what he has learned. In the later volume, he takes a number of sermons written for the eye and turns them into sermons ready for the ear. Take one example:

Original sermon

Is God still in control—even when tragedy strikes? Somehow it seems easier to believe God is more in control when things are going our way. After all, isn't that a sure sign we're following God's will? What happens, though, when circumstances don't go our way? Does that mean God has abandoned us? Is God only in control of the good events that transpire in our lives? Can God still be in control of the unexpected?[37]

Before reading on, how would you rewrite this for the ear?

Here is how Jacks moves it from eye to ear.

Rewrite

Tragedy strikes!

The unexpected,
    unwanted,
      unwelcome,
    unthinkable
      has just happened in your life!

---

[34]Jacob Firet, *Dynamics in Pastoring* (Grand Rapids: Eerdmans, 1986), p. 36.

[35]G. Robert Jacks, *Getting the Word Across: Speech Communication for Pastors and Lay Leaders* (Grand Rapids: Eerdmans, 1995).

[36]G. Robert Jacks, *Just Say the Word! Writing for the Ear* (Grand Rapids: Eerdmans, 1996).

[37]Ibid., p. 136.

Everything's out of control:
  you're out of control,
    on the verge of panic,
      absolutely fit to be tied.

How's it all going to end?
How are you possibly going to live through it?
Who on earth can you turn to?
Who has any answers?
Who even cares—except, maybe . . . God.
And so you start to wonder:
Is God still in control?
Does God know how to handle the situation?

Jacks continues in this way through the rest of the sermon. He makes the sermon feel more personal, turning stiff prose into more of a story, changing from passive to active verbs, engaging the listener more directly. I commend his work to you.

Throughout the book Jacks gives what he calls "'Rules for Writing for the Ear." He ends up spelling out fifty, summarizing them for us, humbly saying, "Do with them what you will."[38] Let me list what I think are the especially helpful ones:

Write the way you *talk*, not the way you *write* (his number 3).
Active voice is more alive than passive (6).
Use visual images, drawing pictures with words (7).
Don't use a 50-cent word when a 5-cent word will do (8).
Remove unnecessary occurrences of *that* and *which* (9).
Remove unnecessary or assumable information and get to the point (10).
"People" your ideas—use dialogue for added interest and life—reveal attitudes as well as imparting information (11).
Use contractions where appropriate (14).
Verbs are more alive than nouns (15).
Accentuate the positive (17).
Avoid clichés (20).

---

[38]Ibid., pp. 92-95.

Remove forms of the verb *to be* whenever possible (21).

Give us stories—from life, if possible (22).

Don't overuse adjectives or adverbs (27).

Where possible, replace adjectives with stronger, more colorful verbs (28).

Repetition can be effective in introducing new ideas, reinforcing important ideas, "nailing down" the end of an idea group (29).

Use rhetorical questions to convert a sermon "monologue" into a sermon "dialogue" (30).

Use questions rather than conjecture—invite your listeners to think along with you (31).

Build in musical "tones" for your delivery—bright ideas and darker ones—leading to pitch variation (34).

Listen to the *rhythm* of your ideas—keep it varied (35).

Vary sentence lengths. Are sentences as easy to speak as they are to read (36)?

What's your perspective? *In-scene* (participating) or *outside* (observing) (38)?

Don't spin wheels—keep thoughts moving (39).

Don't qualify everything. *Pecca fortiter (Sin boldly)* (44).

Consider first person *(we, I)* rather than second person *(you)* for a positive tone (45).

Preach like Jesus—show more than you tell (49).

Preach Jesus like a beggar telling another beggar where to find bread (50).

Allow me to add my own "rules of thumb" for enhancing preaching to the ear.

If a numbered format is used, conform it to the listener's expectation. If we say at the beginning of the sermon, "I want to make three points today," the ear is expecting to hear us say, "The first is . . ." and then later, "The second is . . ." and then later, "The third is . . ." We therefore have to deliver on the implicit promise; we cannot say, "The first is," and then later, "And also" and then, "The third is." We will distract our hearers. They will not hear the beginning of our third point wondering if they missed the second.

If we do use this numbered (1, 2, 3) format for the whole of the sermon, when we come to develop one of the numbered subsections we cannot use the same format; we need to switch to something like a lettered (a, b, c) format. If the ear hears, "I will be developing three points today," and then under point two hears, "Now I have three elaborations," the ear gets confused. So we need to keep one format for the whole of the sermon and use another for the sections. If one wants to use the same format in both places one has to help the listener understand this (e.g., "I want to make three points today. Under each point I will make two elaborations"). It may be a bit much, but at least we have told the ear what to expect.

Speak in "breath bites." That is, when writing the sermon, try to write in clauses that we can say with one breath. Write each "breath bite" on a separate line.

Example: "I know that the church of Jesus Christ in the West will have finally come to understand the fullness of the gospel when Pentecost is as big a celebration as Christmas and Easter." I cannot say that whole sentence in one breath. So I write it out on my manuscript this way:

> I know
> that the church of Jesus Christ
> in the West
> will have finally come to understand the fullness of the gospel
> when Pentecost
> is as big a celebration
> as Christmas and Easter.

Here is another example: an introduction to a sermon on Luke 11:5-8.

> "Lord, teach us to pray."
> It is the only thing the first disciples asked Jesus to teach them.
> There is no record of "teach us to lead,"
> or "teach us to heal,"
> or "teach us to counsel,"
> or "teach us to cast out demons,"
> . . . not even "teach us to preach"!
> Just "Lord, teach us to pray."
> Why?

Because the first disciples could see
> that Jesus' leading,
>> healing,
>>> counseling,
>>>> preaching ministry
emerges out of his relationship with the one he calls "Father."
And they could see
> that the key to that relationship is prayer;
>> he is regularly slipping away to pray.
"Lord, teach us to pray." And us too![39]

Do not make your eyes go all the way back to the left hand side of the page in order to finish a sentence. For example:

Not: "What the apostle Paul is telling us is that 'being subject to one
    another' requires the work of the Spirit of God."
But: "What the apostle Paul is telling us
        is that 'being subject to one another'
            requires the work of the Spirit of God."

We want our eyes and mouths to "work in the same direction." It is easy to get lost when our eyes have to shift all the way over to the left when we have been moving to the right.

Limit the number of words printed on any page of the manuscript. Typing the sermon in normal typing format makes for far too many words for the eye to keep track of. We want to be able to look down at the page and instantly see the words we are speaking. Too many words

---

[39]I should tell you that I am able to format my manuscript this way because I write it with pencil or pen—I have for all these years. I understand all the positives of using a word processor, as I am doing right now. But those positives do not outweigh the negatives, and do not match the positives of handwriting. Positives of handwriting include greater freedom in placing letters and words wherever I want them to go and starting the memorization process with more tactile engagement with the page on which the words lay. Negatives of using the word processor for sermon composition include not being as free to place letters and words where my eye-ear coordination faculty wants to put them; forestalling the memorization process as any modification to the sentence moves words around to new places (i.e., a word I originally placed on the right-hand side of the page is now on the left, etc.); having worked with the material in one format on the screen, when printed out it comes to me in a new format—more or less words in front of me—than when I was writing, different color of background (the white on the screen is a different white than the paper). Someone needs to develop a word-processing program for preachers! I would, however, still use a pencil or pen.

makes the eye have to hunt for the words, which in turn affects the way we are saying the words, which in turn affects the way the words are being heard. Not to mention we are losing eye contact with the listeners. At a minimum, double-space and tighten the margins.

Try to word the subpoints in short, easy-to-hear phrases. Ideally we want all of the subpoints to have about the same number of syllables and similar sounding words.

Repeat. Repeat. Repeat. Do so with some variation, of course, so as not to bore the listeners. But repeat nevertheless. It may feel pedantic to the preacher's ears, but it will not to the listener's ears. Remember, we have spent hours on what we have written and are now saying; it is very familiar to us. But the listeners are hearing it all for the first time, and the more help we can give them to catch it, the better.

Practice the sermon by reading it out loud. This helps us know if the words we have chosen sound right; they may look right on paper but do not sound at all right in the preaching moment. Especially practice the transitions.

Order (easy-to-follow flow) and orality (attending to rhetorical devices geared for the ear) must not be underestimated as we move into actually crafting a sermon. These are elements that become increasingly important as we move from textual interpretation to delivering a meaningful, memorable exposition of the text.

THE HOMILETICAL PROCESS

Just as there are four major steps for moving from text to sermon—devotional, exegetical, hermeneutical and homiletical—there are also a series of steps for the actual process of putting together a sermon. I do not know how else to develop this part of the process except by walking through it step by step. And the best way to do this is to number the steps. I do so not because the process unfolds in a numbered way but so that I can later refer back to specific steps as the process continues.

1. Construct a preliminary outline of the sermon. As Bryan Chapell observes, "the ear expects symmetry."[40] Whether we use numbers (1, 2, 3)

---

[40]Chapell, *Christ-Centered Preaching*, p. 126.

or letters (a, b, c) or other kinds of unarticulated movement indicators will not matter in the end.[41] What matters is that the listener senses a symmetry, a flow, an unfolding, a feeling that "this is going somewhere."

2. Write a tentative conclusion. Where would you like the listeners to be at the end of the sermon? What do you want to see happen for them? This, of course, is a function of what the Holy Spirit is seeking to do through the text.

3. Write a tentative introduction. The introduction serves to move into the main point of the text, which is the main point of the sermon. It also subtly begins to prepare the hearer for the conclusion, which is why we write them in tandem.

4. Rewrite the conclusion in light of the introduction. Try to make sure the trajectory of the conclusion is the trajectory of the introduction.

5. Write out the main point, the major homiletical statement.

6. Write out each of the subpoints. Of course, we must make these consistent with the main point. (See the sample outlines earlier in this chapter.)

7. Write out the transitions. Craft the statements that move from one section of the unfolding sermon to the next. It is worth spending a good amount of time on these. Preachers can bring a whole lot more substantive teaching into the sermon if the transitions are clear. Even if one ends up, after writing out the sermon, not actually using a manuscript, one should have the transitions clearly in mind, having sounded them out a number of times to make sure they really do move the sermon forward.

8. Now flesh out the rest of the sermon. Write it out even if you are not going to take the written pages into the pulpit with you. Writing clarifies our thinking and gives the sermon precision. And we know how much we can say in the allotted time.

9. Set the work aside for a while. Let it rest for twelve to twenty-four hours. Do other things; use other parts of the brain, heart and body.

10. Come back and read the sermon, out loud if possible, to see how it

---

[41]David Buttrick, *Homiletic: Moves and Structures* (Philadelphia: Fortress, 1987).

sounds. Note the mix of verbs: see how it sounds. Do the words and phrases and sentences flow naturally? If not, rework them so they do.

11. As you read it out loud, attend to any sentences or paragraphs that have even a hint of being a diversion or tack-on. Ruthlessly eliminate extraneous material. (We might want to keep it on file for another time.)

12. If any sentences sound too complex for your ear, they will to the listener's ear too, so rewrite them. Make them into smaller units, using two or even three small sentence fragments. As we have noted a number of times in this book, the problem is that we write the first time for the eye; but we have to get the words into a mode for the ear.

13. Again, set the work aside for a while. At least for a few hours. (Again, starting on Saturday night is simply not going to work!)

14. Come back and read it again to assess if it now flows smoothly. If it does not, make whatever adjustments are necessary.

15. Without notes, try to sketch out the outline of the sermon on one side of a half-sheet of paper or on the white board. If we cannot remember the outline without the notes, our hearers will definitely not be able to do so.

16. Go back and rephrase the outline (step 6) and the transitions (step 7) in light of this experience.

17. Read the whole sermon out loud again. About now we will begin to think or feel things like, "This is all too obvious," or "They already know all this," or "They will say, 'We pay you to give us this?'" This is because we have worked so hard on the material and it is for us all too obvious. But it is not so for the hearers. If the sermon is faithfully expounding the text and following a nice, clear order, our hearers will think or feel, *This is so fresh,* and, *It's like I am hearing this for the first time.* Trust the work the Spirit has been doing with us through the whole process.

18. Read the whole sermon out loud again. Especially sound out the transitions to see if they are clear.

19. Set all the work aside again.

BACK TO THE ORIGINAL STEP: DEVOTIONAL AGAIN

Go to sleep, trusting the Lord of the text with the sermon on his text. Wake up. Have some quiet time. Exercise. Eat a healthy meal. Pray: "I surrender all my work to You, the Lord of the text."

Recite the memorized text, which will be "read" while holding the Bible. Reread the manuscript.

Step up before people who are dying to hear a living word from the living God.[42] Pray: "O Lord, I want these people to think well of me. But more than that, I want them to think well of you." Really? Yes. I was taught to pray this way by the Welsh Presbyterian preacher Peter Joshua. He had retired from a very fruitful preaching ministry that had a significant impact on Billy Graham, among others. He and his wife, Margery, were worshiping in the church where I was just beginning to preach. (This was 1970.) Apparently he saw something in me that made him want to spend time with me to pass on to me what the Lord had taught him. At that time, people were responding to my preaching in positive ways, and I was afraid it would go to my head. I confessed to Dr. Joshua—I could not call him Peter—that I wanted people to like me and to say good things about my sermons. I told him that I was trying to overcome the pride but was not making the kind of progress for which I was praying. He then told me that humility is not a function of putting one's self down but of lifting Jesus Christ up. Humility in preaching comes not by taking ourselves out of the picture, but by putting ourselves in the right place in the picture, under Jesus, pointing to Jesus. Then he said, "As you walk up the steps of the pulpit next time, say, 'Lord I want these people to think well of me.'" "What?" I asked aghast! And then he said, "And then pray, 'But more than that, I want them to think well of you,' and you will be free." He was right. And free I have been. And so will you.

Those are just some of the human mechanics of participating with the living God as God works the miracle of transformation through preaching.

How is your sermon on your text developing?

---

[42]I will develop this in chapter ten, "Standing in the Mystery."

7

WALKING THE SERMON
INTO EVERYDAY LIFE

Implication and Application

I WANT NOW TO DO WHAT I CAN TO lift a horrible burden off of preachers. It is the burden of "applying the text" to the everyday life of the listeners. Yes, we can, and we should, try to help people understand the text's radical implications. But applying the text is not the preacher's responsibility.

I know that what I have just said seems to fly in the face of standard homiletical teaching. I might even stand alone in this assertion. But I cannot say otherwise. For preachers are carrying a burden they are not called to bear. The human mechanics of participating in the divine transformation of the world do not include "applying the text."

Think with me about the word *application* (or *apply*) and then about the word *implication* (or *imply*). The two words reflect two different approaches to life. The difference is not simply a matter of semantics. Dictionary definitions begin to highlight the distinctions. *Application:* the act of applying. *Apply:* to put to use for some practical purpose.[1] *Implication:* a logical relationship between two propositions. *Imply:* involve or indicate by inference, association, or necessary consequence.[2] *Apply* conveys the idea of making something happen. The preacher says, in effect, "You have heard the truth, now make it happen in your lives by

---

[1] *Webster's Seventh New Collegiate Dictionary,* s.v. "application" and "apply."
[2] *Webster's Seventh,* s.v. "implication" and "imply."

doing this." *Imply* conveys the idea of accepting the logical inherent consequences of the truth;. "Let the truth work its full impact in your life." Application, to my mind, is too mechanistic, too modernistic, too humanistic (in the sense of humanity as the measure of all things). Implication is more dynamic, more relational, more empowering. Apply suggests, "You make it happen." Imply suggests, "This is what necessarily happens."

The fact of the matter is no one can apply the text but the Lord of the text; he is the only one who can "make it happen." To expect preachers to apply the text for their listeners is to ask them to play God. Have you ever thought about it this way? Preachers can "imply the text," suggesting and showing the necessary, inherent, logical consequences for life which the text is declaring. But a preacher cannot call the listeners to make the text relevant to their lives. The only thing the preacher can do is enter into the new reality announced and described, and by the power of the Spirit of the text, "live into" the new reality.

I do not think I am playing a semantic game here. I think we are talking about two very different understandings of how God works to transform us. The claim is often made that unless the listeners are helped to apply the text, the text has no effect in their lives (I have heard this many times). This is simply not true. The claim reflects an inadequate understanding of the nature of God's Word. God's Word not only informs the listener, leaving the listener to perform it; God's Word performs, working on and in the listener. "You accepted it [the preached message] not as the word of men, but for what it really is, the word of God, which also *performs its work* in you who believe" (1 Thess 2:13, italics mine).

I repeat: the pressure to apply is a modernist pressure, not a biblical pressure. William Willimon observes that most congregations love hearing preaching with this application emphasis. The only problem, he says, is that such preaching is not biblical preaching. The "subtext" of so much of this must-apply preaching is, "*You are gods unto yourselves. Through this insight, this set of principles, this well applied idea, you can save yourselves by yourselves.*"[3] In this mode, "God is humanity spoken in a resonate, upbeat

---

[3]William H. Willimon, introduction to *The Word in This World: Two Sermons by Karl Barth,* ed. Kurt I. Johanson, trans. Christopher Asprey (Vancouver, B.C.: Regent College Publishing,

voice backed up with PowerPoint presentation."[4]

This is why Richard Lischer tells preachers not to worry that all of our words are not remembered; people are not going to take in and absorb all we say in the sermon, even a short sermon. We need not worry about people remembering, "for the words are needed only as long as it takes for them to form Christ in the hearers."[5] Isn't that good? And isn't that liberating? No biblical text tells us, "Go, form Christ in yourselves in light of what you have heard." Rather, the Spirit of the text says, "I will form Christ in you."

Let me put it another way. Truth is self-authenticating.[6] One does not need to "defend" the truth: articulate, clarify, rephrase, but not defend. So too, truth is self-applying. One does not need to make truth work. Whatever is not consistent or congruous with truth ultimately does not work and cannot stand.

Consider the events of and around the first Christian sermon recorded in Acts 2. It is pure kerygma, pure proclamation. Peter is explaining, or accounting for, the unusual phenomena: wind, flames of fire, people hearing the gospel in their own languages. Peter stands up, Bible in hand, turns to the prophecy of Joel and says, "This is that." "This is what was spoken of through the prophet Joel: 'AND IT SHALL BE IN THE LAST DAYS,' God says, / 'THAT I WILL POUR FORTH OF MY SPIRIT ON ALL MANKIND'" (Acts 2:16-27). Peter continues citing the whole text, leading up to his main point: because God has raised from the dead the Jesus who was crucified and seated him on the throne of the universe, he can now pour forth "this which you both see and hear" (Acts 2:33). Peter then brings his sermon to its end, declaring, "Therefore let all the house of Israel know for certain that God has made Him both Lord and Christ—this Jesus whom you crucified" (Acts 2:36). And that is it. No further elaboration, no attempt to apply the truth. He just puts it out there. And sits down. Peter has done his job.

The people are "pierced to the heart." As I have been saying, some-

---

2007), p. 7. Italics original.

[4]Ibid.

[5]Richard Lischer, *A Theology of Preaching: The Dynamics of the Gospel* (Nashville: Abingdon, 1986), p. 79.

[6]I learned this from watching Earl Palmer preach; it explains the winsomeness of his ministry.

thing always happens. The people say to Peter (and to the rest of the apostles with him), "What shall we do?" (Acts 2:37). The burden of "doing something" about what was preached did not lie on Peter. The Spirit through the Word brought about a piercing conviction, causing hearts to cry out, "What shall we do?"

What shall we do? One word: repent. That is the application and implication of the kerygma. Turn around, think around *(meta-noeō)*, change your mind, see things from God's perspective. And when you do, be baptized. That is, enter into the new reality brought about by God making the crucified Messiah Lord. It is the only thing we can do: the word Peter preached calls for a massive reorientation, moving us away from all false ways of understanding reality (especially away from all false ways of understanding Jesus) and moving us into God's way of understanding reality (especially into God's way of understanding Jesus). The most logical response to the gospel in Peter's sermon is to repent and begin to live in a whole new reality.

You can see then that we, in the Western world anyway, have a faulty view of discipleship. If I am hearing us correctly, this is what we believe: We are walking down the road, a road of our own choosing. The risen and ascended Jesus comes to us and intersects our lives. He offers us all the blessings and challenges of living with him in the kingdom of God. We like what he offers, so we "accept" him; we "receive" him. And we continue walking down our road, assuming that we will begin to experience kingdom life on that road. But soon we are disappointed; things are not working like the Word suggests they should. Some of us walk away from the call; some of us just try harder to make things work. But they do not. For the simple reason that when the risen and ascended Jesus intersects our lives and calls us to follow him into the kingdom life, he calls us onto a different road. We thought we could confess him as Lord and Savior and keep living the way we did when we were following other lords and would-be saviors. It does not work. The blessings of the kingdom only come on a new road. "Repent, get off the highway you are on, and follow me down a different path."

Much "application" of texts turns out to be proposing ways for people to live for Jesus while continuing to live for other lords. As N. T.

Wright once put it, "It is not enough to say one's prayers in private, maintain high personal morality and then go to work to rebuild the tower of Babel."[7] The application the gospel calls for has huge implications. The gospel calls us to line up with the new reality created by the death of, resurrection of, ascension of, out-pouring of the Spirit by and coming again of Jesus of Nazareth.

Maybe a story would help at this point.

It was Christ the King Sunday, November of 1985. I was pastoring Union Church of Manila. Things were heating up. Ferdinand Marcos, the president of the Philippines, a corrupt dictator being propped up by the United States, had, on *Larry King Live,* declared that he was willing to hold an election to show the world that he had the country's support. Mrs. Cory Aquino, wife of Senator Benito Aquino whom the Marcos forces had assassinated in August of 1983, took up the challenge and ran for president against Mr. Marcos. Things were quite tense, to say the least.

On that Christ the King morning, I preached a sermon on Daniel 2. I titled it "The Preview." I showed how the vision in Daniel 2, a vision played in the subconscious of Nebuchadnezzar, king of Babylon, was a kind of "theology of history." Through the vision and Daniel's God-given interpretation of the vision (Dan 2:22-23), God was declaring the gospel of the kingdom. Nebuchadnezzar kept seeing this giant statue, representing exalted human empires, being knocked over and crushed by this stone "cut out without hands" (Dan 2:34, 45), with the wind blowing away the remains like chaff (Dan 2:35). Though it was a terrifying dream, it was an act of mercy and grace. For God loved that pagan leader enough to play "The Preview" in his mind and bring a prophet who could explain it. The stone represented the kingdom of God always pressing in on the world, ever advancing against all that is inconsistent with the kingdom.

I concluded the sermon that Sunday saying, "Nothing will ever stop the coming and advancing of the kingdom of King Jesus. Nothing. Nothing. Nothing." And I sat down. You could have heard a pin drop;

---

[7]N. T. Wright, *The Challenge of Jesus: Rediscovering Who Jesus Was and Is* (Downers Grove, Ill.: InterVarsity Press, 1999), p. 11.

the silence was palpable. And so was the sense of the presence of the Great King.

Unbeknownst to me, sitting in the congregation were two men from Washington, D.C. One was a C.I.A. agent; the other was an "image-maker" hired by President Marcos to help change his image in the Western press. The image-maker, accompanied by the C.I.A. agent, was to meet with Mr. Marcos the next morning, Monday morning. As the image-maker tells it, during the silence after the sermon, he felt "this presence," and he began to tremble inside. He said, he "heard a voice" say to him, "All you are to do tomorrow morning when you meet with Mr. Marcos is read Daniel 2." The image-maker said he was constrained by the conviction. He knew he could do nothing else. So, on Monday morning after Christ the King Sunday, he did it. He met with Mr. Marcos and read him the "theology of history." Three months later, the so-called People Power Revolution toppled Mr. Marcos's rule. I saw the Lord of the text himself work out the implications of the text. I did not have to come up with any application. Any application would have felt trite. Indeed, in that setting I did not suggest the application. The Lord of the text did it himself.

Does this mean that we are not supposed to give, in the sermon, any word of exhortation, any imperative, any concrete steps to take? No. For many texts do exactly that. It's just that we are to give any such imperative, any steps to take, in the context of the text's own inherent implications.

I learned this while preaching Jesus and his Sermon on the Mount. If Peter's Pentecost sermon is pure kergyma, Jesus' Sermon on the Mount is pure exhortation. Or is it? It is if the Sermon is separated from the context in which Jesus first (and always) preaches it. But if the Sermon is heard in the context Jesus preaches it, it is also kergyma, gospel.

The context for the Sermon on the Mount is Jesus' first sermon. It is very short, only two clauses: "Repent, for the kingdom of heaven is at hand [or, has come near]" (Mt 4:17). Jesus comes on the scene, as we saw in chapter two of this book, announcing the wonderfully good, good news that the long-awaited reign of God is breaking into the world in and because of him. Immediately, as all three Synoptic Gospels show, Jesus begins to do mighty deeds: he frees people from the grip of the demonic, he repairs people's broken bodies, he heals people of all kinds of illnesses. And he then preaches his great Sermon. The point? Just as Jesus' deeds are signs that the kingdom is breaking into the world in and because of him, so also the attitude and behaviors Jesus describes in his Sermon are signs that the kingdom has broken into ordinary people's lives. Jesus' deeds are pictures of what the kingdom is all about, and so too are the kinds of people he describes in his Sermon. This is crucial to see. Separate the Sermon from its context and it becomes either frustrating idealism ("Who could ever live up to that?") or crushing legalism ("I must do this or I will never be pleasing to the King"). But hear the Sermon in the context in which Jesus preaches, and the Sermon becomes an irresistible invitation to the only really workable way of life there is.

Really? Yes.

Take note of the people's response to the Sermon. Matthew tells us, "The result was that when Jesus had finished these words, the multitudes were amazed at His teaching, for He was teaching them as one having authority, and not as their scribes" (Mt 7:28-29 NASB modified). Authority. The Greek is *exousia*. Made up of two words: *ek*, the preposition meaning "out of," "out of the center of," and *ousia*, the feminine noun related to the verb "to be." *Ek-ousia* therefore conveys the idea of "out of the center of being." The people hear Jesus preach what goes against just about everything they think they know about life, and their response is, "These words come out of the very center of being." The implication is, "These words are the real thing, these words are describing things the way they really are." And what were they to do but do them? They had been introduced to a new world, and they needed only to "live into" that new world by living the way of the new world.

Jesus is not in his Sermon legislating a new morality; he is not moralizing. Rather he is announcing the good news of the kingdom and describing what that kingdom looks like in everyday life. In the Sermon, Jesus is showing us what happens when the kingdom breaks into human lives, individually and corporately. Or, to use the language of the apostle Paul, Jesus is describing what happens when the

Holy Spirit comes and takes up residence in human lives (the Spirit is for Paul the personal embodiment of the kingdom). Or, to use the language of the apostle John, Jesus is describing what happens when human beings are born again from above. The kingdom comes, the Spirit comes, people are born anew, and they begin to live the life Jesus portrays in his Sermon.

Thus E. Stanley Jones can say that when we first read the Sermon,

> We feel it is trying to give human nature a bent it will not take; something for which human nature was not made. Chesterton says that on first reading you feel it turns everything upside down, but the second time you read it you discover that it turns everything right side up. The first time you read it you feel it is impossible; the second time you read it you feel that nothing else is possible.[8]

The Sermon comes with authority, *ek-ousia*, out of the center of reality. And the only logical thing to do is simply to do it.

Our task as preachers, as I have been trying to show throughout this book, is to open the text in such a way that the text itself does what only the text can do.

The question, therefore, is not "How should we apply the word?" The question is "Where is the word leading us?" and "Will we cooperate and enter in?" The question is not "What do I the preacher want people to do as a result of hearing this word?" The question is not even the one we worked with in the last chapter, legitimate as it is, "What do I want to see happen in people's lives as a result of hearing the word?" The question is "What do I want to see God do as a result of people hearing the word?" Even better, "What does God want to do?"

Again, we are not just playing a semantic game. We are wrestling with a tension between two different worlds: the world as it seems to be, centered in and dependent upon the human person, or the world as it is, centered in and dependent upon the living God. It is the tension Paul identifies in his letter to the Galatians: "Having begun by the Spirit, are you now being perfected by the flesh?" (Gal 3:3). Having begun the new life by receiving the Spirit "by hearing with faith" (Gal

---

[8]E. Stanley Jones, *The Christ of the Mount* (Nashville: Abingdon, 1931), p. 14.

3:2), are we going to live this new life by trusting our own resources? Applying the text, as in, "We need to make this work in our lives," is seeking to be perfected by the flesh; it is throwing people back on themselves to actualize salvation. The actualization of salvation is the work of the Spirit, with whom we are called to cooperate.

Or, to put it yet another way, it is to turn gospel into law. It is very subtle. Helmut Thielicke helps me here. He observes that when, in our preaching we hold Jesus Christ up as an example and call people to imitate him (think WWJD), we have changed the gospel into law. Yes, we look to Jesus to give us the power to be like him, but essentially we are still living by law and are looking to him as a means to that end; "redemption is thus the means to an ethical end."[9] "Imitation piety," applying the text by trying to do what Jesus does, "no longer views Christ as the one who redeems us from the curse of the law and who represents the divine repenting"; it makes us the ones who redeem.[10] "Imitation piety" subverts the good news and "links my salvation to my achievement in imitating Christ and using the power granted to me in redemption. Thus the gospel itself becomes a source of assault. Instead of being our consolation it brings us into judgment."[11] Why? "Attention is directed all the time on the self instead of on the salvation event outside the self which Christ has accomplished on and to us. . . . We are looking at ourselves. We measure the level of our discipleship. We are condemned to a new curving in on ourselves."[12] That is the problem— "curving in on ourselves"; in Luther's words, "throwing ourselves on ourselves." Applying the text, in the sense given above, throws us onto ourselves instead of throwing us onto Christ.

Thielicke works with Luther's great insight that Jesus is "not model but prototype."[13] The difference makes all the difference in the world. Jesus as model calls us to do our best to be like him. Jesus as prototype, as archetype, calls us to join him in his vicarious humanity, to realize

---

[9]Helmut Thielicke, *The Doctrine of God and of Christ*, vol. 2 of *The Evangelical Faith*, ed. and trans. Geoffrey W. Bromiley (Grand Rapids: Eerdmans, 1977), p. 194.
[10]Ibid.
[11]Ibid., p. 195.
[12]Ibid.
[13]Ibid.

that he is who we were created and are being redeemed to be; indeed, who we now are in him. I do not "live up" to him; I live "into" him. He makes me like himself.

In my experience, when people say, "I need more application in the sermon," they mean, "Can you illustrate this in another way so I can understand it better?" or, "Can you show me what living the new reality looks like Monday to Friday?" They are not really asking for "how-to steps." They simply want more help to navigate the new world into which they implicitly realize they are being called. They are asking the question C. S. Lewis says is the key to illustrating truth: "What is it like?" Lewis, as we know, is a master illustrator, describing the "saved world" in such a way that we say, "Of course—how else could it be and how else would a human want to live?"

Let me now suggest that the "practical" question we are to ask of any text we are preaching is this: What is the reality into which the text is introducing us? Once we know the answer, the implications are, I think, obvious.

Take an example: Matthew 6:19-34. Read the text, asking yourself, How does the Jesus of this text see the world? and, How is he inviting me into it?

> Do not store up for yourselves treasures on earth, where moth and rust destroy, and where thieves break in and steal.
>
> But store up for yourselves treasures in heaven, where neither moth nor rust destroys, and where thieves do not break in or steal;
>
> for where your treasure is, there your heart will be also.
>
> The eye is the lamp of the body; so then if your eye is clear, your whole body will be full of light.
>
> But if your eye is bad, your whole body will be full of darkness. If then the light that is in you is darkness, how great is the darkness!
>
> No one can serve two masters; for either he will hate the one and love the other, or he will be devoted to one and despise the other. You cannot serve God and wealth.
>
> For this reason I say to you, do not be worried about your life, as to what you will eat or what you will drink; nor for your body, as to what you will put on. Is not life more than food, and the body more than clothing?

Look at the birds of the air, that they do not sow, nor reap nor gather into barns, and yet your heavenly Father feeds them. Are you not worth much more than they?

And who of you by being worried can add a single hour to his life?

And why are you worried about clothing? Observe how the lilies of the field grow; they do not toil nor do they spin, yet I say to you that not even Solomon in all his glory clothed himself like one of these.

But if God so clothes the grass of the field, which is alive today and tomorrow is thrown into the furnace, will He not much more clothe you? You of little faith!

Do not worry then, saying, 'What will we eat?' or 'What will we drink?' or 'What will we wear for clothing?'

For the Gentiles eagerly seek all these things; for your heavenly Father knows that you need all these things.

But seek first His kingdom and His righteousness; and all these things will be added to you.

So do not worry about tomorrow; for tomorrow will care for itself. Each day has enough trouble of its own. (Mt 6:19-34)

I chose this text because it appears to be pure exhortation, full of commands (nine, on my counting). So we could think that any sermon on it should "apply the text" by leaving people with the commands. Clearly, the central command of the text is the one repeated three times, "do not be anxious" (Mt 6:25, 31, 34). And the way Jesus works with it illustrates what I have been trying to convey in this chapter. Let me show you what I mean.

Notice that the first "do not be anxious" is introduced with "Therefore" (Mt 6:25). You know the rule: when you come across a *therefore* you are to ask, "What is the *therefore* there for?" It is there for a reason. I think the reason is this: anxiety (the mark of our age) does not just happen in people's lives; it emerges out of decisions we are making about what I will call "fundamental movements of the human heart," about which Jesus speaks in the verses before the *therefore* in Matthew 6:25. He identifies three fundamental movements of the human heart. Number one (Mt 6:19-21): we all treasure treasures; we all seek to find some security against the uncertainties of the future. Number two (Mt 6:22-23): we all have a vision of reality through which we assess the people, circumstances and events of our lives.[14] Number three (Mt 6:24): we all serve some sort of god, either the living God or some sort of mammon (the word derived from the Aramaic word *amon*, meaning "that in which one puts trust," only one form being money). Jesus does not simply tell us to stop being anxious; he helps us understand why we are anxious. We have made wrong decisions about one or all of these movements of the heart. We are anxious because, first, we are treasuring treasures on earth, a very unstable kind of investment against the future, since such treasures are easily negated by rust ("time's corrosions") or moths ("nature's corrosions") or thieves ("humanity's corrosions").[15] We are anxious because, second, our vision of reality is clouded (for whatever reason) and we cannot see the Rock of Ages in the middle of all the upheaval and change. We are anxious because, third, we are serving some sort of mammon and our hearts know, if only subconsciously, that no form of mammon can hold up under the weight of life (speaking of idols, see Is 41:7, "The craftsman . . . / fastens it with nails, / So that it will not totter"). The Jesus of this text is introducing us to the world as it is, a world in which our decisions in one area of life have implications in others, if not in all. In speaking the command in the way he does, he is not merely commanding; he is also, and primarily, showing us how our hearts work and calling us to attend to them.

Furthermore, Jesus does not command us not to be anxious without telling us how. And this he does by further introducing us to the world as it is with him in it. He speaks three other commands. Number one (Mt 6:26): look at the birds of the air. Literally, "start looking" at the birds of the air, the implication being something like, "Quit focusing on what makes you anxious and start looking at the birds. The birds know something you keep forgetting; they know someone you keep

---

[14]I know the exegesis of Charles Talbert, arguing that Jesus is likely working with the Old Testament use of "good eye, evil eye" as indicators of people's orientation toward possessions: "good eye" denotes generosity, "evil eye" greed. *Reading the Sermon on the Mount: Character Formation and Ethical Decision Making in Matthew 5-7* (Grand Rapids: Baker Academic, 2004), pp. 122-23. And I agree with his work on this. However, I do not think that it means we cannot also understand the words metaphorically, namely, that Jesus is speaking of the eye as one's worldview, which, of course, is affected by whether one is generous or greedy.

[15]F. Dale Bruner, *The Christbook* (Waco, Tex.: Word, 1984), p. 260.

forgetting. They know the heavenly Father, your heavenly Father. They know that your heavenly Father cares and can be counted on to take care of those he loves. If the Father loves birds for goodness' sake, do you not think he loves you? You are looking in the wrong direction: start looking at the birds."

Number two (Mt 6:28): look at the flowers. Again literally, "start looking" at the flowers, the implication being something like, "Quit focusing on what makes you anxious and starting looking at the flowers. Notice how exquisitely and extravagantly God clothes them. Do you not know this God? Do you not realize that if this God cares for transient flowers he can be counted on to care for you? You are looking in the wrong direction: start looking at the flowers. See with the flowers the hand of the great gardener who cares for you."

And number three (Mt 6:33): seek first the kingdom and righteousness of God. Literally, "keep on seeking." It is a call to keep on channeling all the emotional energy of anxiety away from seeking all that other "stuff" (which the Father knows we need) to instead seeking to live in the reign of God and all the right relatedness of it. The implication is therefore: "If you want to be 'anxious' for anything, be so for God's rule to come and for getting to live in the restored relationships it involves."

Charles Talbert asks then, suggesting the implication of the whole text, "Which is the real world, the world of our anxiety or the world of which birds and flowers are images?"[16] He then quotes Robert Tannehill: "Our involvement in these structures of care [treasures, masters, etc.] is too deep to be uprooted by a simple command. . . . A change could only take place if we were to see the world in a fundamentally new way."[17] The text "induces a sense of strangeness about our life and a sense of the presence of something more, something deeper, which offers an alternative for action and makes finally unimportant our structures of care. . . . This opens a new possibility for life."[18]

---

[16]Ibid., p. 129.
[17]Robert Tannehill, *The Sword of His Mouth*, Semeia Studies 1 (Philadelphia: Fortress, 1975), p. 67.
[18]Ibid., p. 66.

Do you see what the Jesus of this text is doing? Not just applying truth. But opening up the truth so that when we see it we cannot but walk in it. And then we find that we are no longer anxious!

Jesus does that in and with every text.

Again (and again and again), the burden to "make it happen" does not belong to the preacher. The responsibility does not belong to the hearer. The responsibility belongs to the text, to the God of the text. He is the one through whom the preaching of the text reorients us into his reality. "If you abide in My word, you are My disciples indeed. And you shall know the truth, and the truth shall make you free" (Jn 8:31-32 NKJV).

Thanks be to him!

8

The Person of the Preacher

Truth Through Personhood

THE MOST ESSENTIAL OF THE HUMAN mechanics of participating in the divine transformation of the world is the preacher. We have established that it is the living God who speaks the transforming word. But the living God has chosen to speak the transforming word through human beings. The preacher preaches through preachers.

Methodist Episcopal Bishop William A. Quayle, in 1910, asked if preaching is "the art of making a sermon and delivering it." And he answered, "Why, no, that is not preaching. Preaching is the art of making a preacher and delivering *that*."[1] Do you agree? "It is no trouble to preach," Quayle continues, "but a vast trouble to construct a preacher."[2] "A sermon is not a piece of carpentry, but a piece of life—a spacious heart, a spacious brain, a spacious sympathy talking out loud."[3] The "business of preaching is not with the preaching, but with the preacher."[4]

I say yes and no. Yes, there is a sense in which we preachers need to be made. And, no, there is a sense in which we are given, we are a gift. Yes, a vision of who God is in Jesus, and what God has done, is doing and will do in Jesus, needs to be made. Yes, character traits of Jesus

---

[1]William A. Quayle, *The Pastor-Preacher* (1910; reprint, Pasig City, Merto Manila, Philippines: LifeLine Philippines, 1984), p. 363. Italics his.
[2]Ibid.
[3]Ibid., p. 367.
[4]Ibid., p. 364.

himself need to be made in us, character traits consistent with the message we are preaching about Jesus. Yes, the ability to do exegesis and hermeneutics, the ability to craft clear, faithful, compelling messages needs to be made. But when God uses a person to preach, God knows the person being used. That is, there is something already there; there is something about the person, both innate and potential, that God reckons useful for the work of proclamation (and the other verbs of participating). God does not call the person we will one day be; God calls the person we are right now. Yes, we need to be redeemed from all kinds of consequences and expressions of sin in us (and thank God this is exactly what God in Jesus comes to do). But there is—even in our not yet fully redeemed state—a givenness. And it is this givenness that we bring to participating in God's transformation of the world.

I would wholeheartedly agree with William Quayle if he had used the verb *mold*. "Preaching is the art of molding a preacher and delivering that along with the message of the text." *Mold* allows for the fact that God employs the givenness of the preacher while acknowledging the need for further development. As God enables us to mold a sermon and deliver it, so God molds a preacher and delivers him or her.

The most quoted definition of preaching, in the Western world anyway, is that given by the Puritan preacher Phillips Brooks (who composed the Christmas carol "O Little Town of Bethlehem") in his 1877 Yale University "Lectures on Preaching."[5] Preaching, he said, is "truth through personality." William Willimon affirms this description, adding that it "strikes experienced preachers as essentially right."[6] Brooks writes, "Preaching is the communication of truth by man to men" and women, and by women to men and women.[7] "It has two essential elements, truth and personality. . . . Preaching is the bringing of truth through personality."[8]

When you read Brooks you realize he used the word *personality* in a wider sense than we do in our time. The word *personhood* better conveys

---

[5]Phillips Brooks, *Lectures on Preaching* (New York: E. P. Dutton, 1877), p. 5.
[6]William Willimon, *Pastor: The Theology and Practice of Ordained Ministry* (Nashville: Abingdon, 2002), pp. 157-58. After nearly forty years of preaching, I agree!
[7]Brooks, *Lectures*, p. 5.
[8]Ibid.

his conviction. *Personhood* encompasses what he meant by *personality* but also includes other dimensions of the human being, such as our physical constitution, our life experiences, the ways in which the Holy Spirit has gifted us, and our historical, cultural and geographical contingencies. Preaching is truth through personhood.

In this chapter I want to emphasize that we have to honor "the ecology of our personhood."[9] We are who we are, and that is going to come through to people no matter how much we might want to keep ourselves out of the preaching moment.[10] Put more positively (that is, in a manner more consistent with the grace of God), God honors the ecology of our personhood. After all, much of it is God's handiwork! God honors the way we are put together, the way we relate to God, others and ourselves, the way we interact with the world, seen and unseen. "For You formed my inward parts; / You wove me in my mother's womb. / . . . My frame was not hidden from You, / When I was made in secret, / And skillfully wrought in the depths of the earth" (Ps 139:13, 15). God honors this ecology, and so must we.

Indeed, this is part of how God exercises sovereign leadership over the church. When God wants to do a particular work among a particular group of people in a particular place, God calls a particular preacher with a particular ecology of personhood. Failing to honor who the preacher is may disrupt God's purposes. Trying to be who we are not gets in the way of the unique work God wants to accomplish.

In 1993, I became the senior pastor of Glendale Presbyterian Church in Glendale, California. The majority of people attending Sunday worship had some role in the film and entertainment industry; Glendale housed the world headquarters for Hanna-Barbera, ABC, Disney, DreamWorks and MTV. After I arrived and realized that most of the people who would hear me were into the flashy, hip, cool and cutting-edge, I began to think that I needed to change the way I preached. I thought I maybe ought to develop a new style of communicating. It was

---

[9]I first heard this term from Ken Shigematsu in a sermon at Tenth Avenue Alliance Church, Vancouver, B.C., May 2007.

[10]See Andre Resner, *The Preacher and the Cross: Person and Message in Theology and Rhetoric* (Grand Rapids: Eerdmans, 1999) for an in-depth study of the person in the communicating moment.

then that the Lord helped me see what he had taught me twenty years earlier, when I began to preach at Saint John's Presbyterian Church in West Los Angeles, California, and wondered if I needed to change to fit that context. The Lord showed me again that if he had wanted someone with the "film and entertainment style" he could have called him or her. But he called me and wanted me to be me, because his purposes for those particular people at that particular time required someone with my personhood. During my first year there, I invited a number of actors and actresses to meet with me, partly to find out how I could better serve them in their challenging vocations, but also to find out why they would come to hear someone like me preach. Their uniform answer was, "We live our lives in a make-believe world. What you preach and the way you preach breaks through the illusion and brings us into the real world." Honoring the ecology of our personhood honors God's purposes through us.

In this chapter I want to explore three dimensions of personhood that are especially at work in preaching: temperament, woundedness and Spirit gifting.[11] They are intricately intertwined in us. The apostle Paul exhorts Timothy, "Pay close attention to yourself and to your teaching; persevere in these things, for as you do this you will ensure salvation both for yourself and for those who hear you" (1 Tim 4:16). We are to "pay close attention" to who we are in temperament, woundedness and Spirit-gifting because the preaching of the gospel—"your teaching"—is wrapped up in the personhood of the preacher—"yourself."

TEMPERAMENT

We are to pay close attention to our temperament. In using this term I mean the complex configuration of one's character traits, thought processes, emotional responses, behavioral patterns, perceptions, attitudes, needs and longings. This complex configuration is a "given." It is who we were created to be; it is the way we were created to live in the world. We are to preach out of who we are. Many of us, thinking

---

[11]I am using the phrase "Spirit gifting" instead of spiritual gifts to emphasize that it is the Holy Spirit's gifts we are talking about and because "gifting" is more dynamic than the static noun "gifts."

that a preacher must be only one kind of person (usually an unrealistic, idealized person), spend enormous energy turning ourselves inside out to do this work. We need not do so, for God knows whom he calls to participate in the work of transformation and calls us to be ourselves.

There are many ways of understanding and articulating all this. One many have found helpful is the Taylor-Johnson Temperamental Analysis (TJTA).[12] Although especially designed for premarital counseling, it opens up for preachers ways of self-understanding. The test frames human personhood in terms of a series of juxtapositions: nervous vs. composed, depressive vs. light-hearted, active-social vs. quiet, expressive-responsive vs. inhibited, sympathetic vs. indifferent, subjective vs. objective, dominant vs. submissive, hostile vs. tolerant and self-disciplined vs. impulsive. (You can see why I said temperament and woundedness are deeply intertwined, for a number of the TJTA temperament traits are not due to our creation but to the consequences of the Fall of creation; more later.)

Another helpful tool is the Birkman indicator.[13] Although used to help people understand how they function in a business context, it too opens windows on how preachers do their work. The tool explores how we relate to individuals and how we relate in groups; how we relate to structures and authority; what kind of incentives we need to work well; our preferred pace of action; how we deal with change; whether we like to work alone or with others; whether we prefer action and then reflection, or reflection and then action.

Yet another helpful resource for self-understanding is the widely used Myers-Briggs Type Indicator.[14] It is the work of Katharine Briggs and her daughter, Isabel Briggs Myers, who adapted the insights of Carl Gustav Jung (1875-1961), wanting to make his insights into the human person more accessible to the larger population. Their motive

---

[12]Robert M. Taylor and Lucile P. Morrison, *Taylor-Johnson Temperamental Analysis* (Thousand Oaks, Calif.: Psychological Publication Co., 1984).

[13]See www.birkman.com.

[14]Isabel Briggs Myers with Peter B. Myers, *Gifts Differing* (Palo Alto, Calif.: Consulting Psychologists Press, 1980); Isabel Briggs Myers and Mary H. McCaulley, *Manual: A Guide to the Development and Use of the Myers-Briggs Type Indicator* (Palo Alto, Calif.: Consulting Psychologists Press, 1985); David Keirsey and Marilyn Bates, *Please Understand Me: Character & Temperament Types* (Del Mar, Calif.: Prometheus Nemesis Book Company, 1984).

was to help people understand why they do the things they do and thus to help them make wiser choices. Jung looked at us humans and saw a number of different "archetypes," or configurations of tendencies and perspectives. Myers-Briggs suggests eight basic "preferences" (especially under stress—which for us is the preaching moment!) that make up the archetypes of the human family. They gather these preferences into four pairs: (E) extroversion and (I) introversion; (S) sensing and (N) intuition; (T) thinking and (F) feeling; and (J) judging and (P) perceiving. The first pair has to do with how we are energized for living: (E) extroversion, we like to be with people most of the time, we are energized by the outer world of people, things and activities; (I) introversion, although we enjoy people, we prefer (and need) time alone, we are energized by the inner world of thought and ideas. The second pair has to do with how we approach life and assess reality: (S) sensing, we use the five senses, we observe the facts and like data and finding order; (N) intuition, we use the "sixth" sense, we can see and hear without the senses, looking for associations and patterns and meaning. The third pair has to do with how we process what we learn through either sensing or intuiting: (T) thinking, we think out what we have gathered, we analyze and reason it out; (F) feeling, we feel out what we have gathered, we try to own what we learn, we need to have integrity with what we learn. Myers-Briggs is not suggesting that thinkers do not feel or feelers do not think; it is just that thinkers prefer thinking out reality, while feelers prefer feeling out reality. The fourth pair has to do with what we then do with what we have gathered and processed: (J) judging, we act on it all, we make decisions and go for it; (P) perceiving, we process it all, wanting to make sure we have taken in all the possible input and considered all the possible courses of action. How wonderfully diverse we are![15]

All of this helps us understand the complexity of the preaching moment. The preacher comes at the event from one set of preferences, while the hearers come from that set and many others. It is incumbent

---

[15]I intentionally used the pronoun *we* throughout because Myers-Briggs argues that we all have the capacity to live from all these tendencies; it is just that we have preferences, which we automatically act from under stress.

on preachers to be themselves while appreciating that the majority of the listeners are working out of a very different configuration. Thankfully, we have at our disposal a host of research into this complexity.[16]

Working with the insights of TJTA, Birkman, Myers-Briggs and other temperament sorters, let me suggest how they inform preachers' self-understanding.[17] I can identify at least five different temperamentally shaped preachers. I call them faithful exhorters, spontaneous activists, orderly logicians, passionate visionaries and creative artists.

Faithful exhorters. Preachers of this type value the past and, consequently, tradition. They relate to God, therefore, by remembering the past (in the sense of both "recall to mind" and "participate in") and by projecting themselves into the past. They prefer the highly exhortative books like Matthew and James. They feel duty-bound to speak only what the Bible says, and they call people to uncompromising obedience: "we do this because the Bible says so." They have the unique capacity to enter a text and almost immediately sense what was going on in it. Take Mark 1:16-20 for example, the calling of the four fishermen. Faithful exhorters are able to smell the sea air and the fish, to feel the sea breeze, to hear the yelling on the beach as fishermen try to haul their catch to the shore, etc. And as preachers, they are able to help the rest of us do the same. Preachers of this type naturally communicate in an orderly way (even preferring printed outlines) and naturally use concrete, sensually vivid language—all unto calling people to faithfulness.

Spontaneous activists. Preachers of this type value the present and therefore openness and spontaneity. They relate to God in the now and by doing: theirs is an informal, hands-on spirituality. They prefer

---

[16]See Lloyd Edwards, *How We Belong, Fight, and Pray: MBTI as a Key to Understanding Congregational Dynamics* (Washington, D.C.: The Alban Institute, 1993); W. Harold Grant, Magdala Thompson and Thomas E. Clarke, *From Image to Likeness: A Jungian Path in Gospel Journey* (Mahwah, N.J.: Paulist, 1983); Otto Kroeger and Janet M. Thuesen, *Type Talk: or How to Determine Your Personality Type and Change Your Life: Based on the Myers-Briggs Indicator* (New York: Delacorte, 1988); Roy M. Oswald and Otto Kroeger, *Personality Type and Religious Leadership* (Washington, D.C.: The Alban Institute, 1988).

[17]What I develop has been influenced by the work of Chester P. Michael and Marie C. Norrisey, *Prayer and Temperament: Different Prayer Forms for Different Personality Types* (Charlottesville, Va.: Open Door, 1984). They present fascinating research on the correlations between personality type and preferred ways of praying that have significant implications for preachers and preferred ways of preaching.

the more dynamic books like Mark (which uses the adverb *immediately* thirty-six times) and Proverbs, and they enjoy the Sermon on the Mount. They find standing behind a pulpit with a manuscript very confining. In their sermons they get right to the point and want to move people into action as soon as possible. (If you are a spontaneous activist, you found chapter five of this book very tedious if not outright boring.)

Orderly logicians. Preachers of this type value the mind and therefore, logical progression of thought. They relate to God through logic, reading and writing prayers, asking probing questions. They think out their experiences and can quickly articulate their evaluations of their experiences. They prefer the carefully crafted books like Romans, Deuteronomy and Luke. As preachers they are very precise with words and sermon flow. They are freest when they work with a well-crafted manuscript.

Passionate visionaries. Preachers of this type value the future; they are always seeking meaning and focusing on possibility. In relating to God, they crave authenticity. They need regular time of stillness and silence in order to bring their passionate feelings in line with the gospel. They prefer the more mystic texts like John, Isaiah and Revelation. As preachers they are able to size up a group of people quickly, adjusting the tone, if not vocabulary, of the sermon to speak into the lives of the hearers. They have the capacity to stand in just about anyone else's shoes and see, hear, feel or think the world from their perspective.

Creative artists. Preachers of this type value sight and sound. They make sense of the world, and their experience of the world, through audio and visual means. They prefer the parables, the poetry of the prophets and the visions in Revelation. They have the capacity to "paint" vivid pictures with words; they prefer, however, to literally "paint" and let the painting (or song or film or sculpture) speak for itself.

Where do you find yourself in this rubric? To some extent every preacher can identify with each of the categories. And to some extent each of us needs to try to understand the other types; after all, any audience is going to be comprised of all the types, and we want to connect as widely as possible. Which preachers do you know who embody these different ways of being and living? Most importantly, what do you need to pay close attention to about your temperament in order to be the preacher you were created to be?

WOUNDEDNESS

We are to also pay close attention to our woundedness. We all come at life, at relationships, at work and, therefore at preaching, out of wounds we have suffered, especially in the early years of life. Around these wounds have emerged patterns of dealing with the pain. These wounds are always there, some painfully so, most unconsciously or subconsciously so. We could try to ignore them, but they will affect the preaching moment anyway.[18] This is just the way it is. The glory of the gospel is that God does heal these wounds, and while in the process of healing, God works with them for the sake of the truth.[19]

This theme is worthy of an entire book, and people with greater insight into the human person than myself have written such works.[20] Some of us live out of the need to fill the deep, painful void at the center of our souls. Some of us live out of the need to control the world around us. Some of us live out of deep anxiety, not knowing whom or what we can really trust. Some of us live out of deeply rooted perfectionism, feeling we have no worth unless our work is done perfectly. Some of us (the majority of preachers?) live out of the need to please people, always making sure that what we do finds favor in other people's eyes.

All of these wounds hit at the issues of identity and worth. If my life is anything like the norm, we will, to one degree or another, revolve

---

[18]See Paul Johnson, *Intellectuals* (New York: Harper & Row, 1988), and Susan Howatch, *Glittering Images* (New York: Fawcett Crest, 1989).

[19]Three good examples: Jonathan Edwards, E. Stanley Jones and A W. Tozer. See George M. Marsden, *Jonathan Edwards: A Life* (New Haven, Conn.: Yale University Press, 2003); Stephen A. Graham, *Ordinary Man, Extraordinary Mission: The Life and Work of E. Stanley Jones* (Nashville: Abingdon, 2005); and Lyle Dorsett, *A Passion for God: The Spiritual Journey of A. W. Tozer* (Chicago: Moody Press, 2008).

[20]See especially the work of Archibald Hart, *Healing Life's Hidden Addictions* (Ann Arbor, Mich.: Servant, 1990); Henri Nouwen, *The Wounded Healer: Ministry in Contemporary Society* (Garden City, N.Y.: Doubleday, 1972); David Seamands, *Healing for Damaged Emotions* (Wheaton, Ill.: Victor, 1991).

around these issues all of our lives.[21] Preachers, therefore, perhaps more than others, need to regularly receive gospel preaching; we need regularly to hear again that in Jesus Christ we have been brought into his status as the Son of God, and that we have been adopted by his Father as real daughters and sons, and that we too hear the Father say, "You are my beloved." We, more than others, need to hear again and again that our worth is not determined by our work but by God's gracious choice that we be his own (Eph 1:3-14).

And we need to hear again and again that the Spirit of God is at work healing the wounds and also that by his grace, the wounds become the place out of which he enables us to preach. Out of the deep void some of us experience can come the preaching of the fullness of life into which the triune God calls us. Out of the deep need to control can come the preaching of the secure hold of the Sovereign Shepherd. Out of the anxiety can come the preaching of the Lord who has our best interest in mind and can provide for all our needs. Out of the crippling perfectionism can come the preaching of the perfect unconditional love for creatures who never can be and never need be perfect. Thanks be to God that even our wounds can be used to bring about transformation for others.

May I suggest that before reading any further you take some time to pray about any woundedness of which you are aware? And may I commend to you a prayer composed by C. Baxter Kruger, a passionate lover of the Trinity?[22]

> Father, in the freedom of your endless love and in the safety of your embrace, I acknowledge to you that something happens to me and I get lost in the darkness.
>
> Instead of living in your joy, I get crippled inside. Instead of receiving your love, my soul is disturbed. I become needy. I shut down and withdraw. I become self-centered, angry and frustrated. I hurt those I love in my pain. I waste time and life. I am embarrassed. I am scared to look

---

[21]I am finding help in the work being done around the so-called Enneagram, an ancient attempt to understand the "down-sides" of our human ecology. See especially Richard Rohr and Andreas Ebert, *The Enneagram: A Christian Perspective* (New York: Crossroads, 2002).

[22]C. Baxter Kruger, blog entry on perichoresis.org (accessed via secure site).

at myself. Forgive me for blaming others for my problems. Speak to my soul, Father. Tell me again that there is more to me than I know.

Help me believe that my existence, my life, my future is part of yours. Help me see that facing my life and my hurt means liberation and full-ness, not death.

Jesus, give me your eyes. Help me to see myself as you do. Holy Spirit, bear witness to my soul that I belong to Jesus and his Father forever. Show me where and when and how I am not receiving Jesus' Father's love. Show me how my fear is attached to people and places, events and smells and things. Deliver me from the triggers and associations of evil. Forgive me for what I have done and said, not done and not said to your children. Amen.

SPIRIT GIFTINGS

We are to pay close attention to how God has gifted us for ministry. Here is the good news for us wounded preachers: in our brokenness, Jesus Christ has wired each of us to function in the world for his glory. Jesus, by whom and for whom we were made, and by whom and for whom we are being redeemed, has uniquely wired each of us to live and serve in unique ways. It is the gospel part of the ecology of our personhood.

Wired. *Gifted* is the more usual term. *Charismatized* is the more literal biblical term; *charismatized*, from *charisma*, meaning "gift of grace." Every member of the body of Christ in the world has been char-ismatized, graciously endowed by the Holy Spirit to perform a unique function in the church and in the world. That gifting goes so deep within us that I use the term *wired*, suggesting that the gifting is con-stitutive of our being. It is not so much that we have a gift; rather it is that we are a gift.

The apostle Paul exhorts us "not to think more highly" of ourselves than we ought to think (Rom 12:3). What he means is that none of us is to think that we are gifted by the Holy Spirit to do everything that Jesus calls the church to do in the world. (One of the wounds many preachers bear—the need to be omni-competent in order to feel worthwhile.) Rather, "think so as to have sound judgment, as God has allotted to each a measure of faith" (Rom 12:3). We are to embrace the way we have been wired and not try to be everything the church and world need preachers to be.

Consider the following fun parable by Bruce Bugbee, founder and president of Network Ministries International.[23]

> It wasn't too long after creation that the animals got together to form a school. They wanted the best school possible, offering their students a well-rounded curriculum of swimming, running, climbing and flying. In order to graduate, all the animals had to take all the courses.
>
> The duck was excellent at swimming. In fact, he was better than his instructor. But he was only making passing grades at climbing and was getting a very poor grade in running. The duck was so slow in running he had to stay after school every day to practice. There was only little improvement, because his webbed feet got so badly worn. With such worn feet, he was only able to get an average grade in swimming, but average was quite acceptable to everyone, so no one worried much about it . . . except the duck.
>
> [The rabbit was at the top of her class in running. But after a while,] she developed a twitch in her leg from all the time she spent in the water trying to improve her swimming.
>
> [The squirrel was] a peak performer [in climbing, but was constantly frustrated in flying class. His body became so bruised from all his hard landings that he didn't even do very well in climbing, and he ended up with poor marks in running.]
>
> [The eagle] was a continual problem student. She was severely disciplined for being a non-conformist. [For example, in climbing class she would always beat everyone else to the top of the tree,] but insisted on using her own way to get there.

By now you are getting the point of the story. Each of the animals had a particular expertise. When they did what they were designed to do, they excelled. When they tried to operate outside their areas of expertise, they were not nearly as effective. Think about it for a moment. Can ducks run? Sure they can! Is that what they do best? No!

The point is to free the ducks for the water, the squirrels for the trees and the eagles for the sky.

Not all preachers are made alike. Each of us has been wired in unique

---

[23]Bruce Bugbee, "Do You Have the Right People in the Right Places for the Right Reasons?" *CRM* March/April 1995, pp. 18-20.

ways. We can learn from each other. But we should not try to imitate each other.

There are many resources available to help us discover our unique way of serving in the world, and thus of preaching. The one I have found most helpful (as I try to understand how I have been wired as a preacher, and as I help other preachers understand how they have been wired) is that developed by Glen A. Thorp, with whom I served for a number of years in Los Angeles.[24] He takes the tack that in Romans 12:6-8 the apostle Paul is identifying seven major ways of doing ministry, or, more in line with the emphasis of this book, seven different ways of participating in the ongoing ministry of the risen and ascended Jesus. Why seven? Could it be that in Scripture seven is the number of completeness, and that the seven wirings somehow represent or embody the essence of the Spirit's gifting of the church? The seven are prophecy, service, teaching, exhortation, giving, leading and mercy.

> And since we have gifts that differ according to the grace given to us, let us each exercise them accordingly: if prophecy, according to the proportion of his faith; if service, in his serving; or he who teaches in his teaching; or he who exhorts, in his exhortation; he who gives, with liberality; he who leads, with diligence; he who shows mercy, with cheerfulness (Rom 12:6-8 NASB modified).

Thorp makes the case that what we have in Romans 12 are ingrained motivations for ministry. In 1 Corinthians 12 we have gifts as manifestations of the Spirit's ministry; in Ephesians 4, we have gifts as offices of ministry. In Romans, Paul is speaking of seven different motivations the Spirit has built into members of the body of Christ. These motivations are so deeply ingrained that, again, I refer to them as wirings constitutive of who we are in Jesus.

What Thorp argues, and I agree with him, is that all seven motivated persons can preach. But each of them will preach out of a differ-

---

[24]Glen A. Thorp, *Freed and Equipped for Ministry: A Critical Study of Spiritual Gifts and Their Use Within the Church* (D.Min. diss., San Francisco Theological Seminary, San Francisco, Calif., 1980). I will not be quoting directly from his paper as I have worked with the material so long now that it has been restated in my own words. I owe the genesis of the ideas, however, to Dr. Thorp.

ent motivation. All seven could take the same text, and because they automatically work out of their wirings, they will hear seven different sermons. The same truth is heard in seven different ways. And that is just fine.

Let us work our way through the list of seven four times: first, briefly suggesting what Paul means by each term; second, suggesting the sorts of words and phrases each wiring tends to use; third, suggesting the passion of each motivation; and fourth, suggesting the texts of Scripture to which each motivation is drawn and would likely most often want to preach.

Round one: meaning.

Prophecy. As we have already said, the verb means to "speak forth." This motivational gifting is the ability to speak a fresh word from the living God. Of all the motivations it cannot be exercised at will. It is under the direct and immediate control of the Holy Spirit, which is why the Old Testament prophets regularly said that the word of the Lord "came upon me." Sometimes prophesying happens in preaching; most of the time preaching is teaching or exhortation (or one of the other verbs we looked at in chapter four). The prophetic word may be a word of warning, a word of comfort, a word of demand, a word of wooing. Whenever it comes people know it is the word of God.

Service. The word Paul uses is *diakonia,* from which we get the word *deacon.* Although all disciples of Jesus are called to be servants, what Paul is referring to here is a unique motivation to serve. Persons with this wiring are keenly aware of temporal needs around them. They walk in a room and are immediately aware of concrete things that need to be done, and they go to it.

Teaching. This motivation involves the careful, systematic interpretation and application of Scripture. The desire is to impart information, to help people understand the word spoken by the apostles and prophets. "Why do we need theology?" Clark Pinnock asked rhetorically. "Because Christianity is a missionary religion, and if we are going to get the message out, we had better get it right!"[25] This wiring seeks to

---

[25]"Why Do We Need Theology?" *Christianity Today,* March 27, 1981, p. 68.

protect and pass on "the faith which was once for all handed down to the saints" (Jude 3).

Exhortation. The word Paul uses here is *paraklēsis,* from the verb *parakaleō,* and related to the word Jesus uses for the Holy Spirit, *paraklētos.* The Holy Spirit has been called in alongside to do a number of things for Jesus' disciples: convict, convince, comfort, counsel, kick in the pants. Those with this motivational gifting desire to come alongside people to help in whatever ways are needed in the moment. Charles Cranfield says the purpose of this wiring is "to help Christians to live out their obedience to the gospel."[26]

Giving. All Christians are called to give of their financial resources. What Paul is referring to here are special kinds of givers, persons motivated to give in generous ways. Are they motivated to give away their own resources? Or, as John Calvin thought, are they "charged with the distribution of the public property of the church"?[27] Whichever, they delight in giving liberally, hoping thereby to be a catalyst for more giving by others.

Leading. The word used by Paul is a military term related to the verb that means "to stand up before others." The motivation here is to step up to the head of the line and get things moving in one direction. Another word for this is *administration:* people graciously managing people and resources to meet the needs of people. The desire is to see the kingdom of God advance in the world.

Mercy. It is the key word of the three chapters before Romans 12. The mercy of God is God doing for us what we cannot and never could do for ourselves, and what, because of sin, we do not deserve to have done. Persons with this motivational wiring have a huge capacity to feel for and with others. It is the desire simply to be there for others as Jesus is there for us.

Round two: other words. Here we'll look at the sorts of words and phrases that tend to reveal these diverse motivations, providing an-

---

[26]C. E. B. Cranfield, *A Critical and Exegetical Commentary of the Epistle to the Romans,* International Critical Commentary (Edinburgh: T & T Clark, 1979), p. 623.

[27]John Calvin, *Calvin's New Testament Commentaries: The Epistles of Paul to the Romans and Thessalonians,* trans. R. Mackenzie (Grand Rapids: Eerdamans, 1973), p. 270.

other window into different modes of preaching.[28]

Prophecy. Some of the most frequent phrases these people use in preaching include "Seeing reality as it really is" and "Knowing God as God really is" (as the hymn goes, "naught be all else to me save that Thou art"). These persons are always thinking in terms of potential and possibilities: "It doesn't have to be this way," they regularly remind us. They have a need to tell others what they see: the joy of seeing it is not complete without others also seeing.

Service. These people quickly recognize "the concrete needs" of people. They value being detail-oriented and organized. "No task is beneath your dignity as a disciple of the Great Servant." They do it all with a joyful spirit.

Teaching. They are precise, systematic, able to balance individual texts with "the whole counsel of God." "Well, that is not exactly what the text says; notice . . ." They seek faithfulness to the text. They enjoy research. They delight in seeing "the light go on" in others.

Exhortation. From these people we hear again and again, "Relationships matter." They enjoy the one-on-one, the side-by-side. "Comfort the disturbed, disturb the comfortable." They see the Christian life as a "walk," and enjoy helping people take the next step in the journey. "Walk the walk." "Be who you are in Christ."

Giving. Such disciples never say, "We do not have the funds." They are not ashamed to talk about money. "The surest statement of faith is not your reciting of the Creeds but what you do with your money." They enjoy watching other ministries begin and thrive.

Leading. We hear them regularly saying things like, "shape up the troops," "fulfill the vision," and "we are in this together." They are willing to make hard decisions and suffer the relational consequences. "No pain, no gain."

Mercy. They are not afraid to enter into another's pain. "Something in that person draws out of me the compassion of Jesus" (Glen Thorp regularly said this). "No one cares how much we know until they know how much we care." "It matters not why the other is in trouble; all that

---

[28]Here I am most indebted to the work of Glen Thorp.

matters is that they are in need." And, "just be there for others."

Round three: passion. Each of the different wirings comes at life and, therefore, at preaching out of a passion inherent to each motivation.

Prophecy. To see and help others see.

Service. To see to it that needs are met.

Teaching. To understand and help others understand.

Exhortation. To come alongside and help others take the next step.

Giving. To make resources available.

Leading. To see that the job gets done.

Mercy. To be there for others, mediating the compassion of Jesus.

Round four: biblical texts. Each of the different motivations likes to live in and preach particular portions and genres of Scripture. The following is what each wiring seems most drawn to and, therefore, what each will likely choose to preach.

Prophecy. First and Second Kings, where God raises up the prototypical prophets, Elijah and Elisha. Isaiah, the great visionary, the prophet of the mind of God. Jeremiah, the pleading prophet, the prophet of the heart of God. Habakkuk, who was told to "hang in there" when he could not see what God was doing: "The vision . . . will not fail. / Though it tarries, wait for it" (Hab 2:3). The Revelation, where we see Jesus Christ in all his glory and victory. Ephesians, especially chapters 1–3, the indicative of grace. And John, who joyfully declares, "We saw His glory" (Jn 1:14).

Service. Exodus, where we see God provide for the physical needs of his people as they make their way to the Promised Land. Haggai, the prophet who cares about the specific, concrete (literally) needs of the temple. First Timothy, addressing everyday issues like decision-making processes, budgeting and caring for widows. And Luke, where we find Jesus meeting the needs of hurting people and then calling us to join him in such service (i.e., the women who funded Jesus' itinerant ministry, the parable of the good Samaritan).

Teaching. Deuteronomy, the "second telling" of the law, where Moses systematizes former teaching. Judges, where Israel struggles to discern and live by revealed truth. Isaiah, Israel's greatest theologian. Romans, where Paul more systematically lays out the gospel of God. Hebrews, the massively brilliant articulation of the finished work of Jesus the High Priest. And Matthew, wherein Jesus' words and deeds are collected in five orderly teaching sections.

Exhortation. First and Second Corinthians, where the inherent consequences of obedience and disobedience are developed for us. Proverbs, the cry of Wisdom to learn from her, to develop skill in everyday living. Amos, the prophet who wants to move people on to the next level of maturity and obedience. Ephesians, especially chapters 4–6, the imperative of grace. James, with his emphasis on "doing the word." And Matthew and Luke, where Jesus comes alongside and exhorts people to move on.

Giving. Exodus, where the generosity of God is so wonderfully displayed, enabling a million plus people to make their way across a hot and dry desert. Second Samuel to First Chronicles—the life of David, the generous giver. Philippians, where Paul celebrates the Lord who provides. And Luke, with Jesus' parables of the generous grace of God and with the stories of those who provided for the work of the kingdom.

Leading. Ezra and Nehemiah, where God directs and empowers leaders to rebuild the destroyed Jerusalem. Daniel, whom God raises to significant leadership in a foreign land. Exodus, where Moses has to rise to leadership. Joshua, the reluctant leader, and "Be strong and courageous." First and Second Timothy, one leader coaching another leader. And Mark, because of that repeated word "immediately" . . . "and immediately Jesus."

Mercy. Genesis 12–50, where we see God's merciful ways with the dysfunctional families of Abraham, Isaac and Jacob. Hosea, the prophet of the second chance. Psalms, the prayers for mercy. Philemon, where Paul makes an appeal "for love's sake" (Philem 9).

What amazingly creative diversity! How could there possibly be only one type of preacher?

Where do you see yourself in all this? Which of the motivations best describes you as you take on the work of preaching? Thus, the apostle Paul exhorts us, "kindle afresh the gift of God which is in you" (2 Tim 1:6). Wholeheartedly embrace the unique motivation God has worked in you. Again, this is not to think too highly of ourselves (Rom 12:3). Thinking too highly of ourselves means thinking we are wired in every way. Embracing our unique wiring is to have sound judgment.

God honors the full ecology of our personhood—temperament, woundedness, Spirit gifting—and so must we. Parker Palmer puts it so well: "The God I know does not ask us to conform to some abstract norm for the ideal self. God asks us only to honor our created nature, which means our limits as well as potentials."[29] In my experience, burnout in ministry does not result from overworking; burnout results from not honoring who we are and instead trying to be who we think we ought to be. And in my experience, joy comes by embracing who we are—though we are not everything we would like to be—and trusting the great Preacher to preach through the preacher he is making, redeeming and molding us to be.[30]

---

[29]Parker Palmer, *Let Your Life Speak: Listening to the Voice of Vocation* (San Francisco: Jossey-Bass, 2000), p. 50.

[30]Again I commend to you the works of Kenton C. Anderson, *Choosing to Preach: A Comprehensive Introduction to Sermon Options and Structures* (Grand Rapids: Zondervan, 2006), and Robert Stephen Reid, *The Four Voices of Preaching Connecting Purpose and Identity Behind the Pulpit* (Grand Rapids: Brazos Press, 2006). Both, in different ways, get at the issues of this chapter.

9

THE LIFE OF THE PREACHER

Living In

THE CALL TO PREACH IS A CALL TO LIVE A different kind of life. Great preaching, the kind that participates in the miracle of Ezekiel 37, will not happen unless, and until, preachers embrace this call and choose to live a different way. Great preaching also requires that churches embrace the implications of a preacher's call and do what they can to free their pastors to obey.

Thus far in this book we have been thinking about the preaching moment, about the communicating-the-gospel moment. In this chapter I want to help us think about the preaching life. As we will see (and as you who have been preaching for some time already know), saying yes to this call logically, and necessarily, means saying no to a lot of other worthy, needed activities. Every yes is a no to something or someone else. If we preachers say yes to everything and everyone who comes our way, we are implicitly saying no to the kinds of priorities and activities inherent in the call to preach. It would be of great help if churches would grasp the dynamics of this call and help ameliorate the diverting demands and expectations that keep us from fulfilling the call. Nevertheless, in the final analysis, only the preacher can say the yes and the required noes.

Therein lies the biggest price to pay in order to effectively participate with the great Preacher in the preaching ministry. Preachers are, for most part, prone to people pleasing. Saying yes to the Preacher,

Jesus, necessarily means saying no to many things traditionally expected of the pastor-preacher. But in fact, pastors often impose those expectations on themselves. Doing so emerges out of our need to be important and (more to the point) to be seen as important. In our insecurity vis-à-vis the busyness of the "important" people of the world, we allow ourselves to be equally busy, handling all kinds of responsibilities, responding to all kinds of requests for our "indispensable" services. Who was it that said, "Professional busyness is a sign of spiritual laziness"? Eugene Peterson, speaking the heart of the matter as usual, says, "Busyness is an illness of spirit, a rush from one thing to another because there is no ballast of vocational integrity and no confidence in grace."[1] James S. Stewart said it even stronger: "Beware the professional busy-ness which is but slackness in disguise."[2] He asks, "What does it all amount to—the whole religious paraphernalia of good works and religious machinery—if there is lacking the intense concentration on the message which is to deliver people's eyes from tears, their feet from falling, and their souls from death, the lonely wrestling with God at Peniel without which no blessing comes?"[3]

What happens in the preaching moment happens, as we have seen so clearly, because of the Spirit and the Word. Yet, what happens in the preaching moment—from the human mechanics perspective—happens because of the way the preacher lives before and after that moment.

In this chapter, I identify eight basic dynamics in the life of the preacher. I articulate them in eight statements beginning "Live in . . ." The first seven are, in varying degrees and in different modes, true of all disciples of Jesus; discipleship is impossible without living them in one way or another. The preacher lives them with even greater intentionality and in larger amounts of time. What is expected of all disciples in order to mature in Jesus is expected all the more of those he calls to preach him.

---

[1] Eugene Peterson, *Five Smooth Stones for Pastoral Work* (Grand Rapids: Eerdmans, 1997), pp. 61-62. He expands on this in *Under the Unpredictable Plant: An Exploration in Vocational Holiness* (Grand Rapids: Eerdmans, 1992) and in *The Contemplative Pastor: Returning to the Art of Spiritual Formation* (Grand Rapids: Eerdmans, 1994).
[2] James S. Stewart, *Heralds of God* (1946; reprint, Vancouver, B.C.: Regent College Publishing, 2001), p. 196.
[3] Ibid., pp. 196-97.

LIVE IN THE GREAT PREACHER

The life of the preacher is lived in relationship with the Preacher. Better, this life is lived in the Preacher, "in Christ," as the apostle Paul put it so many times. "In Christ" is, according to James S. Stewart, the center of Paul's theology because it is the center of his existence.[4] Stewart notes that Paul was a preacher first and a writer second.

> And both spheres—preaching and writing—were ruled by one great fact—the fact of a living, present Lord; and by one all-decisive experience—the experience of union and communion with him. This was the apostle's calling. This was his sole vocation and concern. This was that for which he had been born. He came to bring, not a system, but the living Christ.[5]

All of Paul's theology "is gathered up in the one great fact of communion with Christ."[6] All that Paul preached and taught and wrote are "but radii of the same circle of which union with Christ is the centre."[7] "For me, to live is Christ" (Phil 1:21). "I count all things to be loss in view of the surpassing value of knowing Christ Jesus my Lord" (Phil 3:8). "If anyone is in Christ—a new creation!" (2 Cor 5:17, my translation). "Christ in you, the hope of glory" (Col 1:27). *In* truly is a blessed preposition! We can be in Christ, and Christ can be in us. Paul's powerful, effective preaching of Christ emerges from a life lived in Christ.

He was simply obeying Jesus' command spoken the night before he was handed over to death. In one of the central discipleship texts, John 15:4-5, Jesus says, "Abide in Me, and I in you." Live in me, and I in you. Make your home in me, and I in you. "I am the vine, you are the branches; the one who abides in Me, and I in him or her, bears much fruit; for apart from Me you can do nothing" (NASB modified). He or she can do nothing. Especially preach. From this text, E. Stanley Jones said he learned his one major job in life: abide in Jesus; the rest is his to do. "The business of my life, and the only business of my life, is to abide

---

[4]James S. Stewart, *A Man in Christ: The Vital Elements of St. Paul's Religion* (Vancouver, B.C.: Regent College Publishing, 2002).
[5]Ibid., p. 8.
[6]Ibid., p. 10.
[7]Ibid., p. 12.

in him. All else follows."[8] The call to preach Jesus is first and foremost to abide. Simple as that.

I love what Jones goes on to say about this being "in." Listen: "Being in him we are in everything that is in him. Being in him we are in everything good, everything joyous, everything creative, everything healthy, everything for time and eternity."[9] Do you agree? Being in Jesus means being in everything that is in Jesus: in his love, his light, his life, his holiness, his wisdom, his power, his peace, his hope and on it goes. And when Jesus is in us, everything that is in Jesus is in us: his love, his light, his life, his holiness, his power. On it goes. The call to preach is first and foremost the call to live this double abiding: he in us, we in him.

What we soon discover as we live in him is that he lives in the one he calls "Father" and in the one he calls "the Paraclete." That is, Jesus lives his life in relationship with the Father and the Spirit; Jesus lives his life in the inner life of the triune God. And, wonder of wonders, he, through his death and resurrection, makes it possible to live with him in the inner life of Father, Son and Holy Spirit. It takes my breath away every time I say those words. Imagine: mere human beings, and mere sinful human beings at that, invited to live in—really in—the inner life of the living God.[10] I want to shout it from the mountaintops or, in our urban world, shout it from the high rises: "Jesus includes us in the eternal life of the Trinity!" But before I shout the news, I am to live the news. The life of the preacher is lived in union and communion with Jesus, his Father and his Spirit.

This is what the spiritual disciplines are finally all about: ways of abiding, ways of staying plugged in to the vine. Especially important for preachers are the disciplines of silence, solitude and Sabbath. Since we live by speaking, we need to periodically stop speaking to make sure we are not just talking in an attempt to shape and protect our worlds. "We are so accustomed to relying upon words to manage and control

---

[8]E. Stanley Jones, *In Christ* (Nashville: Abingdon, 1961), p. 67.
[9]Ibid.
[10]I expand on this good news in my *Experiencing the Trinity* (Vancouver, B.C.: Regent College Publishing, 2000).

others. If we are silent who will take control? God will take control: but we will never let him take control until we trust him. Silence is intimately related to trust."[11] Since we live continually interacting with people, we need periodically to stop interacting to make sure we are not just going through the motions. "In solitude, we confront our own soul with its obscure forces and conflicts that escape our attention when we are interacting with others."[12] In the solitude we meet the risen Jesus again, and he heals us to "return to society as free persons."[13] And, along with every disciple, we need to periodically stop (one day of every seven) and shift the focus from our work to the work of the living God, from what our hands accomplish to what God's hands accomplish.[14] It is not so much that we keep the Sabbath, but that the Sabbath keeps us.[15] The point of the Sabbath is seeking and delighting in the God who is Father, Son and Holy Spirit, shifting the focus from what we are doing to what God is doing, so that when we act, we realize that we act with and in the triune God. It is not that the preacher keeps the Sabbath but that the Sabbath keeps the preacher. It is not that the preacher keeps silence but that silence keeps the preacher. It is not that the preacher keeps solitude but that solitude keeps the preacher.[16]

We are to do whatever it takes to live in the great Preacher, Jesus.

LIVE IN THE GOSPEL

The life of the preacher is lived in the gospel. So too is the life of every disciple. We can never get enough gospel. For one thing, we forget the gospel and consistently stand in need of being "stirred up by way of re-

---

[11]Richard Foster, *Celebration of Discipline* (San Francisco: Harper & Row, 1978), p. 88.

[12]Dallas Willard, *The Spirit of the Disciplines: Understanding How God Changes Lives* (San Francisco: Harper & Row, 1988), p. 161.

[13]Ibid.

[14]See Peterson, *Working the Angles*, p. 44-60, and Marva Dawn, *Keeping the Sabbath Wholly: Ceasing, Resting, Embracing, Feasting* (Grand Rapids: Eerdmans, 1989).

[15]I think it was Abraham Heschel who said, "It is not that Israel kept the Sabbath but that the Sabbath kept Israel."

[16]I have learned that I must protect one half-day (minimum) a week to get away just to be still before the Lord. It is not study time (though I might study); it is not rest time (though I might take a brief nap); it is not intercessory prayer time (though I might pray for others during the time). It is time simply to be present in the Presence, to be drawn more deeply into the fellowship of the Trinity. Interestingly, the discipline was much easier to do as a working pastor than as a professor!

minder" (2 Peter 1:13; 3:1 NASB modified). And for another, the gospel is so rich, so large and so grand that none of us will ever fully grasp it. No one will ever be able to say, "Well, I've mastered that; time to move on from the gospel." The call to preach is the call to live in the fullness of what God has done, is doing and will do in Jesus Christ.

To put it another way, before we can preach the gospel we need to have the gospel preached to us. Though that can happen through others, we often must preach to ourselves. D. Martyn Lloyd-Jones put it this way: "I suggest that the main trouble in this whole matter of spiritual depression"—to which preachers are uniquely prone—"in a sense is this: that we allow our self to talk to us, instead of talking to our self. . . . The main art in spiritual living is to know how to handle yourself. You have to take yourself in hand, address yourself, preach to yourself, question yourself."[17] And the question to keep asking ourselves is, "So, what is the gospel?" Regularly take out a piece of paper and write out what you believe the good news to be. Ask, "What is 'finished' on the cross? What has been done that never needs to be repeated and needs nothing added to it?" Ask, "What is the nature of the victory God won in the death and resurrection of Jesus of Nazareth?" Ask, "What changes resulted in and for the universe because of what God did on the cross and in the empty tomb?" Ask, "What does it mean that Jesus is now at the right hand of the Father?" Ask, "So what does it mean that Jesus has poured out the Holy Spirit upon us?" Ask, "Is there anything or anyone who can undo what Jesus has done?" Ask, "What are the consequences for the world knowing that 'Jesus is Lord'?" Ask, "What does that new creation, which is soon to descend to the earth, look like?"

Sin has been overcome. Evil has been overcome. Death has been overcome. The door into the Presence of the Holy God has been opened wide. The principalities and powers have been put in their place. The kingdom of God is breaking into the kingdoms of darkness and death. The chains of oppression are being cut. The way the universe goes together has been forever altered, and altered in the direction of setting captives free. On it goes. Preach it to yourself, until your heart is on

---

[17]D. Martyn Lloyd-Jones, *Spiritual Depression: Its Causes and Cures* (Grand Rapids: Eerdmans, 1965), p. 20.

fire and your mind is racing and your feet start dancing. The life of the preacher is lived in the new reality brought into being by the gospel. Live in the gospel.[18]

LIVE IN THE BOOK

The life of the preacher is lived in the Book, the Bible (as is the life of every disciple). It is the chief way we are empowered to live in the Preacher and in his gospel. "If you abide in Me, and My words abide in you" (Jn 15:7). "The words that I have spoken to you are spirit and are life" (Jn 6:63). The call to preach is a call to live our lives in and from the Book.

Psalm 1 says it best.

Blessed are those
　　who do not walk in step with the wicked
　　or stand in the way that sinners take
　　or sit in the company of mockers,
but who delight in the law of the LORD
　　and meditate on his law day and night.
They are like a tree planted by streams of water,
　　which yields its fruit in season
　　and whose leaf does not wither—
whatever they do prospers.
Not so the wicked!
　　They are like chaff
　　that the wind blows away.

---

[18]Some resources: Elizabeth Achtemeier, *The Old Testament and the Proclamation of the Gospel* (Philadelphia: Westminster Press, 1973); Mortimer Arias, *Announcing the Reign of God* (Philadelphia: Fortress, 1984); Carl F. Braaten, *No Other Gospel! Christianity Among the World's Religions* (Minneapolis: Fortress, 1992); George B. Caird, comp. Lincoln Hurst, *New Testament Theology* (New York: Oxford University Press, 1994); C. H. Dodd, *The Apostolic Preaching and Its Development* (London: Hodder and Stoughton, 1936); Michael Green, *The Meaning of Salvation* (London: Hodder & Stoughton, reprinted by Regent College Publishing, 1998); Richard Hays, *The Moral Vision of the New Testament* (San Francisco: HarperSanFrancisco, 1996); Dorothy Sayers, "The Dogma Is the Drama," in *The Whimsical Christian: 18 Essays by Dorothy Sayers* (New York: Macmillan, 1987); James S. Stewart, *A Faith to Proclaim* (1953; reprint, Vancouver, B.C.: Regent College Publishing, 2002); John G. Stackhouse Jr., ed., *What Does It Mean to Be Saved? Broadening Evangelical Horizons of Salvation* (Grand Rapids: Baker Academic, 2002); John R. W. Stott, *The Incomparable Christ* (Downers Grove, Ill.: InterVarsity Press, 2001).

Therefore the wicked will not stand in the judgment,
    nor sinners in the assembly of the righteous.
For the LORD watches over the way of the righteous,
    but the way of the wicked will be destroyed. (TNIV)

The contrast is between those who spend their time listening to the
latest views and news of human beings and are out of touch with the
living God as compared to those who "day and night" listen to the
views and news of the living God. Psalm 1 often catches me in how I
waste time attending to words that do not ultimately matter, and calls
me back to words that give life. Not that preachers must never listen to
what the "wicked, sinners, and scoffers" are saying. It's just that preachers, as disciples, are not to "walk in the counsel of," "stand in the path
of," "sit in the seat of" those who have nothing to do with Jesus and his
kingdom. Preachers, as disciples, are to "meditate" ("ruminate" is the
word) on God's self-revelation (that is the point of Torah) in creation,
redemption, law and gospel. (See also Psalm 119, the psalm for those
who live and work by words.)

The call to preach is the call to be a student of Scripture. And the
whole point of being a student is listening to the Master. As Eugene
Peterson observes, we can read the Bible and study the Bible but never
really listen. "Oh that My people would listen to Me" (Ps 81:13). "Listen to Me, O house of Jacob" (Is 46:3), "Listen to Me, you stubborn-
minded" (Is 46:12), "Listen to Me, O Jacob, even Israel whom I called"
(Is 48:12), "Listen to Me, O islands" (Is 49:1), "Listen to Me" (Is 51:7).
"Today, if you would hear His voice, do not harden your hearts" (Ps
95:7-8). "Whoever has an ear, hear what the Spirit is saying to the
churches" (seven times in Rev 2–3, my translation). And in the text
for servants of the word, we hear the testimony of the Servant of the
Lord himself: "The Lord GOD has given me the tongue of disciples,
that I may know how to sustain the weary one with a word" (Is 50:4).
That is what we want to be doing when we preach, right? What makes
this possible? The Servant continues: "He awakens Me morning by
morning, he awakens My ear to listen as a disciple. The Lord GOD has
opened My ear; and I was not disobedient" (Is 50:4-5). J. A. T. Mot-

yer, commenting on these verses, says that the Servant's words, earlier described as a sharpened sword and polished arrow (Is 49:2), were not spoken on the spot, so to speak, but, "were the products of prolonged attention, defined here as the discipleship of morning by morning appointment with God."[19] And this morning by morning appointment with God was not a discipline the Servant imposed on himself, but a discipline shaped by "responding to the Lord's disciplined and regular approach to him."[20] Then Moyter writes: "The morning by morning appointment is not a special provision or demand related to the perfect Servant but is the standard curriculum for all disciples."[21] And all the more so for all preachers. The major yes of the preacher's life is the yes to God's wakening us in the morning to listen. "The tongue filled with the appropriate word for ministry is the product of the ear filled with the word of God."[22] Students listen. Preachers listen.

As a preacher I am hounded by what God says to those who thought they were speaking God's word in the days of Jeremiah:

> Thus says the LORD of hosts,
> "Do not listen to the words of the prophets who are prophesying to
> you.
> They are leading you into futility;
> They speak a vision of their own imagination,
> Not from the mouth of the LORD.
> "They keep saying to those who despise Me,
> 'The LORD has said, "You will have peace"';
> And as for everyone who walks in the stubbornness of his own heart,
> They say, 'Calamity will not come upon you.'
> "But who has stood in the council of the LORD,
> That he should see and hear His word?
> Who has given heed to His word and listened?
> "Behold, the storm of the LORD has gone forth in wrath,

---

[19]J. A. T. Motyer, *The Prophecy of Isaiah: An Introduction & Commentary* (Downers Grove, Ill.: InterVarsity Press, 1993), p. 399. Moyter wrote this commentary after three decades of studying and teaching Isaiah. It is a treasure of exegetical insight and deep, deep spirituality.
[20]Ibid.
[21]Ibid.
[22]Ibid.

Even a whirling tempest;
   It will swirl down on the head of the wicked.
The anger of the LORD will not turn back
   Until he has performed and carried out the purposes of His heart;
   In the last days you will clearly understand it.
"I did not send these prophets,
   But they ran.
   I did not speak to them,
   But they prophesied.
"But if they had stood in My council,
   Then they would have announced My words to My people,
   And would have turned them back from their evil way
   And from the evil of their deeds. (Jer 23:16-22)

I do not want to speak words of my "own imagination," not even words of my best "Christian-ized" thinking. I want to speak words heard in the council of God, the council into which God invites those who fear him (Ps 25:14), those whom Jesus has made his friends (Jn 15:15). I want to speak the thoughts and feelings and opinions and views and news of the only one whose word gives life. So do you. So we stand in the Presence and listen.

LIVE IN BOOKS

The life of the preacher is lived in books. Not only in the Book, but in books that help us live in the Book. As he is dying in prison, the apostle Paul makes a number of requests of his dear apostolic delegate Timothy. "Bring the cloak which I left at Troas with Carpus" (2 Tim 4:13). Makes sense. "And the books, especially the parchments" (2 Tim 4:13). Imagine that! Even the greatest of all theologians and preachers (next to Jesus, that is) needed books. I like how Charles Spurgeon comments on this fact.

> Even an apostle must read. . . . He is inspired, and yet he wants books! He has been preaching at least for thirty years, and yet he wants books! He had seen the Lord, and yet he wants books! He had a wider experience than most men, and yet he wants books! He had been caught up into the third heaven, and yet he wants books! He had written the

major part of the New Testament, and yet he wants books! The apostle says to Timothy and so he says to every preacher, "Give thyself unto reading."[23]

Especially read biblical theology. Yes, read some of the latest books the cultures are reading. And read some of the books being pushed on the stalls of Christian bookstores. And read some magazines and newspapers and Internet blogs. And read church history and spiritual biography. And read novels. And "read" movies. But especially read biblical theology.[24] It is the kind of literature that drives us deeper into the Book, and the kind of literature that stands the passing of time.

LIVE IN CULTURE

The life of the preacher is lived in the culture. Actually, it is impossible not to do so unless one wants to be a hermit out in the hills. We cannot help but "drink the water" of the particular culture in which God has placed us. As Karl Barth is known for saying, we live with the Bible in one hand and the newspaper in the other. We do need to see movies, listen to music, read what people are writing, attend concerts, listen to debates, go to sporting events, coach Little League or soccer. Such activity automatically helps us connect and helps us speak in ways that connect. But we are not to live in culture at the expense of living in the inbreaking kingdom, a culture itself too. In our desire to connect it is easy to "fall in," so to speak, and no longer have any unique word to speak to the culture. See Psalm 1 again. And Romans 12:2—"Do not let the world around you squeeze you into its mould" (J. B. Phillips). Who was it that said something like, "Read the Times, but more so read the Eternities"? I will say more about this dynamic of our lives in the next chapter.

LIVE IN SUFFERING

The life of the preacher is lived in suffering. Again, it is impossible not

---

[23]C. H. Spurgeon, "Sermon #542, 'Paul—His Cloak and His Books,'" in *Metropolitan Tabernacle Pulpit* (London: Passmore and Alabstar, 1863), p. 9.
[24]I especially commend to you the works of Richard Bauckham, George Caird, Richard Hays, George Ladd, Christopher Wright and N. T. Wright.

to do so given the fallen condition of the world. So let me put it this way: the life of the preacher is lived not trying to avoid suffering but choosing to go with Jesus into his continuing suffering with the world. Yes, he has suffered "once for all" in the atoning sense. Such suffering has ended—"it is finished." Yet he still chooses to be fully in and for the world and to suffer with the world in our ongoing suffering.

On the evening of the first Easter, the risen Jesus "came and stood" in the midst of the disciples, gathered together behind shut doors, "for fear of the Jews" (Jn 20:19). It is my favorite of Jesus' Easter appearances for in it Jesus opens up the nature of ministry in his Spirit. Note what he says and does. He first says to them, "Peace be with you" (Jn 20:19). Then he shows them "both His hands and His side" (Jn 20:20); he shows them his wounds. And then he says to them again, "Peace be with you" (Jn 20:21). He speaks the word of peace; he shows them his wounds; he speaks the word of peace. Peace, wounds, peace. Why in this way? Jesus shows that because of his wounds, we can now have peace. "Having made peace through the blood of His cross" (Col 1:20). And it is in his wounds that we experience peace in this world. Peace comes in the fellowship of his suffering in and for the world. This is why Paul puts it the way he does: "that I may know Him and the power of his resurrection and the fellowship of His sufferings, being conformed to His death" (Phil 3:10). Shouldn't it be "fellowship of His sufferings and the power of His resurrection"? Shouldn't it be moving through suffering to resurrection life? Why the other way around? Because his sufferings are the necessary condition for our peace, and because we experience peace in this present form of existence in Jesus' sufferings.

So, on that first Easter evening, after speaking the second word of peace, Jesus says, "As the Father has sent Me, I also send you" (Jn 20:21). Jesus uses *as* not only in the sense of "now it is your turn to be sent into the world" but in the sense of "in the same way that the Father sent me I send you." If I may paraphrase Jesus: "As the Father sent me into the world to take on the world's sin and pain and bear it as My own, so he is sending you into the world to take on the world's sin and pain and bear it as your own." Which is why Jesus then breathes on the disciples, saying, "Receive the Holy Spirit" (Jn 20:22). We cannot do what we are sent to do in our own strength; we need the Holy Spirit to enable us to enter into the ongoing suffering of Jesus in and for the world. We need the Holy Spirit to enable us to face the sin of the world and, in the name of "the Lamb of God who takes away the sin of the world" (Jn 1:29), speak the word the world is dying to hear: "Your sins have been forgiven" (Jn 20:23 NASB modified). Peace, wounds, peace. It is because of and in the wounds of the Savior that we have and experience peace. "Crown him the Son of God, before the worlds were made; / And ye who tred where He hath trod, crown Him the Son of Man. / Who every grief hath known, that wrings the human breast, / And takes and bears them as His own, that all in Him may rest."[25]

The call to preach is the call to enter into the suffering of the world with the suffering servant. It is this living in suffering that "adds the grace note to life" and preaching.[26] The preacher never has to say anything about this; people implicitly know the preacher knows.

LIVE IN PRAYER

The life of the preacher is lived in prayer. Given everything else we have said, how could it be otherwise? And does not the apostle Paul model this for us? In ten of his thirteen letters in the New Testament, Paul precedes with prayer both his declaration of the indicative of the gospel and his exhortation of the imperative of the gospel.[27] Before Paul speaks to people he speaks to God about people. He thanks God for what God has been doing in people's lives and then prays for God's further work in their lives. Paul could preach so boldly because he prayed so boldly.

It is this dimension of the preacher's life that keeps us going. If we can keep giving thanks for the signs of the kingdom in the lives of the people we serve, and if we can keep interceding for the fullness of the kingdom, we will have the vision and strength to keep announc-

---

[25]A verse of Matthew Bridges' 1851 hymn "Crown Him with Many Crowns," which, sadly, most hymnals omit.

[26]William Barclay, commenting on 1 Peter 5:10, in *The Letters of James and Peter: Daily Bible Studies Series* (Philadelphia: Westminster Press, 1976), p. 273.

[27]Romans, 1-2 Corinthians, Ephesians, Philippians, Colossians, 1-2 Thessalonians, 2 Timothy and Philemon.

ing the gospel of the kingdom. It is when we stop giving thanks and interceding that we begin to lose the graces we need to keep preaching. James S. Stewart is right: "Most failures in the ministry were due, not to lack of visiting or of study or of organizational activity, but to lack of prayer."[28]

Live in the prayers of Paul; let them shape our praying. Let us get down on our knees and pray with Paul that "he would grant you, according to the riches of His glory"—inexhaustible riches—"to be strengthened with power through His Spirit in the inner person; so that Christ may dwell in your hearts"—there is that blessed preposition again!—"through faith; and that you, being rooted and grounded in love, may be able to comprehend with all the saints what is the breadth and length and height and depth, and to know the love of Christ which surpasses knowledge"—if there was ever a preacher's prayer this is it—"that you may be filled up to all the fullness of God" (Eph 3:16-19 NASB modified). Pray like that and watch the tone of your preaching change, and watch what starts happening in people's lives (see also Rom 1:8-10; Eph 1:16-22; Phil 1:3-6, 9-11; Col 1:3-5, 9-12; 1 Thess 1:2-3; 2 Thess 1:3, 11-12; 2:13-14; 2 Tim 1:3-4; Philem 4-6).

Or live in the Lord's Prayer. Pray for God to hallow his name in the lives of those we serve. Pray for God to bring his kingdom into their homes and workplaces "on earth as it is in heaven." Pray for God to work his will, his good pleasure in their relationships and decisions and vocations. Only God can do these things: only God can hallow his name, bring in his kingdom, accomplish his purposes for the world. "Father—do it!" That is what Jesus frees us to pray in his prayer. "Father, we cannot do these things; only you can. So do it!" Pray that God would supply all their needs, all they need to live a full kingdom life and ministry. Pray that God would cancel all their debts, empowering them to cancel the debts of others. Pray that God would rescue them from the temptations of the evil one, especially from his desire to undermine and destroy their confidence in the goodness of the Father. Pray this way and watch how our preaching changes, and watch for

---

[28]Stewart, Heralds, p. 202.

what happens in the lives of our listeners.[29]

Or live in John 17, another prayer of the Lord Jesus. Live in this most sacred of texts where the Son of God, incarnate in our humanity, opens his heart to his Father. I call this prayer "Listening in on the conversation at the center of the universe." From the four Gospels, we know of Jesus' habit of prayer. But for the most part he is usually off by himself, and we do not hear what he is praying. But in John 17, he draws the first disciples, and then us, close by his side and lets us hear everything he prays. The implication is that he wants us to hear his heart so that we can live his heart. Live in Jesus' praying and watch what happens to and in our preaching.

Or live in the Psalms, the great prayer book of the Bible. I have been doing this for so long now I cannot imagine praying without them. John Calvin calls these prayers "an anatomy of all the parts of the soul."[30] Martin Luther says that in these prayers we have "a mirror in which each of us sees the motion of our own souls."[31] After praying these prayers nearly everyday for twenty years, I have come to agree with Martin Luther that in whatever situation we find ourselves there are prayers that fit our case as if they were put their "just for our sake," so that we could not put it better ourselves, "or find or wish for anything better."[32] Pray with the psalmists, and the people who hear us preach will regularly say, "You have been living where I live"—because we have. The psalmists live where everyone lives.[33]

The call to preach is the call to pray. James Stewart says there are two specific consequences for preaching from our praying. On the one hand, people will be blessed. On the other, "When you look into their faces on the Sunday, as you lead their worship and proclaim to them

---

[29]See my *Fifty-Seven Words That Change The World: A Journey through the Lord's Prayer* (Vancouver, B.C.: Regent College Publishing, 2003).

[30]John Calvin, *Commentary on the Book of Psalms*, trans. Arthur Golding, rev. and ed. T. H. L. Parker (Grand Rapids: Eerdmans, 1949), 1:334.

[31]Martin Luther, *Word and Sacrament I*, Luther's Works (Philadelphia: Fortress, 1960) 35:255-56.

[32]Ibid.

[33]The two most helpful resources for praying the Psalms that I have found are Eugene Peterson's *Answering God: The Psalms as Tools for Prayer* (San Francisco: Harper & Row, 1989), and Charles Hadden Spurgeon's *Treasury of David*, 3 vols. (Grand Rapids: Zondervan, 1966).

afresh the all-sufficient grace of Christ, that background of your hidden intercessions, of your pleading for them name by name, will lift your words and wing them with love and ardour and reality."[34] We need never say a word about praying for people; they will implicitly know that, before we stepped up to speak to them about God, we spoke to God about them.

LIVE IN PREPARATION

The preacher's life is lived in preparation. Constant preparation. Always thinking, listening, attending, planning. I have already hinted at this in previous chapters when I said that there is no way (except by a huge miracle) that we can stand up before people on Sunday morning with a "home cooked meal" if we start the preparation process on Saturday night. Preparing the sermon (as well as preparing the preacher) takes time—in fact, blocks of time. It cannot be rushed.

I encourage fellow preachers to think of preparation in two modes: the weekly and the yearly. Weekly: spread out the process so that you are working on the sermon every day, not just one day. Yearly: always have in mind a tentative text for the Sunday one year hence. Let me show you what I mean.

Weekly. Begin the process on Monday. If it is the day you take off, still take some time in the late afternoon to read the text, if only devotionally. (This text will have been chosen and much of the study on it will have been done beforehand, as we will see in a moment.) On Tuesday tackle exegesis, beginning with the hardest issues first. As you go about other activities in the day, your mind will be processing what you studied. So keep a piece of paper at hand, or an index card in your pocket or purse, for example, to write down what you will inevitably be thinking. On Wednesday, finish up any exegetical work, come to terms with the big idea and move into the hermeneutical process, thinking in particular about how to illustrate what the text is saying. Again, keep a piece of paper at hand; your mind is going to be working on this even as you counsel or lead committee meetings or make hospital calls. On

---

[34]Stewart, *Heralds,* pp. 203-4.

Thursday, move into making an outline of the sermon, trying to have it sketched out by dinnertime. On Friday morning, write out the sermon (even if you are not going to use the manuscript on Sunday). Try to be done by noon. And again, as you go about your duties the rest of the day, keep a piece of paper at hand, as now your mind will be in a highly creative mode and will be "tweaking" everything. On Saturday, take time to read the sermon out loud at least two times. The first time, sit at your desk, or in the backyard, and read it looking down at the pages. See how it sounds. Make any adjustments. The second time, read it looking down only to get the first line of the sentences and looking up to speak without reading. It is amazing how the mind can do this; you are actually memorizing the words. Set it all aside. Enter into a more restful mode for Saturday evening. (An introvert is speaking here.) Then on Sunday, enter into the flow as articulated in chapter six. Spreading the work throughout the whole week gives our minds and hearts the space they need to be spacious.

Yearly. Try to live one year ahead at all times. We may not end up actually doing what we tentatively planned. That is okay. The goal is to always be in process, moving forward. It is easier to switch tracks on a moving train than to get one up and running.

I encourage preachers to work with what is commonly called the Christian Year.[35] I am aware that many churches no longer honor this centuries-old tradition. But I think they are missing out on a great gift. The intent of the Christian Year is to make sure that in a year's time, we keep coming back to the essentials of the gospel. Robert Webber called the Christian Year calendar "a chronological confession of faith."[36] I call it "the cyclical gospel," a way to let Jesus and his good news shape the rhythm of the year instead of simply being shaped by current events or the preacher's best Christianized thinking. The Christian Year breaks the twelve months up into seven major seasons (some traditions further

---

[35]See, for example, Ronald Allen, *Interpreting the Gospel* (St. Louis: Chalice Press, 1998), pp. 104-9; Robert Webber, *Blended Worship: Achieving Substance and Relevance in Worship* (Peabody, Mass.: Hendrickson, 1996), and *Worship Old and New*, 2nd ed. (Grand Rapids: Zondervan, 1994); Marva Dawn, *Reaching Out Without Dumbing Down: A Theological Worship for the Turn of the Century* (Grand Rapids: Eerdmans, 1995).

[36]Webber, *Blended Worship*, p. 136.

refine one or two of these). The seven seasons are not of equal length, but are of equal value in terms of announcing and living the gospel.[37] They are minimally:

Advent (four Sundays before Christmas Day): a time to focus on and celebrate the comings (plural) of Jesus; his first coming in the events taking place around Bethlehem; his second coming in all his glory, bringing about the new heaven and new earth.

Christmas (Christmas Eve, Christmas Day and the Sunday after Christmas): a time to focus directly on the "The Invasion," as C. S. Lewis called it.[38]

Epiphany (five to eight Sundays, depending on the date of Easter, beginning the first Sunday after January 6, for Orthodox Christians): a time to focus on and celebrate the earthly life and ministry of Jesus, his "appearing," and thus the appearing of the kingdom of light and life and love. This is a great time to preach from one of the four Gospels. (One of the sad facts of our time is that most disciples of Jesus know their way around the Ikea Catalog or Microsoft Windows Program better than they know their way around the simple facts of Jesus' life, teaching and ministry.)

Lent (the five Sundays before Palm Sunday): a time to focus on the death of Jesus and on the discipleship implications of his death, that dying and rising again is not just a once-for-all event but is the pattern of our lives in Jesus.

---

[37]The story of how the form of the Christian Year developed is beyond the scope of this chapter. Simply put, the Year is basically built around two dates: Passover, the specific date of which is a function of the movements of the moon, and December 25, the date chosen in A.D. 360 by Liberius, bishop of Rome, for the birth of Jesus; the church co-opted the old Roman festival Saturnalia, dedicated to Saturn, celebrating universal freedom and the return of the unconquerable light. "Easter, by its Passover connection, forms a link with the Jewish liturgical calendar, which is lunar; Christmas was fixed on 25 Dec. by the fourth century, coinciding with the winter solstice in the Roman calendar, and is thus a link with the Roman civil year which began on 1 Jan., and is solar." "Year, liturgical," in *Oxford Dictionary of the Christian Church*, ed. F. L. Cross and E. A. Livingstone, 3rd ed. (Oxford: Oxford University Press, 1997), p. 1772. Paul Jewett called the whole year "The Trinity Cycle": "God is the Father who sent His Son (Christmas cycle); God is the Son who died and rose again (Easter cycle); God is the Holy Spirit who is poured out upon the Church (Pentecost cycle)" (in an unpublished essay for Jewett's course in systematic theology at Fuller Theological Seminary, 1971).

[38]C. S. Lewis, *Mere Christianity* (New York: Macmillan, 1952), pp. 32-36.

Holy Week (Palm Sunday, Monday to Wednesday, Maundy Thursday, Good Friday, Silent Saturday and Resurrection, or Easter Sunday): a time to focus on "the week that changed the world." Palm Sunday presents the paradoxical King, not the King we expected but certainly the King we need. Monday to Wednesday, Jesus teaches in the context of conflict with "religion." Maundy Thursday (from the Latin *mandatum*, meaning "command") focuses on Jesus' washing of the disciples feet and his command to love one another in the same self-emptying way.[39] Good Friday focuses on the passion of Jesus. Good? Had we been there would we have used the word *good?* Ugly Friday or Evil Friday or Dark Friday. But good? This is perfect time to go deeper into his death and thus deeper into God's good news for the world. Easter Sunday proclaims the defeat of death, the Father's vindication of his Son, the emergence of the last Adam, the new human, the head and progenitor of a new human race, "The First Day of the New World." What a day to preach! As Richard Lischer rightly claims, "Christian preaching was born in the resurrection. . . . Let the reminder for preachers be: only because of the resurrection does Christian preaching assume the significance and importance so desperately claimed for it."[40]

Eastertide (six weeks): a time to focus on what it means to live in light of Jesus' resurrection. In this period Ascension Day provides the time to focus on the meaning of Jesus' ascension to the right hand of the Father, that he lives and reigns as Lord.

Pentecost (fifty days after Easter, Pentecost Sunday celebrates the coming of the Holy Spirit, the season of Pentecost continuing to Christ the King Sunday, the climatic Sunday of the year, usually the Sunday after American Thanksgiving): a time to focus on the person and work of the Spirit and the life he breathes us into. As I said in chapter six, the church of Jesus Christ will have finally understood his gospel when Pentecost is as big a deal as Christmas and Easter. (Tragically, too many evangelical congregations are not even aware of this great day of the year.)

---

[39]Do not preach John 13 without consulting Lesslie Newbigin's commentary *The Light Has Come: An Exposition of the Fourth Gospel* (Grand Rapids: Eerdmans, 1982), pp. 170-71.
[40]Richard Lischer, *A Theology of Preaching: The Dynamics of the Gospel* (Nashville: Abingdon, 1986), p. 31; "Preaching, to be *preaching*, reenacts and participates in the defeat and victory of Jesus" (p. 43).

What you do next is take this calendar and, having spent time praying and listening, plan series of sermons for each season.[41] I advocate preaching series for three reasons: one, we stay in one section of the Bible for a number of weeks, teaching people how to read the Bible; two, it forces us preachers to deal with texts and issues we might otherwise skip over; and three, it creates the environment wherein the one leading the church is the Word and not just the pastor with his or her agendas and needs. You can, of course, plan a series that begins in one season and keeps moving through the next; a series in the Sermon on the Mount, for instance, that would neatly begin in Epiphany and continue through Lent. What I do is create a file for each season series, with smaller files for each of the Sundays of the season; a series in the temptation story, for instance, with a separate file for the introduction, first round, second round and third round.

Now, you can do this in two ways. One is to take a week or two during the summer break and plan out the whole year. The only problem is that the fall series (or spring, if you are serving in the southern hemisphere) will come too quickly for you to do much advanced reading and praying. So the other way is to set the series for next year's season at the end of this year's season; to be planning ahead all the time, not just once a year. So, for example, on Sunday evening of the last Sunday of Advent 2015 you plan the series for Advent 2016. On the Sunday evening of Lent 2016 you plan the series for Lent 2017. And so on. I usually get home late from church on Christmas Eve, actually very early Christmas morning. It is then that I sit down, for just a moment, and tentatively plan for next Christmas Eve. Why then? Why not wait a few weeks or months? Late Christmas Eve is the best time because, one, all the sounds and smells and sights of the celebration are fresh in my senses, and, two, I know what I did not preach for lack of time and wished I could have. As I walk home after worship on Easter Sunday, I tentatively plan for next Easter. Why then? I do this for the same

---

[41]If you do not use this calendar in your congregation, you can divide up the whole year around natural "high holy days." In the northern hemisphere, the year would begin the Sunday after Labor Day. So start with the long period that comes after it, stretching to Christmas. The next big date is New Year's, so begin the Sunday after it and plan up to Easter.

reasons: my mind and heart are full of the music and pageantry of the day, and I am aware of the "so much more" of Easter that I could not even hint at for lack of time.

All this advanced planning then gives you a mental closet in which you can hang all your thinking, listening and reading in the coming year. You have fifty-two hangers on which to drape the various experiences of life. You begin to see everything—birthdays, anniversaries, elections, deaths, tragedies, sporting events—through the lens of the gospel. Your mind begins to gather and sort all the input and reflections around Jesus and his good news. And you are being changed.

Some examples might be in order.

Example A

Advent 2020: Luke 1–2
  Songs of Salvation
  1. Luke 1:45-55: Mary's *Magnificat* (Magnifies)
  2. Luke 1:67-79: Zacharias's *Benedictus* (Blessed Be)
  3. Luke 2:14: the angels' *Gloria* (Glory Be)
  4. Luke 2:29-32: Simeon's *Nunc Dimittis* (Now Departs)

Christmas Eve 2020: Luke 2:1-20:
  When Caesar Augustus Thought He Ruled the World

Sunday after Christmas 2020: Luke 2:41-51
  My Father's Business: Preparing for a New Year

Epiphany 2021: Encounters with Jesus: Portraits of Grace (Luke)
  1. Luke 5:1-11: A Fisherman
  2. Luke 6:11-17: The Widow's Only Son
  3. Luke 7:36-50: A Pharisee and a Woman of the Street
  4. Luke 18:35-43: A Blind Man
  5. Luke 19:1-10: A Tax-Collector
(If there are more than five Sundays, work with more encounters.)

Lent 2021: The Call to Discipleship (Luke)
  1. Luke 9:18-27: Who Do You Say That I Am?
  2. Luke 9:51-62: When Loyalties Conflict
  3. Luke 10:1-20: Laborers in His Harvest
  4. Luke 14:15-24: Flimsy Excuses

    5. Luke 14:25-35: Cannot or Will Not?

Palm Sunday 2021: Luke 19:28-44
    The Things That Make for Peace

Maundy Thursday 2021: Luke 22:7-23:
    Until

Good Friday 2021: Luke 23:32-38
    Father, Forgive Them

Easter Sunday 2021: Luke 24:1-12
    Just As He Said!

Eastertide 2021:
    Living in Easter Space
    1. Luke 24:13-35: Opening Eyes
    2. Luke 24:13-35: The Book and the Table
    3. Luke 24:36-43: A Bodily Resurrection
    4. Luke 24:44-49: Opening Scripture
    5. Luke 24:50-53: The Posture of Blessing

Pentecost Sunday 2021: Acts 2:1-13
    Wind and Fire

Pentecost Season 2021 (Up to summer vacation): Galatians 3:1-4;
    5:13-6:8
    A New Life and a New Way to Live It
    1. Galatians 3:1-3; 5:16: Flesh and Spirit: Two Opposite Ways of
       Being Human
    2. Galatians 5:16: Walking by the Spirit
    3. Galatians 5:22: A Different Kind of Love
    4. Galatians 5:22: A Different Kind of Joy
    5. Galatians 5:22: A Different Kind of Peace
    6. Galatians 5:22: A Different Kind of Patience
    7. Galatians 5:22: A Different Kind of Kindness
    8. Galatians 5:22: A Different Kind of Goodness
    9. Galatians 5:22: A Different Kind of Faithfulness
    10. Galatians 5:23: A Different Kind of Gentleness
    11. Galatians 5:23: A Different Kind of Self-Control
(Although each sermon in #2-11 will focus on a different fruit of the

Spirit, taking things this slowly allows one to say how to walk by the Spirit eleven different ways—the real point of the series!)

Pentecost Season 2021 (From summer vacation through the fall): Philippians

Joy from a Prison Cell

1. Background on Paul, his imprisonment and the church in Philippi; present the whole book, speaking it out from memory (takes about 16 minutes).
2. Philippians 1:3-11: He Always Finishes What He Starts
3. Philippians 1:12-20: Crummy Circumstances Advance the Gospel?
4. Philippians 1:21-30: To Live Is Christ
5. Philippians 2:1-11: The Secret of the Universe
6. Philippians 2:12-30: Who Does the Work?
7. Philippians 3:1-11: All Things Loss for This
8. Philippians 3:12-16: Apprehended by Christ
9. Philippians 3:17-21: Eagerly Awaiting a Savior
10. Philippians 4:1-9: The Mind at Peace
11. Philippians 4:10-23: The True Patron

Christ the King Sunday 2021: Philippians 2:5-11

So *That* Is What It Means to Be King?

(Revisiting the hymn and going deeper and, thus, wider.)

Example B. This time starting the planning from the fall and working through the following year.

Pentecost Season 2030 (Starting in the fall): Genesis 1–3:

What It Means to Be Human

Three sermons in Genesis 1

1. Recite the text from memory. The Song of Creation
2. Order out of Chaos, Fullness out of Void
3. In Our Image

Three sermons in Genesis 2

1. A Fourfold Relational Harmony
2. The One Command
3. Man and Woman

Three sermons in Genesis 3

1. Enter the Tempter

2. How the World Fell Apart

3. Protected from the Tree of Life

Christ the King Sunday 2030: Daniel 2
The Preview (of History)

Advent 2030: Matthew 1
1. Matthew 1:1-17: The DNA of the Savior (His Surprising Genealogy)
2. Matthew 1:18-20: Beginning Again: The Meaning of the Virgin Birth
3. Matthew 1:20: The Strange Thing Happening to You Is of the Holy Spirit: The Angel Speaks in a Dream
4. Matthew 1:23-25: He Really Is All His Names Imply

Christmas Eve 2030: Isaiah 9:2-7
Such Names for a Child!

Sunday After Christmas: Galatians 4:4-7
In the Fullness of Time

Epiphany and Lent 2031: Abraham and Sarah
In the Footsteps of Saving Faith
1. Genesis 12:1-3: Blessed to Be a Blessing
2. Genesis 12:4–13:4: Up and Down, but Always Forward
3. Genesis 13:5-18: Lead by the Eyes: Be Careful Where You Look!
4. Genesis 15:1-6: Just Say "Amen"
5. Genesis 15:7-21: The Greatest Assurance
6. Genesis 16:1-6: Engineering God's Plan
7. Genesis 16:7-16: The God Who Sees
8. Genesis 18:1-15: Why Do You Laugh?
9. Genesis 18:16-33: Pressing In
10. Genesis 20:1-18: Not Again?
11. Genesis 22:1-19: Ultimate Risk, Ultimate Discovery

Palm Sunday 2031: Matthew 21:1-17
Behold Your King

Good Friday 2031: Matthew 27:45-54
No More Separation!

Easter Sunday 2031: Matthew 28:1-10
The Verbs of Easter: Come, See, Go, Tell

Eastertide: Pentecost 2031 (up to summer vacation): Ephesians 1–3
In Christ: The Wonder of Grace
1. Background: Paul, his circumstance, the church in Ephesus (and the larger Lycus valley); present the whole book from memory (takes about 20 minutes)
2. Ephesians 1:3-14: Part I: Every Spiritual Blessing!
3. Ephesians 1:3-14: Part II: More of Every Spiritual Blessing!
4. Ephesians 1:3-14: Part III: Even More of Every Spiritual Blessing!
5. Ephesians 1:15-23: Open the Eyes of Our Hearts
6. Ephesians 1:19-22: Altered Structures of Reality
7. Ephesians 2:1-10: But God!
8. Ephesians 2:11-22: The New Humanity
9. Ephesians 3:1-13: The Unfathomable Riches of Christ
10. Ephesians 3:14-20: Living in the Trinity
11. Ephesians 3:20-21: Why It All Happens

Pentecost Season 2031 (from summer vacation through the fall): Ephesians 4–6
In Christ: The Walk of Grace
1. Therefore (A sermon to review the whole book and show Paul's normal pattern of indicative then imperative, and to argue that we must keep the vision of chapters 1–3 before us as we work through chapters 4–6)
2. Ephesians 4:1-16: Preserving the Unity of the Spirit
3. Ephesians 4:17-24: Changing Clothes
4. Ephesians 4:25-32: Do Not Grieve the Spirit
5. Ephesians 5:1-2: Imitators of God?
6. Ephesians 5:3-14: Children of Light
7. Ephesians 5:15-21: The Filling of the Spirit
8. Ephesians 5:21: Mutual Submission: The Miracle of the Spirit
9. Ephesians 5:21-33: Grace at Work in Marriage: Ladder of Hierarchy or Circle of Servanthood?
10. Ephesians 6:1-4: Grace at Work in the Family
11. Ephesians 6:5-9: Grace at Work in the Marketplace
12. Ephesians 6:10-24: Dressed to Stand

Christ the King Sunday 2031: Psalm 96–99
Say Among the Nations: 'Our God Reigns!'
(Or, Confessing Jesus as Lord in Dangerous Times)

Advent 2031: Matthew 24–25
On Living in Waiting
1. Matthew 24:1-44: No Further Warning
2. Matthew 24:45–25:13: Ready or Not, Here He Comes!
3. Matthew 25:14-30: Putting Money in the Bank: Not a Good Idea
4. Matthew 25:31-46: Welcoming Jesus in His Strange Disguises

Christmas Eve 2031: Matthew 2:1-12
Magnetic: He Even Draws Stars to Himself!

Sunday After Christmas: Matthew 2:1-6
Should Herod Have Been Nervous?

Isn't this fun? One last example showing how to preach one whole book in a year, in this case the Gospel of John.

Example C
Advent: John 1:1-18
1. John 1:1-2: The Self-Expression of God
2. John 1:3-5: Before Bethlehem
3. John 1:9-13: Welcome Home
4. John 1:14-18: Beholding Glory

Christmas Eve: John 1:14
If the Real Story Be Told

Sunday After Christmas: John 1:19-51
What Have We Gotten Ourselves Into?

Epiphany: John 2–4
All Things Made New
1. John 2:1-11: The Prototypical Miracle
2. John 2:13-25: Fit for Glory
3. John 3:1-21: From *Bios* to *Zoe*
4. John 4:1-45: The Woman Who Became a Well
5. John 4:46-54: Your Son Lives

Lent: John 18–19
He Reigns from the Tree

1. John 18:1-11: Not a Helpless Victim
2. John 18:12-27: Religion on Trial
3. John 18:28–19:16: Politics on Trial
4. John 19:17-30: That the Scripture Might Be Fulfilled
5. John 19:30: What Is Finished?

Palm Sunday: John 12
   The Theater of Glory

Maundy Thursday: John 13
   Surprise!

Good Friday: John 19:38-42
   A Secret Disciple

Easter Sunday: Eastertide: John 20–21
   1. John 20:1-10: Through to the Other Side
   2. John 20:11-18: The Gardener Indeed
   3. John 20:19-23: Peace in the Wounds
   4. John 20:24-29: Thomas, Disciple for Our Time
   5. John 21:1-23: He Gave Me a New Past

Pentecost and the Pentecost Season: John 14–16
   In the Absence of Jesus' Physical Presence
   1. John 14:1-3: Preparing for the Wedding
   2. John 14:4-15: The Way Home
   3. John 14:16-24: With You and *in* You
   4. John 14:25-31: Teach You All Things
   5. John 15:1-11: Your True Home
   6. John 15:12-17: I Call You Friends
   7. John 15:17-27: The Spirit and the World: Part I
   8. John 16:1-16: The Spirit and the World: Part II
   9. John 16:17-28: In Travail
   10. John 16:29-33: I Have Overcome!
   11. John 17: Listening in on the Conversation at the Center of the Universe
   12. John 17: Continued
   13. John 17: Ccontinued

Pentecost Season (through the fall): John 5–11
   Never Did a Man Speak the Way This Man Speaks

1. John 5: Jesus and the Sabbath: I Am Working
2. John 6: Jesus and Passover: I Am the Bread of Life, Part I
3. John 6: I Am the Bread of Life, Part II
4. John 7: Jesus and Tabernacles, Part I: Living Water
5. John 8: Jesus and Tabernacles, Part II: I Am the Light of the World
6. John 8: Jesus and Tabernacles, Part III: I Am I Am
7. John 9: Jesus and the Religious Leaders: I Am the Light of the World—Again
8. John 10: Jesus and Dedication (or Hanukkah): I Am the Good Shepherd
9. John 11: Jesus and Death: I Am the Resurrection and the Life
10. John 11:47–12:11: So, What Are You Going to Do?

You can see from these examples how living in advance preparation causes us to live in the fullness of the gospel. I have said for many years that the person who benefits most from God calling me to preach is myself. What a life! Living in the gospel day in, day out, year in, year out. I have also said over the past few years that none of us has enough Sundays (or Saturdays or Wednesdays) to preach all that needs to be preached. I guess that is why God calls so many preachers.

I imagine that by now you have two questions. First, do I always stick to the plan? No. The Lord can and does change the plan. But when he does he is working with someone who is immersed in the Word. Second, what do you do about crises that come along? First I ask if what has been laid out might not actually, in the providence of God, speak to the crisis. On the Sunday after 9/11 I did not need to change the text at all—it spoke a very powerful word into the fear most people were feeling. Yet there are times when the plan has to be altered, in which case I work with another text for a Sunday or two, and then go back to the plan.

The call to preach is the call to live a different kind of life. A life lived in the Preacher, in his gospel, in his Book, in books, in culture, in suffering, in prayer and in advanced planning. It is all part of the glory of preaching!

Alexander M'Laren was one of the most effective preachers Scotland, the home of great preaching, ever heard. It was said of him that he was "neither priest nor philosopher, but messenger and proclaimer." He had the capacity to analyze a text in a way that, after seeing what he saw, one would not want to see it any other way. And he had the ability to shape the "consummate sentence" and deliver it with ease and grace. In his eulogy of M'Laren, W. Robertson Nicoll makes this observation: "If ever any one was apprehended by Christ Jesus in the early years, it was Alexander M'Laren. . . . Never was any one more profoundly loyal to the lessons of the morning. He desired no other and no better thing than that the end of his life should circle around the beginning, only with a deeper conviction and a stronger love at last."[42] Is that not your desire? Then Nicoll says this, a fitting conclusion to this chapter on the life of the preacher: "Those who observed him recognized that he drank from fountains older than the world, and for him they were always running fresh."[43]

Make it so for me, Lord, and for us who read these words. Amen.

---

[42]W. Robertson Nicoll, *Princes of the Church* (London: Hodder and Stoughton, 1921), p. 245.
[43]Ibid., p. 246.

PART THREE

THEORETICAL
FOUNDATIONS AGAIN

10

STANDING IN THE MYSTERY

The Space in Which We Preach

HAVING DONE ALL OUR PREPARATION, we are ready for the sermon work to become a sermon. A prepared sermon does not become a true sermon until it is spoken. The sermon "happens" when we stand up before other people, Bible in hand, and say what God is saying in the text of the day.

We stand up to stand in. We stand up to stand in a particular place (with all that it entails) at a particular time (with all its challenges and fears and longings) before particular people with particular life experiences. And when we do, we stand in all that particularity in a mystery. When we are finally ready to stand up and preach, we stand up to stand in a space, in an event, in a happening over which—in the final analysis—we have no control, the nature and dynamics of which wecannot explain. We stand up to stand in a mystery.

I am using the word *mystery* in the sense that the New Testament does. Not as something which only elite, super-bright, super-spiritual people can access after all kinds of elaborate ritual. But rather as something, although ordinarily not immediately obvious, that has been revealed by God and can be known and experienced by anyone who is willing to trust God. I am using the word in the sense of "open secret."[1]

---

[1]The title of one of Lesslie Newbigin's books on the mission of the triune God in the world. *The Open Secret* (Grand Rapids: Eerdmans, 1978). "I shall therefore begin by looking at the Christian mission in three ways—as the proclaiming of the kingdom of the Father, as sharing in the life of the Son, and as bearing the witness of the Spirit" (p. 31).

It is nothing esoteric, yet it is something we would not discover on our own, something we do not make happen and cannot completely articulate to everyone's satisfaction. "Mystery is not the absence of meaning, but the presence of more meaning than we can comprehend."[2] To stand up to preach is to stand in a mystery.

In this chapter I want to do two things. First, I want to try to open up the dynamics of the mystery in such a way that, second, we can become more comfortable (in the traditional meaning of the word, *com:* with, *forte:* strengthen) taking our stand in the mystery.

Why speak this way? Well, step back with me for a moment.

You may have noticed that I have not referred to postmodernity in any serious way in this book. I am writing in 2008. You may be reading in 2009 or 2015 or (if the book is still in print) in 2055. Being aware that many Christian preachers in 2008 are saying that postmodernity is the ruling philosophical construct of the day, you may be wondering why I have not brought it up and wrestled with its implications for preaching.

I have intentionally not brought it up. Not that I am afraid to do so. I actually think that postmodernity, in its rejection of the unrealistic demands and arrogance of modernity, has contributed to a new day for the gospel.[3] But I have not intentionally engaged in a discussion about postmodernity for four reasons.

First, I am not yet competent to do so. Thankfully, many who make their living thinking about these kinds of issues feel the same way. Kevin Vanhoozer, for instance, says, "Those who attempt to define or

---

[2]Dennis Covington, *Salvation on Sand Mountain* (New York: Addison-Wesley, 1995), pp. 203-4.

[3]See David Lose, *Confessing Jesus Christ: Preaching in a Postmodern World* (Grand Rapids: Eerdmans, 2003), pp. 1-62, for a brilliant analysis of the issues involved. Postmodernity, he argues, challenges the modernist demand for certainty based on "hard data." Those who chose, with postmodernity, to let go of that kind of certainty and live "with the tension of uncertainty," he says, "are free, free to believe, to speak, and to act on the basis of their convictions. Ultimately, therefore, what we surrender is not truth, but the ability to prove truth; not speech, but the right to have the last word; not faith, but unambiguous certainty; not hope, but a future secured by modernist foundationalism. . . . In this sense, post-modernity renders Christians a tremendous service by clarifying the essential nature of our faith, as we realize and recall that Christian claims can rest upon *no* ultimate foundation, not even that of nonfoundationalism. Rather, Christianity exists solely by confession, the conviction and assertion of revealed truth apart from any appeal to another criterion; we live, that is, always by faith alone" (p. 62). A good Lutheran stand!

to analyze the concept of post-modernity do so at their own peril."[4] In fact, David Tracy, a leading thinker on the postmodern condition, argues that "there is no such phenomenon as post-modernity," just many different postmodernists.[5]

Second, it seems to me that the postmodern construct is an interim construct. It is a reaction to the abuses of modernity (which held up facts as the only source of knowing, human beings as the measure of all things, oppression of ideologies, etc.), and thus, is an extreme swing of the pendulum, so typical of us creatures. In time the pendulum will level back to some middle ground, to a way of thinking and being not yet emerged. Given the volatile nature of our time, the world may pass through a number of other interim arrangements before we settle on a scheme of things that will lead the world for the next long season. Preachers need to be sensitive to the issues postmodernity raises and poses, but we need not adjust our whole way of knowing, being and acting. "This too shall pass," my grandmother would wisely say. We need not give in to the pressure of having to jerk our whole understanding of preaching around to accommodate what cannot finally sustain itself.

The third reason I have intentionally not brought up the matter is more important. As a matter of fact, postmodernity is not as dominant a construct and condition as we are often made to think. It may be dominant in certain parts of the world, in the so-called secular West, for instance (and the rich, educated West, at that). But it is not the ruling ideology in the East or South. That is, it is not the dominant worldview of the new centers of Christianity. Talk to preachers in Asia or Africa and the challenges are very different, post-postmodernity. Believers in those parts of the world have always had to live with the

---

[4]A range of perspectives: Kevin J. Vanhoozer, ed., *The Cambridge Companion to Postmodern Theology* (Cambridge: Cambridge University Press, 2003). This is a superb resource, pulling together the thinking of a wide range of scholars. See also Stanley J. A. Grenz, *A Primer on Postmodernism* (Grand Rapids: Eerdmans, 1996), and Brain D. McLaren, *A New Kind of Christian: A Tale of Two Friends on a Spiritual Journey* (San Francisco: Jossey-Bass, 2001); Richard J. Middleton and Brian J. Walsh, *Truth Is Stranger Than It Used to Be: Biblical Faith in a Postmodern World* (Downers Grove, Ill.: InterVarsity Press, 1995); Graham Johnston, *Preaching to a Postmodern World: A Guide to Reaching Twenty-First-Century Listeners* (Grand Rapids: Baker, 2001); John H. Wright, *Telling God's Story: Narrative Preaching for Christian Formation* (Downers Grove, Ill.: IVP Academic, 2007).
[5]Quoted. in Vanhoozer, *Cambridge Companion*, p. 1.

challenge of competing "metanarratives." You have always had to dig deep and find reasons to follow Jesus as Lord that are not found in the dominant worldview where you live. You have always had to understand and communicate the Christian story in worlds dominated by truly oppressive "deep stories." When I met with students in Sweden a few years ago, they were wrestling with the horrendous fall-out of having lived with earlier forms of postmodernity. When I met with students in Armenia, sitting around a table a few feet from where a statue of Lenin once stood, they were wrestling with very different issues, ones to which Western postmodernity had nothing to say. They simply wanted to know more about Jesus; they wanted to know Jesus. And they were willing to pay whatever price they had to pay to do it, be it financial, intellectual or social. Postmodernity does not shape the way of life for our brothers and sisters in Beirut and Nazareth or in Baghdad and Tripoli. I do not mean to be blithely dismissing the matter; I feel the presence of some of the aspects of postmodernity all the time, especially in post-everything Vancouver, Canada. Yet I offer us preachers a reminder that postmodernity is only one ideology with which we have to converse in communicating the gospel. If there was an ideology demanding our understanding in 2007, it was radical, fundamentalist Islam. If you are living in the West reading this in 2050, you probably deal with different challenging issues.

The fourth reason I have intentionally not brought up the matter is the most important, a reason I have framed as carefully as I know how: in dialoguing with any ideology that questions or challenges the gospel there is the very real possibility that we may "fall in" to that ideology. Not in any wholesale way, but enough so that we actually subtly begin to lose touch with essential dimensions of the gospel. I did this in dialoguing with the demythologizing project of the Bultmanians.[6] In trying to make Jesus and his gospel make sense to worldviews out of sync with Jesus and his gospel, it is possible to subtly undermine the gospel. I fear this is happening more than we care to know in the present rush to make the gospel comprehensible to the postmodern frame

---

[6]As I shared in chapter three of this book, "Where Does It Happen?"

of reference. A number of preachers I respect, in being absorbed with engaging the phenomenon, also begin to embody it. There is that edge of postmodernity in their preaching, a subtle arrogance, for instance, over those who still want to advocate that Jesus is the only way to God; there is a kind of suspicion about the church's desire to know and live "the truth." I think that preachers must beware of this kind of subtle captivity to ideologies.

This caution about being too concerned to make Jesus and his gospel make sense to any "world" grew in me, in part, because of my having unconsciously become a "closet demythologizer." But most of my concern comes because of reading a book titled *Without God, Without Creed: The Origins of Unbelief in America* by James Turner, then professor of history at the University of Michigan.[7] Turner asked the question, Why, for all the religious heritage of the United States of America, indeed, for all the specifically Christian heritage, did unbelief emerge as a fully viable option for Americans? The conventional answer was that religious belief basically collapsed under the pressure of new scientific discoveries and massive social change. Agreeing that such pressure is a factor, Turner proposes another very surprising answer. Turner writes, "Though both science and social transformation loom large in the picture, neither caused unbelief. To believe that either did, I now think, is to stand the problem of unbelief on its head, to give credit to the blueprint but ignore the architect who drafted it, and ultimately to distort the history of Western religion from the sixteenth century through the nineteenth."[8] Then what caused unbelief in a world steeped, supposedly, in belief? "Put briefly, unbelief was not something that happened to religion. On the contrary, religion caused unbelief."[9] What? How could that be? Here is Turner's thesis and the reason why I am bothering to bring it to our attention as preachers: "In trying to adapt their religious beliefs to socioeconomic change, to new moral challenges, to novel problems of knowledge, to the tightening standards of science,

---

[7]James Turner, *Without God, Without Creed: The Origins of Unbelief* (Baltimore: Johns Hopkins University Press, 1985). Thomas Gillespie, then president of Princeton Theological Seminary, recommended it to me at a gathering at Whitworth College, Spokane, Washington, 1986.
[8]Ibid., p. xiii.
[9]Ibid.

the defenders of God slowly strangled Him."[10] How could that be? Certainly they did not do it intentionally. Turner continues, "If anyone is to be arraigned for deicide, it is not Charles Darwin but his adversary Bishop Samuel Wilberforce, not the godless Robert Ingersoll but the godly Beecher family" (a prominent American family of preachers in the nineteenth century).[11] The story is, understandably, complex. Hoping not to overly simplify the argument, it comes down to this: in trying to make the Christian faith make sense in terms of "novel problems in knowledge" and "the tightening standards of science," preachers subtly adopted the presuppositions of the new way of thinking. They presented the Christian faith in terms of those presuppositions, and inadvertently, reduced the Christian faith to those presuppositions, thus reducing the Christian faith to less than the biblical gospel. In particular, preachers inadvertently preached the God of natural law, the Deist god who winds up the universe like a clock and lets it go on its own.[12] Since this god can only be known by intellectual assent to rationally verifiable "facts," preachers began to defend the faith by appealing to "demonstrable" propositions. The gospel became something to which one assents intellectually (which is a dimension of faith), and the gospel became "principles to live by." Lyman Beecher, says Turner, "unwittingly aped Jefferson when he called the Bible 'a Code of Laws' and claimed that its 'real meaning' lay in the 'laws of a moral government' contained in it."[13] Faith was no longer personal trust in a person. The gospel was no longer news about what that person, the God revealed in Jesus, did, is doing or will do. "God helps those who help themselves" becomes the basis of Christian living. So Turner concludes, and I quote him at length because he speaks a word of warning to preachers in any age living under any ideology:

> The crucial ingredient, then, in the mix that produced an enduring
> unbelief was the choices of believers. More precisely, unbelief resulted
> from the decisions that influential church leaders—lay writers, theolo-

---

[10]Ibid.
[11]Ibid.
[12]Ibid., p. 73.
[13]Ibid., p. 84.

gians, ministers—made about how to confront the modern pressures upon religious belief. . . . And the choices, taken together, boiled down to a decision to deal with modernity by embracing it—to defuse modern threats to the traditional bases of belief by bringing God into line with modernity.

Whatever the wisdom of hindsight, this strategy was far from contemptible. Anyone who believes in God will want that belief, that God, to have some bearing on the world in which we breathe, think, live, and die. . . .

In tailoring belief more closely to human understanding and aspiration, however, many religious leaders made a fatal slip. They were not wrong to think that any significant faith would have to express itself in moral practice. But they often forgot that their God's purposes were not supposed to be man's. They were not mistaken in believing that any resilient belief must ground itself in human thought and experience. But they frequently forgot the tension that, by definition, must exist between an incomprehensible God and the human effort to know Him. They were hardly fools to insist that any God must be lord of this world, but they did not always remember that this world could not define Him. They forgot, in short, that their God was—as any God had to be to command belief over the long term—radically other than man.[14]

Yet perhaps, after all, there is really only one lesson here. The universe is not tailored to our measurements. Forgetting that, many believers lost their God.[15]

Turner's insights sober me. One might argue that Turner may have over-reached somewhat in his conclusions. And one might charge me with inadequately conveying his conclusions. But the point still remains: in our desire to connect, to be relevant in our preaching, we may lose the very message we seek to announce.

Three of my contemporaries express it this way:

What we first thought of as our humble, self-effacing attempt to articulate the gospel in a "responsible and contemporary way" was a simple demonstration that we had submitted to the powers-that-be. We had given up the battle too soon. *In bending over backward to speak to the*

[14]Ibid., pp. 266-67.
[15]Ibid., p. 269.

"modern world," we fell in. In our dialogue with contemporary culture, the traffic moved in one direction. It was always contemporary culture rummaging around in the gospel, telling the gospel what it could and could not believe. This is a project in which we have lost faith.[16]

The danger of this happening is even greater in "bending over backward to speak" to the postmodern world, for postmodernity has fundamentally lost faith in nearly everything. "Words make worlds," contrary to the postmodern suspicion about words having any real meaning and influence.[17] "As Walter Bridgman has told us pastors, if we will not let the gospel use us to create a new world, then all we can do is service the old one."[18] Oh Lord, do not let us go astray.

When I quoted these three pastors, I omitted the first sentence of the paragraph, which I now cite: "We are learning that *it is all conversion.*"[19] I take them to mean that we are always in need of conversion, of "thinking again," or turning around. We are always in need of repenting. No human constructs, not even religious human constructs, can ever fully summarize, capture, encapsulate and embody Jesus and his gospel. "No one form of knowing can possibly navigate the labyrinth of reality."[20]

> "For My thoughts are not your thoughts,
>   Nor are your ways My ways," declares the LORD. (Is 55:8)

We do our best to understand the gospel, and we do our best to help others understand (or stand under) the gospel; we work at coming up with connections and analogies; and then we realize that the closer we get to the heart of the gospel, the more it becomes virtually impossible to illustrate from any frame of reference. Our speaking, by necessity, becomes more and more apophatic, speaking in terms of what something is not, or is not like. In saying this I am not affirming all that comes with apophatic theology, theology by the Via Negativa ("Nega-

---

[16]Martin B. Copenhaver, Anthony B. Robinson and William H. Willimon, *Good News in Exile: Three Pastors Offer a Hopeful Vision for the Church* (Grand Rapids: Eerdmans, 1999), p. 56, emphasis added.

[17]Ibid.

[18]Ibid.

[19]Ibid., emphasis in original.

[20]Turner, *Without God, Without Creed*, p. 269.

tive Way"). What I am saying is that the further we move into the very center of the gospel, the more cultural precedents are unable to help us articulate what has been revealed. The incarnation, for example. "It is like . . ." Like what? Like nothing that has ever happened before or since.

For example, I spent four years in Manila, Philippines, four of the best years of my ministry. I came to love the Filipino people (we adopted one as our daughter!). I have said that if my becoming a Filipino would help raise that lovely people group to the status in the world they deserve, I would do it: I would change the color of my skin, the shape of my face, the way I look at the world, the way I relate. I would become Filipino flesh and blood. It is the closest analogy I can come up with for the incarnation. And yet it is miles apart from the truth. Yes, in one sense I would be becoming what I was not; but I would not in any way change my essential way of being. I would still be human, just a different kind of human. In the incarnation, God became what God was not (and was not in any way, shape or form). Any analogy at best only points to the mystery and moves us in the direction of having to say, "Like—yes—but not wholly like."

Or the resurrection, for another example. "It is like . . ." Like what? Like a butterfly emerging from a cocoon, as I used to hear preached when I was a young boy. Really? The analogy does point to the fact of continuity between the body of Jesus on Good Friday and the body of Jesus on Easter Sunday. But the analogy misses the essence of the event. Butterflies emerge from a cocoon as the result of a natural process built into the larva. Resurrection is not the result of a process built into the human body, not even into the body of God Incarnate. Resurrection is a brand new act, bringing into being a brand new reality, something that had never been before and for which there simply is no analog in any worldview. "Jesus and his gospel are like . . ." Yes. And "Jesus and his gospel are not like . . ." Not like anything in any human construct of reality. The gospel, the incredibly good, good news, comes up against all human ways of knowing, thinking, feeling, being and acting. It calls for a massive turning toward a whole new way of knowing, thinking, feeling, being and acting.

Sometimes, when I read the sermon manuscript early Sunday morning, I am overcome with a profound sense of inadequacy. Sometimes I am overcome with a sense that I am really silly to say what I plan to say; that I am woefully naive, that folks will judge me to be unrealistic or uneducated or just plain stupid. I mean, listen to what we are saying when we stand before our contemporaries. "There is a God, a living God." How do you know? And who gives you the right to make such a claim? "This God made the world." What? You say that in the face of "incontrovertible evidence" that the world evolved into being out of a long, natural process? "This God made us humans; indeed, we are made in this God's image." Now you are reaching, now you are "nuts" (as my neighbor said to me one day). "This God likes us humans and attends to us more than mothers and fathers attend to their little ones." How sentimental and out of touch with the "real" world. "This God became a human being, one of us, in the person of the baby lying in the manger in Bethlehem." You are really nuts; what are you on? "This God lived the only truly human life ever lived and invites us to follow him into his way." "This God got crucified." Whoa. "On a Roman cross. And that act turns out to be the pivotal act for all of history. That act has implications for every human being who ever lived, lives or will live." One particular man, who you say is God-in-our-flesh, dies, and his death affects the whole of the human race? Listen to yourself; you are losing it. "In this one particular man, God-in-our-flesh, death did not have the last word; it only had the second to the last word. This one particular man goes through death and emerges on the other side alive, the New Human, the head and progenitor of a whole new human race." Wait a minute! "And one day he is going to come again, and he is bringing with him a whole new creation, where there will no longer be any sickness or sorrow or death." You are frying all my sense of reality; I have never heard anything like this. Either you are really off your rocker, or . . .

What worldview (cultural and/or philosophical) "gets" all this? None. We only "get it" when we turn and believe what finally fits no human worldview. We make a turn that is nothing short of a miracle.

Therefore, our posture in preaching has to be, by necessity, one of invitation. Even when we are heralding ("Here ye, hear ye") or prophesying ("Thus says the Lord"), we invite people, if not in words then in tone and affect, to consider Jesus and his gospel. We acknowledge that he and the gospel may not make immediate sense on their terms. So be it. "Come and see." Jesus said the words to two of John the Baptist's disciples who asked, "Rabbi, where are you staying?" "Come and see" (Jn 1:39 NKJV). Philip says the words to Nathaniel who asked, "Can anything good come out of Nazareth?" "Come and see" (Jn 1:46). The unnamed woman at the well said the words when she went back to her village after meeting Jesus: "Come, see a man who told me all the things I have done; this is not the Christ, is it?" (Jn 4:29). "Come, look, listen, investigate, ask questions."

We do so with the whimsical joy of Dorothy Sayers, who, realizing how foreign and how challenging the gospel can sound to our contemporaries, encouraged us to still say it. Christian theology can make its own case in the marketplace of ideas; the grand Story can hold its own amidst all the competing stories. "The dogma is the drama," this dramatist told us.[21] By "dogma" she meant the content of the gospel:

> The dogma is the drama—not beautiful phrases, nor comforting sentiments, nor vague aspirations to loving-kindness and uplift, nor the promise of something nice after death—but the terrifying assertion that the same God who made the world, lived in the world and passed through the grave and gate of death. Show that to the heathen, and they may not believe it; but at least they may realize that here is something that a man might be glad to believe.[22]

All of this is why I speak of "standing in the mystery." In the face of all of the above (and so much more), we stand up in front of other human beings, Bible in hand, and stand in the mystery.

The mystery has, of course, many, many dimensions. Three are especially pertinent for understanding the preaching event. They are the mystery of the human person, the mystery of the altered structures of reality and the mystery of the work of the Holy Spirit. We can only begin to explore them in this last chapter.

---

[21]Dorothy Sayers, *The Whimsical Christian: 18 Essays by Dorothy Sayers* (New York: Macmillan, 1987), p. 27.
[22]Ibid., p. 28.

THE HUMAN PERSON

When we stand up before other human beings, what do we see? The answer determines so much of what and how we preach. When the authors of the New Testament look out at other human beings they see persons made by Jesus, for Jesus, held together in Jesus, longing for Jesus, only finally human when in relationship with Jesus. The other human beings themselves may not know this; most do not even have a clue; some would be insulted to have someone say this. But the writers and preachers of the Bible take their stand before others in this mystery.

It is the apostle Paul who articulates this most succinctly. Speaking of Jesus as the Son of God, as the "beloved Son" (Col 1:13), Paul writes (no, sings):

> He is the image of the invisible God, the firstborn of all creation. For by Him all things were created, both in the heavens and on earth, visible and invisible, whether thrones or dominions or rulers or authorities— all things have been created through Him and for Him. He is before all things, and in Him all things hold together. He is also head of the body, the church; and He is the beginning, the firstborn from the dead; so that He Himself will come to have first place in everything. For it was the Father's good pleasure for all the fullness to dwell in Him, and through Him to reconcile all things to Himself, having made peace through the blood of His cross; through Him, I say, whether things on earth or things in heaven. (Col 1:15-20)

In 1931, E. Stanley Jones said, "The Christian world has not taken this passage seriously—it has treated it as a rhetorical flourish."[23] So too the Christian world of our day. Yet nothing is more important.[24] Every human being we ever meet has been made by Jesus Christ. Every human being we ever meet has been made for Jesus Christ. Every human being we ever meet is being held together in Jesus Christ. Even those who do not yet believe. Even those who think they hate him. Even those who are telling you that you are crazy to preach what you are preaching. You the preacher know something about every person sitting or standing

---

[23]E. Stanley Jones, *In Christ* (Nashville: Abingdon, 1961), p. 282.
[24]For a thorough exegesis of this hymn, see N. T. Wright, *The Climax of the Covenant* (Minneapolis: Augsburg, 1993), p. 104.

before you that they may or may not know. You know that, having been made by God, the only way to live is his way. You know that, having been made for him, only he can finally fulfill all their longings. Indeed, you know that all their longings are symptomatic of their longings for him. You know that, being held together in him, they find their greatest joy in knowing him and cooperating with him as he works out his will for them. That is, you know that nothing less than Jesus himself will ever satisfy them. Again, they may not know this. And you do not necessarily need to tell them all this at once. But you know this mystery. And, therefore, you speak to them in this mystery.

Furthermore, you know that because Jesus has made your hearers for himself and holds them together moment by moment, he is pursuing them. This means that Jesus Christ has, in the mystery of things, drawn the human beings who sit before us as we stand up before them. The real "seeker" in the situation is not the person who shows up to church, and not even the church, but Jesus himself. This is what is going on in the Zaccheus story. He climbs up in a tree, "seeking to see who Jesus [is]" (Lk 19:3 NKJV modified). And then he discovers that he is not the real seeker; Jesus is. "For the Son of Man has come to seek and to save that which was lost" (Lk 19:10). The story is bracketed by the verb *seek:* Zaccheus seeks Jesus who was seeking Zaccheus.[25] What else explains why people get up out of bed on a Sunday morning, get dressed, walk or travel by auto or bus to a church building, find a seat, and then give attention to the reading and preaching of the Bible? This is why we do not have to "water down" our preaching to reach people; when anyone bothers coming into a church building, he or she is already thinking, if only implicitly, "I am going to hear something I do not ordinarily hear, and I may not fully understand; but I am seeking more than what I presently know and understand." This means that we preachers had better give what they were drawn there to get: the "deep story" of who he is and what he has done, is doing and will do for the world. No matter what else the sermon might be about, the sermon had better give them what

---

[25]I owe the observation to Doug Nason in a sermon at Fuller Seminary's Wednesday chapel.

they were made for: Jesus, and in him, the Trinity and the kingdom.

As a number of people have noted, the common bond with any seeker is not culture but creation. They and we were made by and for the only one who can say, "I am the beginning and the end."

ALTERED STRUCTURES OF REALITY

When we stand up before other human beings we know that the gospel we are about to announce has drastically changed the reality in which we stand. We know all too well that sin, evil and death are at work in the space in which we speak. But we also know that sin, evil and death do not have the place in that space they once had. We know, when we are alive in the gospel, that these forces ranged against humanity have been defeated—not eliminated, not yet, but defeated.

Two New Testament writers say it best:

> When you were dead in your transgressions and the uncircumcision of your flesh, He [God] made you alive together with Him [Jesus Christ], having forgiven us all our transgressions, having canceled out the certificate of debt consisting of decrees against us, which was hostile to us; and He has taken it out of the way, having nailed it to the cross.
>
> When He had disarmed the rulers and authorities, He made a public display of them, having triumphed over them through Him [or, through it, the cross]. (Col 2:13-15)

And

> Therefore, since the children share in flesh and blood, He Himself likewise also partook of the same, that through death He might render powerless him who had the power of death, that is, the devil, and might free those who through fear of death were subject to slavery all their lives. (Heb 2:14-15)

Talk about texts that transform the world! Both are announcing the good news that the coming of Jesus has altered the very structures of reality. Things have really changed. Before Jesus' birth, life, death, resurrection and ascension, reality, life in the universe, went together one way. After his birth, life, death, resurrection and ascension, reality, life in the universe, is configured in another way. When he comes again, it will all be configured in yet another way.

Imagine a basement cellar or a backyard shed. Over the years spiders have moved in and spun their cobwebs. Before you open the door, "reality" in the cellar or shed is configured one way. But after you open the door and stick your hand into the space, "reality" is configured another way. Or imagine a nation going through a political revolution. I know what that is like, for my family and I were caught up in the so-called People Power Revolution of 1986 in the Philippines. Before the revolution, the structures of life in the Philippines were configured one way; after the revolution, the structures of life were configured another way. The challenge after revolutions is learning how to operate in the new reality.

Before the Jesus events (his birth, life, death, resurrection, ascension), reality was configured one way. Sin, evil and death had their place in the universe. But after the Jesus events, reality is configured in a new way. Sin, evil and death do not have the place they once had. Oh, the spiders are still around and still know how to weave their way into the new configuration. The forces ousted in the revolution still exert pressure (see Rev 12–13). But they do not have the place in the structures of reality they once had. Through the Jesus events, the structures have forever been altered. The spiders and forces do not have the hold on us they had before Good Friday and Easter Sunday, Pentecost and Ascension.[26]

When we stand up before other human beings, we know that sin, though still around and still very nasty, does not have the power it once had. Jesus has delivered us from its grip; we do not have to obey its call anymore. We do, but we are no longer beholden to sin (Rom 6:1-22; Jn 8:31-36). When we stand up before other human beings, we know that the powers of evil, the "rulers" and "powers," "the world forces of this darkness," "the spiritual forces of wickedness in the heavenly places" (Eph 6:12), do not have the power they once had. Jesus overcame them in the moment that he died, and he stripped them of their weapons of

---

[26]I will be developing all this more fully in a forthcoming book to be titled *Altered Structures of Reality: Setting the Captives Free.* I will be working with a series of lectures I gave for Founder's Day, Örebro Missionsskola, Örebro, Sweden, December 16, 2002.

fear and accusation.[27] We do not have to obey the powers any more; we no longer need fear their threat of death to those who do not comply with their demands.

> And though this world with devils filled,
> Should threaten to undo us,
> We will not fear, for God hath willed
> His truth to triumph through us.
> The prince of darkness grim,
> We tremble not for him;
> His rage we can endure,
> For lo! his doom is sure;
> One little word shall fell him.
> MARTIN LUTHER, 1529, "A Mighty Fortress."

That one little word is the name Jesus. Evil is still around and tries its diabolical best to destroy Jesus and all he makes and redeems. But evil is no longer what it once was; it is on a leash and has been stripped of its status and authority. And when we stand up before other human beings, we know that death, though still "the last enemy" (1 Cor 15:26), does not have the power it once had. Jesus has overcome death and has taken away its finality. As one of my mentors, Peter Joshua (whom I mentioned in chapter six), used to say, "When death stung Jesus Christ, it stung itself to death." So, "Oh death, where is your victory?" (1 Cor 15:55, quoting Hos 13:14)

This means that we can walk into any space and say to sin, "You have no hold on Jesus. And because these people and I are his, you have no hold on them or me." We can walk into any space and say to evil, "You have no authority over Jesus. You must submit to him. And because these people and I belong to him you have no final authority over us." And we can walk into any space and say to death, "You have no grip on Jesus. And because these people and I belong to him, you have no final grip on them or me. They and I are not going to be intimidated by you

---

[27]See Gustav Aulen, *Christus Victor: An Historical Study of the Three Main Types of the Idea of Atonement* (New York: Macmillan, 1969). We are living in a time when we need to recover this aspect of the work of Jesus Christ; see Robert Webber, *Ancient-Future Faith: Rethinking Evangelicalism for a Postmodern World* (Grand Rapids: Baker, 1999), esp. pp. 49-61.

anymore. We are going to listen to Jesus and do what he tells us to do no matter what you say."

We stand up to preach in the midst of sin, evil and death. But we stand up in the midst of it all in the mystery that because of the Savior and Lord of all, sin and evil and death are not what they once were and cannot do what they once did.

THE WORK OF THE HOLY SPIRIT

When we stand up before other human beings to do this audacious thing we call preaching we do not stand up alone. Oh, sometimes it feels like we are alone. And sometimes the feeling is terrifying. But in the mystery of things, we are not alone at all. When we stand up before other human beings to speak in the name of Jesus, we stand in the company of his Holy Spirit. We stand in his Spirit and in all his Spirit is doing.

This is the great mystery of the preaching moment. And one could write books on it, on him and his work. Let me give an all too brief overview.

The Spirit has been and will work with the text. He has inspired the words, the ideas, the tone, the trajectory.[28] He has superintended its composition and safe transmission. He can open up its meaning. He will affect an encounter with the living Word, bring news, adjust our worldview to that of the text and empower a new step in the "obedience of faith." He can overcome any inability to comprehend, any resistance to what is declared, any fear to follow.

The Spirit has been and will be working with the preacher. He has been opening the text to us and opening our hearts and minds to what he opens. He has been helping us see how the text goes together. He has been helping us organize our thoughts and craft the flow of thought. He has been convincing us of the truth of the text, convicting us of the way we do not believe and live in the truth. He has been sharing his passion for the Jesus of the text. He has been sharing his passionate love for those who will hear our exposition. Blessed be his name.

---

[28]This is what Jesus promises in the coming of the Paraclete. See John 14–16.

The Spirit has been and will be working in and with the hearers. He has, before we stand up before them, been melting hardened hearts, softening stubborn wills, clearing cluttered minds, mending broken spirits. He will make the Jesus of the text real to them. He will be suggesting ways they ought to live the text, ways the preacher never even considered. He will be offering the very life of the living God to them!

The Spirit will work with the dynamics of communication. Consider the following diagrams. The first is what most speakers assume is going on in the preaching moment. The second is what many preachers will assume. The third is what some preachers will recognize about the moment.[29] The fourth points to the mystery.

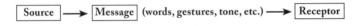

Figure 10.1

Most speakers assume they speak a message and the listeners receive it. It would be nice if it were that straightforward.

The speaker speaks a message the listener receives. But the listener also "speaks" back to the speaker (ordinarily nonverbally—eye and head movement, shifting of the body, etc.; although in some cultures, fortunately, this feedback is given verbally—i.e., some African American congregations, many Middle Eastern congregations, many Filipino

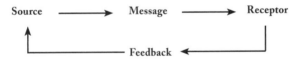

Figure 10.2

congregations).[30] The speaker then, mostly unconsciously, adjusts the message to connect with the listener. The process repeats itself over and over throughout the event. This is why the same sermon preached in two different services results in two different sermons.

---

[29]Gary V. Smith, *The Prophets as Preachers* (Nashville: Broadman and Holman, 1994), p. 110.
[30]We see this going on in the life of Jesus as his audience "interrupts" his speaking with questions and comments, affirmations and criticisms. See John 6.

The speaker speaks a message the listener receives. And the feedback loop begins. But the speaker and listener are not the only actors in the picture. God is working with the speaker and God is working with the listener, which is one of the reasons the same sermon can result in many different sermons in the same service: God is empowering

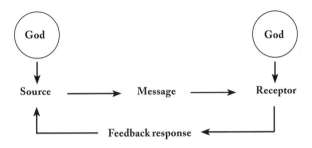

Figure 10.3

the words of the speaker, speaking them in different ways to different people; sometimes God is speaking a word of which the speaker is unaware. This is why, when someone says to us after a sermon, "That was a great word on compassion," and we did not think we were speaking such a word, the wrong thing to say is, "Oh, the sermon was not about compassion but about patience," and the right thing to say is, "Thank God that he spoke to you about that."

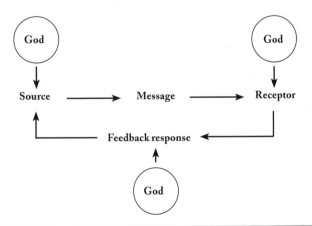

Figure 10.4

The good news is that the Spirit of God is involved in every aspect
of the communication loop. As Fred Rogers, famous as "Mr. Rogers,"
is reported to have said: "The space between my mouth and your ears is
the land of the Holy Spirit." And it is in that out-of-our-reach feedback
loop that we stand when we stand before other human beings and speak
the Word. (See Acts 10:42; 14:3; Hebrews 2:3-4.)

And, as already hinted at, the Spirit is at work quite apart from anything we are doing. This is the real wonder of the mystery in which we
stand. In John 15:26, Jesus says of the Paraclete, "He will bear witness
about Me" (ESV). I had for years taken this to mean that he will help us
bear witness, that as we seek to speak of Jesus in the world, the Spirit
will be present to help us. And he does. But that is not what Jesus is
speaking about in the promise of John 15:26. It was Lesslie Newbigin
who, in his brilliant theological commentary on the Gospel of John,
written while serving in India, helped me see what Jesus is saying; and
it changed the way I understood the preaching moment.[31] We are not
the primary actors in the event.

"It is important to note what is not said," Newbigin begins.[32] "It is
not said that the Spirit will help the disciple to bear witness. That would
make the action of the disciples primary and that of the Spirit auxiliary.
What is said is that the Spirit will bear witness and that—secondarily—
the disciples are witnesses."[33] Newbigin goes on to remind us that it is
not the work of humans to bring other humans to acknowledge Jesus as
he really is; it is always the work of God (Jn 6:44—the Father "draws"
us to Jesus). Then Newbigin writes this:

> What is promised here is that the Spirit will perform His own miracle in
> the hearts and consciences of people so that they are brought to recognize
> Jesus as the one he is. The words, the works and—above all—the suffer-
> ings of the community will be the means by which the witness is borne,
> but the actual agent will be the Spirit who, because he is the Spirit of the
> Father, is the Spirit of truth. When the Lord says to Israel, "You are my

---

[31]Lesslie Newbigin, *The Light Has Come: An Exposition of the Fourth Gospel* (Grand Rapids: Eerdmans, 1982), p. 206.
[32]Ibid.
[33]Ibid.

witnesses" (Isa. 43:10), there is no suggestion that this is a summons to proclamation. Israel is the witness to the majesty and glory of the Lord, not on account of anything that Israel says or does, but on account of those mighty works of which the Lord is the subject and Israel is the object. It is in this sense that the disciples will be witnesses. . . . Their life, their words, their deeds, their sufferings will thus be the occasion, the place, where the mighty Spirit bears his own witness in the hearts and consciences of men and women so that they are brought to look again at the hated, rejected, humiliated, crucified man and confess: "Jesus is Lord." It is the Spirit who is sovereign. The promise to the community of the disciples is not that they will have the Spirit at their disposal to help them in their work of proclamation. That misunderstanding has profoundly distorted the missionary action of the Church and provided the occasion for a kind of missionary triumphalism of which we are right to be ashamed. The Spirit is not the Church's auxiliary. The promise made here is not to the Church which is powerful and "successful" in a worldly sense. It is made to the Church which shares the tribulation and the humiliation of Jesus, the tribulation which arises from faithfulness to the truth in the world which is dominated by the lie. The promise is that, exactly in this tribulation and humiliation, the mighty Spirit of God will bear his own witness to the crucified Jesus as Lord and Giver of life.[34]

That is the mystery. That is the space into which we enter when we stand up before other human beings (some eager, some weary, some afraid, some hostile) and, Bible in hand, try to faithfully say what God is saying in a text.

Yes, we stand in all our hard work. But that is not where we take our stand. Yes, we stand in the ecology of our personhood. But that is not where we take our stand. Yes, we stand in all the relational dynamics between the hearers and us; some positive, some problematic, some negative. But that is not where we take our stand. Yes, we stand in our conviction of the truth of what we are saying; as a woman told Leighton Ford, "I want my friends to hear a preacher who believes at the cellular level what they are preaching."[35] But that is not where we take our

---

[34]Ibid., pp. 207-8.
[35]Leighton Ford, "Evangelistic Preaching in the Twenty-First Century," *Journal for Preachers* 30, no. 4 (Pentecost 2007): 30.

stand. We take our stand in the mystery of the human person, in the altered structures of reality and in what the creative, redeeming Spirit of God is doing with the text, the preacher, the hearers. These are things no one else can do or need do. We take our stand in the mystery of God's incomprehensible love for the world.

So we come back to where we began, to the mystery of divine transformation of the world through the foolishness and weakness of preaching. When the living God speaks something happens . . . always. When the preacher speaks God's speech, God speaks . . . always. When the preacher speaks God's speech, something happens . . . always.

For when the preacher speaks, the preacher is participating in the speaking of the great Preacher.

That is the glory of preaching!

Epilogue

A Sermon

An epilogue is "a concluding section that rounds out the design of a literary work."[1] Thus, it seemed appropriate to "round out the design" of this book on preaching with some preaching—to illustrate how what we have explored comes together in an expository sermon and to actually preach into the lives of preachers.

I have chosen to "deliver" the particular sermon of this epilogue for three reasons. One, it illustrates the most basic of basic homiletical forms, simply taking the first word of the text and continuing one word at a time (not necessarily in strict order).[2] Two, the text, Matthew 11:25-30, has become for me the central text for discipleship; in this text we are taken to the very center of Jesus' call upon our lives. This text is rivaled as "the text" for my life only by the great christological hymn of Philippians 2:5-11, where Jesus reveals what it means for God to be God.[3] And three, I have preached this text and its sermon all over the world and witnessed the Holy Spirit usher people into new freedom,

---

[1]"Epilogue," in *Webster's Seventh New Collegiate Dictionary*, p. 279.
[2]This is quite effective, making for an easy to follow and easy to remember flow. John 1:29—"Behold, the Lamb of God who takes away the sin of the world." Four key terms: Lamb of God, takes away, sin, world. I preach them in reverse order: world, sin, takes away, Lamb of God. John 12:20-33, the center of the Gospel of John. Four words: hour, glorify, grain of wheat, lifted up. Stunning sequence for preaching the heart of the good news. For a masterful example of this approach see Karl Barth's sermon on Matthew 14:22-31 published in *The Word in the World* (Vancouver, B.C.: Regent College Publishing, 2007), pp. 45-61. Pure Word!
[3]You can hear me preach on Philippians 2:5-11 at PreachingToday.com.

hope and joy.[4] The uniform response has been, "Yes. This is life!"

I have presented the sermon in the format I have had in front of me as I preached. Thus, it is written in "breath-bites." Phrases and clauses are indented, key words are capitalized for emphasis, Matthew's words are printed in bold type. As I preached I shuffled the pages right to left. No sentence on my original manuscript continues on a following page. I also use a colored highlighter to mark key transitions (not duplicated here). What I actually had before me was my handwritten manuscript: as I already noted, writing with pencil allows me to freely place words, phrases and sentences on the paper where they can be quickly spotted by the eye freeing me to speak to the ear.

Lord, speak. Your servants are listening.

Text: Matthew 11:25-30

Title: "The Main Thing: Included!"

Occasion: Conclusion to *The Glory of Preaching*[5]

I invite you to now give your attention to two texts.

One is from Stephen Covey, time-management guru.

The other is from Saint Matthew,

---

[4]I have preached variations of it for the people of Glendale Presbyterian Church, Glendale, California; for the people of Fremont Presbyterian Church, Sacramento, California; for the faculty retreat of the School of Theology, Fuller Theological Seminary, Pasadena, California; for the members of a doctor of ministry course I taught at Tyndale Theological Seminary, Toronto, Ontario; for the members of the doctor of ministry courses I taught for Fuller; for the people of First Baptist Church, Beirut, Lebanon; for the people of First Baptist Church, Nazareth, Galilee (one of the highlights of my life—preaching in the same town where the Master preached!); for 300 university students in Yerevan, Armenia: for the people of Chinese Presbyterian Church, Vancouver, British Columbia; for the people of First Baptist Church, Vancouver (I wish you could have been there that day!); for the people of Grace Presbyterian Church, Toronto; for the participants of the Evangelical Homiletical Society Annual Meeting, Trinity Western University, Langley, British Columbia; for the people of St. John's-St. Margaret's Anglican Church, Singapore; for the pastors and fellows of the Pastors Conference of The Trinity Forum Academy, Osprey Point, Maryland; for the 250 pastors and spouses at the Pastors Conference of the Christian and Missionary Alliance churches of British Columbia, Kelowna, B.C.; and for the students of my "Preaching and Worship" classes at Regent.

[5]I set up the manuscript for all my sermons this way: text, title, occasion (with more details to help remember the event).

tax-collector-turned-evangelist.

I am in no way suggesting

that the two texts carry the same weight

or have equal authority!

The text from Stephen Covey

is found on page 34 of his book *First Things First.*

He writes:

"The main thing is to keep the main thing the

main thing."[6]

The text from Saint Matthew

is found in chapter 11 of his book, verses 25-30.

You know the text well.

I am sure you have preached it often.

Through this text

we are drawn into the main thing

that we are to keep the main thing.

(When preaching live, I at this point usually say, "If you are able, would you please stand for the reading of good news?" Once the people stand, I say, "Hear the Word of God.")

"At that time Jesus answered and said, 'I praise You, O Father, Lord of heaven and earth, that You have hidden these things from the wise and intelligent and revealed them to babes. Yes, Father, for thus it was well-pleasing in Your sight. All things have been handed over to

---

[6]A number of the contexts in which I preached would have no working knowledge of Stephen Covey; most contexts in the future probably will not either. So I changed the introduction: "You have no doubt heard, especially if you live in the business world, the saying, 'The main thing is to keep the main thing the main thing.' An architect who heard me use the phrase one Sunday bought me a rock with the words engraved in it: he must have thought I needed to see it every day. And I do. 'The main thing is to keep the main thing the main thing.'" Other contexts call for other modifications to the manuscript; I will not bother to note them.

Me by My Father; and no one knows the Son, except the Father; nor does anyone know the Father, except the Son, and anyone to whom the Son wills to reveal Him.

Come to Me, all who are weary and heavy-laden, and I will give you rest. Take My yoke upon you, and learn from Me, for I am gentle and humble in heart; and 'you will find rest for your souls.' For My yoke is easy, and My burden is light."

Let us pray. "Spirit of the living God: we believe that You enabled Matthew to faithfully remember these words of our Lord, and that You enabled him to accurately record them for us. Will You now, in Your mercy and grace, help us enter into the reality of which they speak? For we pray this in the name of and for the greater fame of Jesus. Amen."

(At this point I invite the listeners to turn to one or two of the people around them and respond to two questions. 1. "As we read this text, what leaped out at you?" 2. "What one question would you like to ask to help you understand this text better"? I find that even the first-time visitor can enter into this since the questions are not threatening, i.e., there are no wrong answers.)

Come.

I once saw a poster that said, "God's favorite word is 'Come.'"

Yes, Jesus says "Go" . . . "Go, make disciples of all the nations."

And yes, Jesus says "Give" . . . "Give yourselves away for the sake

of the city."

And yes, Jesus says "Serve" and "Sing" and "Heal" and "Preach."

But his favorite word is "Come."

Me.

To Me.

Underline the pronoun, **Me.**

Come to Me.

Jesus does not say, "Come to religion."

Jesus does not say, "Come to spirituality."

Jesus does not say, "Come to church."

He does not say, "Come to ministry."

He does not even say, "Come to the divine one."

Raising the question of who he thinks he is!

Come to Me.

He calls us to himself.

While serving as the chaplain of the United States Senate,

Richard Halverson made an observation

illustrating just how easy it is to lose touch with the pronoun.

He observed that Christianity began on Palestinian soil,

as a Relationship with a Person.

It moved on to Greek soil and became a Philosophy.

It moved on to Roman soil and became an Institution.

It moved on to British soil and became a Culture.

It moved on to American soil and became an Enterprise!

Need I elaborate?

Now, Christianity is a Philosophy,

the most coherent and all-encompassing of all philosophies.

And Christianity is an Institution,

the most redemptive and life-giving of all institutions

(or it is supposed to be!).

Christianity is a Culture,

the most inclusive and transformative of all cultures.

Christianity is an Enterprise,

  the grandest imaginable . . .

  the enterprise of restoring the entire universe!

But Christianity is essentially a Person.

  Come to Me.

"The main thing is to keep the main thing the main thing."

  The main thing is a Person.

"Come to Me all who are **weary**."

  All who are weary from the brokenness of life.

  All who are weary from the suffering in the world.

  All who are weary from injustice and pain and sorrow and talk of

    terrorism and war.

  Know anyone like that?

"Come to Me all who are weary and **overburdened**."

  In the English language verbs function in two voices:

    active and passive.

  You may know that in the Greek language verbs function

    in three voices:

    active, passive and what is called the middle.

      Active—"I wash."

      Passive—"I am washed."

      Middle—"I wash myself."

"All who are overburdened."

It is in the middle voice—"overburdened themselves."

"Come to Me all who have overburdened themselves."

Know anyone like that?

For the most part, excessive weariness is our own doing.

"Come . . . and I will give you **rest**."

Oh Lord, can it really be?

Literally, "**I will rest you**."

Is that not a better way to say it?

Certainly more inviting.

"I will rest you."

"I will give you rest"

could lead us to think

that "rest" can be experienced apart from Jesus,

as though rest was a thing Jesus places in our

hands

which we then can carry off on our own.

"I will rest you," suggests the personal involvement of the Rester.

"Come to Me and I will rest you."

Rest.

The word takes us back to the beginning.

Genesis 2:3:

"Then God blessed the seventh day and sanctified it,

because on it God rested from all his work."

What does it mean to say, "God rested"?

That God ceased from all activity?

That God shifted into neutral, so to speak?

No.

"God rested" means God entered into the reason for which God

created.

In the Song of Creation

recorded in Genesis 1

we hear the refrain

"and it was evening and morning."

"It was evening and morning, day one."

"It was evening and morning, day two."

"It was evening and morning, day three."

And day four,

and five,

and six.

But we hear no "it was evening and morning, day seven."

Day seven has no end.

Day seven is why God made the world!

"God rested" means God has entered into the reason

God even bothered with creation.

"God rested" means God has entered into the wholeness willed for

creation.

Come to Me all who are weary and have overburdened yourselves

. . . and I will rest you.

I will lead you into the wholeness for which you were originally

created."

"And you will find rest for **your souls**."

That is where we need it . . . is it not?

In our souls.

Our bodies and brains are weary

because our souls are weary.

What we need is "soul rest."

Come to Me . . . to Me . . . to Me . . .

and I will put your souls at rest.

Please Jesus, please do it!

How? How does Jesus rest us?

Ready?

Take My yoke upon you.

What?

Taking up a yoke will rest us?

It is a startling antidote to weariness, to being overburdened.

The yoke is a symbol for work! For hard work! [See 1 Kings 12:4.]

Did not the Prophet Isaiah tell of the day when a Child would be

born

Who would "break the yoke of the burden" (Is 9:4)?

Taking up a yoke will unburden my overburdened soul?

Taking up a yoke

is what the weary and overburdened people of the first century

least expected![7]

---

[7]F. Dale Bruner, *Christbook* (Waco, Tex.: Word, 1984), p. x.

A leisurely picnic on the banks of the Jordon, maybe.

Or floating in the Dead Sea.

Or a holiday in the hills of Lebenon.

But a yoke?

Yokes are placed on animals' shoulders

    to enable them to carry

    more than they were already carrying!

Come to Me . . . and I will rest you.

Take My yoke upon you . . .

and your souls, you inner being, will find rest.

What gives? What is Jesus getting at?

Ready?

Jesus is telling us

    that we are weary

        because we are wearing the wrong yokes.

Refreshment for the soul comes by "a transfer of yokes."[8]

You see, the question is never, "Will I wear a yoke?"

    The question is always, "Whose yoke will I wear?'

        Every person wears a yoke; there are no yokeless human beings.

        The question is never, "Will I be a disciple?"

        The question is always, "Whose disciple will I be?"

        The question is never, "Will I be pressured by a spirit?"

        The question is always, "Of all the spirits of the age

---

[8]George Buttrick, *The Interpreter's Bible* (New York: Abingdon, 1951), 7:390.

that pressure me,

to which will I yield?"

The question is never, "Will I wear a yoke?"

The question is always, "Whose yoke will I wear?"

Jesus is telling us that we are weary and overburdened because we are
wearing the wrong yokes.

Switch yokes.

Take up Mine.

My yoke is "easy" and My burden is "light."

Easy? Light?

Right, Jesus. Like, I've read the rest of the Story.

Easy? Light?

The billion dollar question is, therefore,

WHAT IS JESUS' YOKE?

WHAT IS JESUS' BURDEN?

He calls it "**My** yoke."

Meaning, it is something he himself wears.

Whatever the yoke is, it is something *he himself* wears.

That is the key.

The yoke he calls us to wear is something he himself wears.

Like "My shirt," something he himself wears.

My yoke.

And the men and women around him could see it . . .

and could see the difference it made in his life.

"My yoke."

And "**My** burden."

Again, something *he himself* bears.

Whatever it is, it is something he himself bears.

The men and women around him could see it too . . .

and could see the difference it made in his life.

"Take up My yoke . . . something I myself wear."

Turns out he has worn it for all eternity!

He wore it before taking on our flesh and blood.

He wore it the whole of his earthly life

from Bethlehem to Calvary.

He wears it even now.

So, what is it?

His new law?

The rabbis of Jesus' day did refer to the "yoke of the law."

So it would be easy to conclude,

as I did for many years,

that Jesus' yoke is his new law,

His new "torah,"

as articulated in his Sermon on the Mount.

But is that what Jesus says?

In particular, is that what he says in the Matthew text?

No.

Then what is his yoke, the yoke that refreshes, the yoke he himself
wears?

IT IS HIS RELATIONSHIP WITH THE ONE HE CALLS
"FATHER."

It is his filial relationship with "Father."

How do we know that?

By honoring the way Matthew has remembered Jesus' words.

Most of us begin where the greeting cards do,

like I have done in this sermon,

with verse 28—"Come to Me."

But that is not where Matthew begins.

He begins at verse 25—

"At that time, Jesus answered and said,

'I praise You, O Father'"—

And goes on the express his trust in his Father's wisdom and
sovereignty.

And to express the mystery of the living God:

that there is within the Being of the one God

a fellowship,

a community,

a reciprocity,

a relational intimacy of knowing and revealing.

Jesus' call of "Come to Me, take My yoke upon you"

emerges out of his prayer

"O Father, Lord of heaven and earth, I praise You."

Jesus' call "take My yoke"

emerges out of his worship,

> **"I praise You that You hid these things**
>
> **from the wise and intelligent**
>
> **and revealed them to babes."**

Jesus' call emerges out of his praising the Father,

> **"Yes, Father, for thus it was well pleasing in Your sight."**

Jesus' call emerges out of his affirming,

> **"All things have been handed over to Me by My Father."**

Jesus' call emerges out of his declaring,

> **"No one knows the Son, except the Father;**
>
> **nor does anyone know the Father, except the Son,**
>
> **and anyone to whom the Son wishes to reveal the Father."**

Do you see that?

The picture the test suggested to me most of my life was this:

Jesus calls me to himself,

    and then,

holding something in his hands,

says to me,

> "Here, I've got this yoke for you to wear . . . and it will rest
> you."

The picture the text now suggests to me is this:

Jesus is praying . . .

Jesus is worshiping . . .

Jesus is in conversation with the one he calls "Father."

He then turns to us

FROM WITHIN THE CONVERSATION,

from within the RELATIONSHIP,

from within the INTIMACY;

He turns to us and says, "Come."

"Come to Me . . .

take up the yoke you see Me wearing right now.

See it?

See my yoke?

My yoke is my relationship with my Father.

And I am calling you to join Me in it."

It takes my breath away!

The text begins with Jesus the Son in communion with the Father.

Jesus really likes being in communion with the Father.

Jesus really likes his Father.

A huge understatement!

It is the secret of Jesus' identity and ministry;

we cannot understand Jesus

apart from his passion for his Father.

He is praising his Father,

He is delighting in his Father,

He is trusting his Father.

 And doing so in a context

  that would seem to call for everything

   but praise, delight, trust.

  The cities of Chorozin, Bethsaida and Capernaum

   were rejecting his preaching of the gospel of the kingdom!

   Some were accusing him of being in cahoots with the devil.

   Some thought he was out of his mind.

   Some wanted to stone him.

Yet there he is,

 praising his Father,

  delighting in his Father,

   trusting his Father.

And he turns to the disciples,

 and says,

  "Come to Me."

Implying,

 "Come into my praising, into my delighting, into my trusting."

Take My yoke upon you.

Jesus' yoke is his relationship with his Father.

And his burden?

 His burden is pleasing his Father.

 Jesus lives to please the Father

—nothing less, nothing more.

As we hear him say in John's Gospel,

"I only do what I see My Father doing,

I only say what I hear My Father saying."

Jesus lives his whole career

—if we can use that word of him—

for an Audience of One.[9]

And he calls us to do the same—

to live for an Audience of One.

Yes, the needs of broken humanity pull at Jesus,

at his guts *(splanchna)*.

But the needs do not set the agenda.

Yes, he cares about what the people around him are asking of him.

But the requests do not shape the rhythm

of his day-to-day existence.

He does not look for the approval of Scribes and Pharisees,

of the Doctors of the Law and Masters of Spirituality.

He does not look for the blessing of the Sadducees and Chief Priests,

of the Intelligentsia and Religious Technicians.

He feels no need to please Herod or Pilate;

whether the power structures

affirm him or not is not his burden.

He is not driven to please his disciples,

---

[9]I owe the phrase to Steve Hayner, the former president of InterVarsity Christian Fellowship.

or his brother or sisters,

or even his mother.

"Did you not know I had to be about My Father's business?"

Spoken at the age of twelve, the words shaped his whole career.

He is driven

—if we can use that word of Jesus—

to please the Father.

Period.

Come to Me all who are weary.

Take My yoke upon you.

Bear My burden.

And you will find rest for your souls.

For My yoke is easy.

And My burden is light.

Easy? Light?

Maybe for You, Jesus.

But for us? Easy for us? Light for us?

Yes, he says.

Yes?

Yes.

Why?

Because it was for this that we were created and are being redeemed!

"My yoke is *easy*."

The Greek word is *chrestus*,

related to the word *Christos*,

Christ.

The yoke of *Christos* is *chrestus*.

Chrestus means "kind" when referring to people.

It means "well fitting" when referring to things.

"My yoke is *chrestus*,

well fitting for Me . . .

because My whole identity and existence are in the Father.

And well fitting for you . . .

because you were created for

and are being redeemed for

the same identity and existence."

"The main thing is to keep the main thing the main thing."

The main thing is the RELATIONSHIP at the center of the universe.

A relationship between a Father and a Son.

A relationship so pulsating with Life

that the relationship itself

is a Breathing,

a Spirit,

a Person,

the Holy Spirit.

OUT OF that relationship we were made.

FOR that relationship we were made.

Long before we came on the scene,

    the relationship was there.

        The triune God was there.

        Infinitely happy being God.

        Not lonely.

        Not needy.

And one day—

    if we can say "day" before time came into being—

    the Father says to the Son,

        "This is too good to keep to Ourselves.

            Let Us make creatures in Our image

                to enjoy what We enjoy."

So God made us!

And when we were so foolish as to turn away from such a Life . . .

    and run off on our own . . .

        God did not give up.

        God came after us.

        God came down.

            All the way down.

            In our flesh.

            And calls us,

                "Come . . . to Me . . .

                    and I will bring you back

                        into that for which the Father and I

                            made you."

Isn't this good?

A number of years ago, I "accidentally"

[though I suppose a Presbyterian ought not use the word!]

stumbled upon a book

by the great Scottish theologian Thomas Torrance.

One of his lesser-known works, *Trinitarian Perspectives*.[10]

And I read a line

that has turned out to be

THE single most important theological discovery

of my journey thus far.

I suppose I should have gotten it in Seminary decades ago,

but I did not.

On the first page of the book,

Torrance writes things like this:

"The doctrine of the Trinity

is the central dogma of Christian theology,

the fundamental grammar of our knowledge of God."

Isn't that good?

"Because the doctrine of the Trinity

gives expression to the fact

that God had opened himself to us . . .

in such a way

that we may know him in the inner relations of his divine Being,

---

[10]Thomas F. Torrance, *Trinitarian Perspectives: Toward Doctrinal Agreement* (Edinburgh: T & T Clark, 1994). All the quotes are from p. 1.

and have communion with him in his divine life

as Father, Son and Holy Spirit."

I am liking what I am reading,

so I continue.

Through the reconciliation worked out at the cross, says

Torrance,

God "has established an intimate

two-way relation between Himself and us

and us and Himself,

making Himself accessible to us . . .

and giving us entry into

the inner fellowship of God's life."

Wow!

Or "glory."

Then I read this line:

"God draws near to us

in such a way

as to draw us near to Himself

within the circle of his knowing of Himself."

I almost dropped the book!

I was stunned.

Tears began to flow.

I wanted to get up and dance . . .

and fall down and kneel.

"God draws near to us."

THAT would be wonderful enough.

But there is more!

"God draws near to us

in such a way as to draw us near to Himself."

THAT too would be wonderful enough.

I could live the rest of life on that alone.

But there is more!

"God draws near to us

in such a way as to draw us near to Himself

within the circle

of his knowing of Himself."

THAT is what Jesus means by his yoke!

Jesus' yoke is the circle . . .

the circle of the Trinity's self-knowing.

And wonders of wonders . . .

Jesus calls us to join him in it!

Thus can Dallas Willard say,

"It is being included in the eternal life of God

that heals all wounds

and allows us to stop demanding satisfaction.

What else matters of a personal nature

once it is clear that you have been included?"[11]

---

[11]Dallas Willard, *The Divine Conspiracy* (San Francisco: HarperSanFrancisco, 1998), p. 341.

"Take My yoke upon you.

    My yoke is easy . . .

        it fits well."

It is the only yoke that fits the human species well.

"And My burden is light."

    Light?

    Pleasing God the Father is "light"?

    For You Jesus.

    But for us?

Yes, he says.

    Infinitely lighter than trying to please our earthly fathers and

        mothers.

    Really?

    Yes!

    For what pleases the Father?

    What pleases the Father is throwing ourselves on the Son.

    What pleases the Father is throwing ourselves

        on the finished work of the Son.

    What pleases the Father is opening ourselves up to the Spirit,

        and welcoming the Spirit's companionship and indwelling.

Take my yoke upon you.

    You get so weary

        because you are wearing the wrong yokes.

You are overburdened

because you are bearing the wrong burdens.

Switch yokes . . . switch burdens.

Wear My yoke . . . bear My burden.

And you will find rest for your souls.

And we are not left

to figure out how to do it,

how to wear his yoke.

In his incarnation,

Jesus the Son

lives out his relationship with the Father

on human terms.

Learn from Me, he says.

Meaning, "Watch Me live out trust and intimacy."

He models for us

what the easy yoke and light burden look like 24/7.

In his overall lifestyle,

in the rhythm of his day and week,

Jesus shows us how to enter into

and work from

the embrace of the Father.

Learn from Me.

It also means "Let Me show you the Father."

Jesus is saying to us—

or to me, anyway—

> "Your problem is that you do not know the Father.
>
> I tell you . . . you can trust My Father . . .
>
> even when your preaching
>
> of the gospel of the kingdom
>
> is being resisted."

> "Come . . . enter my praising the Father.
>
> Come . . . enter my trusting the Father.
>
> Come . . . join Me
>
> in simply doing what I see the Father do . . .
>
> and saying what I hear the Father saying."

For I am gentle and humble of heart.

> I will not berate you for your self-imposed overburdening.
>
> I know why you get yourself in such a state.
>
> I know why you chose to live for other gods
>
> and wear other yokes.
>
> Come, and let Me lead you out of your old ways
>
> and into My way.

So Bernard of Clairvaux

> of the twelfth century could sing:
>
> "O blessed burden that makes all burdens light!
>
> O blessed yoke that bears the bearer up!"

"The main thing is to keep the main thing the main thing."

"Come to Me,

    you who are weary from the harsh realities of life,

    and have overburdened yourselves trying to please everyone else.

    Take up My yoke . . .

        join Me in the circle . . .

            enter into My intimacy with the Father.

So that you also

    can live

        and work

            and preach

                out of a soul at rest."

Name and Subject Index

Scripture Index